Can You Name That Team?

*A Guide to Professional Baseball,
Football, Soccer, Hockey, and Basketball
Teams and Leagues*

David B. Biesel

The Scarecrow Press, Inc.
Lanham, Maryland, and Oxford

SCARECROW PRESS, INC.

Published in the United States of America
by Scarecrow Press, Inc.
A Member of the Rowman & Littlefield Publishing Group
4720 Boston Way, Lanham, Maryland 20706
www.scarecrowpress.com

12 Hid's Copse Road
Cumnor Hill, Oxford OX2 9JJ, England

Copyright © 1991 by David B. Biesel
First paperback edition 2002

British Library Cataloguing in Publication Information Available

The hardback edition of this book was previously cataloged by the Library of Congress as follows:

Biesel, David B., 1931-
     Can you name that team? : a guide to professional baseball, football, soccer, hockey, and basketball teams and leagues / by David B. Biesel
        p. cm.
     Includes indexes.
     ISBN 0-8108-2458-2 (alk. paper)
       1. Athletic clubs—United States—History. 2.   Athletic clubs—United States—Names—History. I.   Title.
     GV583.B49 1991
     796.06'0973—dc20   91-26356

Jacket design: Karl Steinbrenner
Composition: Toni Sortor

ISBN: 0-8108-4552-0   (paper)

Table of Contents

Table of Contents

Introduction

This book is divided into three main sections, each of which contains the names of more than 950 teams in 38 professional leagues in baseball, football, soccer, hockey, and basketball.

The first section is an alphabetical list by the city, state (or province), or regional designation used by the team. Thus, there are entries for Alberta, Carolina, Chicago, Homestead, Jersey, Minnesota, Milwaukee, New Jersey, Southern California, etc. Teams that have taken a state or regional designation (Tri-Cities Blackhawks, Carolina Cougars, Southern California, etc.) are listed under these regional designations.

Some readers may be aware that the Texas Rangers (AL) play in Arlington (TX), the Minnesota Twins (AL) played in Bloomington (MN), and that the New York Giants (NFL) play in East Rutherford (NJ)—but few will remember what city (or cities) the Carolina Cougars (ABA), Minnesota Fighting Saints (WHA), New England Whalers (WHA), or North Hudson Thourots (ABL-2) called home. Nor would many of today's readers be aware that the Tri-Cities team represented the cities of Moline (IL), Rock Island (IL), and Davenport (IA). Hopefully, there are enough cross-references to aid the reader in locating a team. If not, a quick check of the nicknames in Section 3 should locate the designation under which the team is listed.

There are only two entries in Section 1 that do not follow the rule stated above of city, state, or regional designation. These entries are the Oorang Indians and Hilldale. A third team, the Cuban Giants, is the only team listed in Section 1 that did not play in one of the leagues listed in Section 2. However, the influence of the Cuban Giants on the names of many of the Black baseball teams was so great that an exception was made for them.

Also, some teams became well known without using their city designation. Two of these, the Racine Cardinals and the Lincoln Giants, could be confusing, because they contain the names of cities (Racine, Wisconsin, and Lincoln, Nebraska). These, and such teams as Cole's American Giants, are found at the end of the listings for the city in which they played.

Thus, there is a (Chicago) listing, after Chicago, which contains the Racine Cardinals and Cole's American Giants. The (New York) Lincoln Giants follow the New York listing, as does the Jamaica St. Monicas.

The entries in Section 1 contain information, whenever possible, on how the team got its name. If the team is obscure or short-lived, I have tried to provide some data about it. Perhaps others will be able to fill in some missing information in time for the next edition.

The choice of the name used by many of the earlier teams is obvious. City or state nicknames (Keystones, Buckeyes, Quakers, etc.), or in some cases, just the city name (Hudson, Brooklyns, Hartford, etc.) were used by many of the early teams. Some of the early baseball teams had nicknames that referred either to the color of their stockings (or uniform), to the social club their members belonged to, or fire house (Mutuals, etc.) in which they were organized. In basketball, many of the earlier teams had commercial or company names or took their names from the facility in which they played.

In the early years of professional football, the pros were frequently referred to as the post-graduate game. The sport did not enjoy the degree of acceptance that it does today and, in.fact, some of the top college coaches were dead set against the professional game. Therefore, many of the early pro football teams chose names (Rams, Bulldogs, Lions, Wolverines, etc.) that were used by the better college teams in an attempt to trade on the fan enthusiasm for the college game. Many teams in both pro football and basketball adopted the name of the local baseball team in order to gain easy recognition. There have been Dodgers, Giants, Indians, and Reds in football and baseball. In Pittsburgh, the name Pirates has been used not only for the baseball team, but for football, basketball, and hockey teams.

In the early years of professional sports, sports writers were often guilty of picking several names and using them all in the same story, thus adding to the confusion.

For example, when Philadelphia entered the American Basketball League (ABL-1) in 1926, despite the fact that the Cleveland team had a well-known name, the writer for the Philadelphia *Inquirer* initially referred to the Cleveland team as the Indians (using the name of the Cleveland American League baseball team). Then, for variety, he referred to the team as the Braves and Redskins, sometimes in the same paragraph.

The Philadelphia team had itself used the name of the local National League baseball team, the Phillies, until it was changed by owner Jules Aaronson to Warriors in midseason. Even after Aaronson decided to change the team's name to Warriors, the newspaper ads for the team games referred to them as the Phillies.

Section 2 is a genealogy of the teams in each league, where they came from and where they went. Thus, you can trace a team such as the Rochester Royals (now the Sacramento Kings) by looking at either the National Basketball Association (NBA), or National Basketball League (NBL) listing and, in each case, trace the team through all the leagues and cities it played in and the various names it played under.

If you thought that the Atlanta Hawks (nee St. Louis Hawks and Milwaukee Hawks) were originally the Tri-Cities Blackhawks, as most sources indicate, you will find that the team started as the Buffalo Bisons and moved in mid-season (1946/47) to the Tri-Cities location.

Whenever possible, the attempt has been made to show the continuity of a franchise. Did a team move or did a franchise fail and get purchased by someone who moved it? The answers are not always clear, especially with the early basketball teams. While a number of sources now show the Minneapolis Lakers as originally being the Detroit Gems, there is some question as to whether this "change" occurred after the Detroit team had already folded and the defunct franchise rights were purchased by a group of Minneapolis businessmen. The Laker entry in Section 2 does not show the Detroit Gems as their predecessor, but the reader is welcome to question the judgment of the author.

For some teams, especially those that changed names or locations frequently, their listings will seem to dominate the league listing. But each listing is complete, even if there are several in sequence (e.g., see the Brooklyn NL listing or the New York Jewels of the ABL-2). The intent has been to help the reader locate a team under any of its names and to have its complete history without going back and forth to other lists.

Although some baseball teams put their team name on their uniforms as early as 1905, many went by their city name on the uniform until the 1920s and 1930s. Thus, while some nicknames were well-established, others, such as the Brooklyn NL club, were not. The Brooklyn entry will point out this problem. At various times in the 1900-1932 period, the team was referred to as the Superbas, Robins, and Dodgers (with Infants a 3-year also-ran). In fact, frequently all three names would be used in the same newspaper article. Therefore, the reader should be aware that up through the 1930s, for all sports, many team names were in the process of evolution. The names in Section 2 are the ones that seem to have the dominant role at the time.

Section 3 is an alphabetical listing of the names that appear in Sections 1 and 2. Thus, the reader can find out how many teams have shared the same name in the leagues that are listed in this book. However, since each appearance of a team in a league is listed in Section 2, the same team will show up more than once in Section 3.

For example, the first listing in Section 3 is the ABCs, and there are four listings below it. The four listings are the same team. The Indianapolis ABCs (as both the Section 1 and Section 2 entries will indicate) played in three leagues and were in one of those leagues twice. Another example is the Buffalo All-Americans. This team was in the American Professional Football League (APFA), which became the National Football League (NFL). Thus, Buffalo has two listings under All-Americans. When a team appears in the same league two or more times, the inclusive years of each appearance will be shown.

Finally, there is an index to personal names and other data that are within the entries in Section 1. This index refers the reader directly to the specific entry, not to a page number.

This edition is complete as of 1991. There are new franchises planned for 1992 and beyond, and teams will move or fold. These changes will appear in the next edition, and we plan to add other leagues such as the high minor leagues (AAA and AA classifications) in baseball, football's Dixie League and Pacific Coast League, the early professional leagues of basketball, etc. The reader's comments and suggestions will be welcomed and appreciated.

Acknowledgments

To compile a useful reference work, an author needs two valuable aids: the trait of dogged persistence and the blessing of extremely knowledgeable colleagues.

Dogged persistence is needed to sort through miles of newspaper microfilm and voluminous files of media guides, programs, press releases, and the other documentation in the hope of getting small pieces of useful data. Any author can supply this first requirement.

The second aid requires the greatest of luck and in that respect I have "stood on the shoulders of giants" in sports research. It is impossible to list them all, but some must be mentioned.

I want to thank Tom Heitz, the librarian at the Baseball Hall of Fame, and his staff for all their assistance. The facilities and files at the Hall of Fame were of great help, especially a document entitled "The History of Major League Club Nicknames," which was compiled by Bill Deane with the help of many others. Among those who contributed were William Vaules, Mary Armstrong, Scott St. John, Paul Cunningham, Helen Stiles, Dennis Hernandez, Wallace Philips, Jeff Kernan, and John Tortorello. Because of its extensive collection, I was able to research other sports besides baseball and the Baseball Hall of Fame.

The on-going research done by members of the Society for American Baseball Research (SABR) is of great value to any researcher. I am particularly indebted to Marc Okkonen, Dick Clark, Harold Dellinger, Chuck Hershberger, and Cliff Kachline.

In doing football research, one cannot proceed very far without following in the tracks of Bob Carroll, Bob Gill, Joe Horrigan, Bob Braunwart, Brian Butler, and other members of the Professional Football Research Association (PFRA). The PFRA publications have been a major help in sorting out the confusion of the early days of professional football in America.

To research soccer teams would have been very difficult without the help of Colin Jose, who has written a history of the North American Soccer League and is currently researching other soccer leagues. Colin took time from his writing to provide me with much helpful data. Also, I want to thank Lois Emanuelli, curator of the Soccer Hall of Fame at Oneonta, New York, and Jim Baker, deputy director of operations for the Major Soccer League (formerly the Major Indoor Soccer League).

Wayne Patterson at the Basketball Hall of Fame has been of great help, as has Ed Bass of the Basketball Old-Timers of America. The front office staffs of many of the current teams, in all sports, were most helpful in supplying information.

I also appreciate the assistance given to me by the librarians at the New York Public Library (especially the microfilm division on 43rd Street) and the public libraries in Elizabeth (NJ), Trenton (NJ), Newark (NJ), Troy (NY), and Middletown (CT). Grateful acknowledgments go to my local libraries in Bergenfield and Dumont (NJ), and, most especially, to June Lewin, the former director of the Haworth Public Library, who obtained many hard-to-find books and periodicals for me.

To a very special friend and colleague, Bill Himmelman, the NBA historian, I can only hope that someday I can repay his friendship and assistance. Bill helped not only by sharing his encyclopedic knowledge of basketball but also by reviewing the other areas of the book. If there are errors, they are mine, but Bill has made the book far better for his comments, data, and suggestions. Also, Karel deVere, Bill's right hand in statistical research, provided considerable assistance.

I have often wondered why authors I have known always end the acknowledgments by thanking their spouse. Now I know. I doubt that the work would have been completed without my wife's patience and help. Diane is an elementary school librarian who is totally organized and loves to work with the young and confused. I'm not young, but I can be totally confused and disorganized. Despite a complete lack of knowledge of sports, she was able to make order out of the chaos of our study, to find any document I'd sworn I had lost, and to be of constant good cheer. All authors should marry a librarian!

Section 1

Team Names

AKRON (OH)

Firestone Non-Skids (NBL) 1937/38-1940/41
Firestone Non-Skids (MBC) 1936/37
Firestones (MBC) 1935/36
Firestones (NPBL) 1932/33
  Teams sponsored by the Firestone Tire and Rubber Company. Non-Skids was the name of a specific tire produced by the company.

Goodyear Regulars (MBC) 1936/37
Goodyear Wingfoots (NBL) 1937/38-1941/42
Goodyears (NPBL) 1932/33
  Teams sponsored by the Goodyear Tire and Rubber Company. Regulars and Wingfoots were specific tires produced by the company.

Indians (NFL) 1926
  This team had been known as the Pros in 1925 and changed its name to Indians. Although the reason is unknown, many football teams of the era used names that reflected the American Indians (e.g., Indians, Braves, Chiefs).

Pros (APFA) 1920-1921
Pros (NFL) 1922-1925
  The Pros were officially the Akron Professional Football Club and the shortened form of professional was adopted by the fans and sports writers. The name also appeared on the team jersey.

ALBANY (NY)

Albany (ML-1) 1927/28
  The team was one of many of the early basketball teams that was known only by its town or city name.

ALBERTA (Ontario)

Oilers (WHA) 1972/73
  The Oilers started their first season in the WHA as the Alberta Oilers, a name they selected in a Name the Team contest. However, before the first season was over, the Edmonton-based team changed its name to the Edmonton Oilers. The Edmonton region is to Canadian oil as Houston is to American oil. Both Edmonton (Drillers) and nearby Calgary (Boomers) had teams in the NASL that reflected the booming growth of the oil industry in this region.

The Edmonton Oilers of the WHA retained their name when they joined the NHL for the 1979/80 season.

ALTOONA (PA)

Pride (UA) 1884
  A short-lived team in the Union Association that dropped out with a 6-19 record and was replaced by Kansas City. Some references were made to the team as Unions (a reference to the league) or Ottawas (an Indian tribe). The term Pride was occasionally used as an indication of civic pride for teams, and since this was Altoona's first entry into a major league, such may be the case here.

ANAHEIM (CA)

Amigos (ABA) 1967/68
  The Amigos got their name in a Name the Team contest. The name, which is Spanish for "friend," was suggested by Tom Voigt, an Anaheim resident. The Anaheim team moved to Los Angeles and became the Stars in 1968/69.

ANDERSON (IN)

Duffey Packers (NBL) 1946/47-1948/49
Packers (NBA) 1949/50
  This team was sponsored by Duffey's, Inc., a meat-packing plant in Anderson. The driving force behind the team was I. W. "Ike" Duffey, who was secretary-treasurer of the company and became president of the National Basketball League (NBL). He also served as first chairman of the Board of Governors of the National Basketball Association (NBA). At various times, the team was known as the Anderson Chiefs, because the company had been known as the Chief Anderson Meat Packers.
  When the Packers entered the NBA, they dropped the commercial name "Duffey" but were still supported by the company.

ARIZONA (AZ)

Outlaws (USFL) 1985
  The Arizona Outlaws of 1985 were a merger of the Arizona Wranglers (1984) and the Oklahoma Outlaws (1984). *See* Oklahoma Outlaws (USFL).

Wranglers (USFL) 1983

Wranglers is another term for cowboys, a name that had been used by Dallas and Kansas City in the NFL. The USFL needed a stronger team for the southwestern market and so the weak 1983 Arizona Wranglers became the 1984 Chicago Blitz and the more powerful 1983 Chicago Blitz became the 1984 Arizona Wranglers.

Wranglers (USFL) 1984

This team, the Chicago Blitz of 1983, merged with the Oklahoma Outlaws (1984) to become the Arizona Outlaws. *See* Oklahoma Outlaws (USFL).

ATLANTA (GA)

Apollos (NASL) 1973

Black Crackers (NAL) 1938

Atlanta's white minor-league team was called the Crackers. The black team adopted the name. Although the term can be used in a derogatory manner, its use by the baseball teams was to indicate a "native or resident of Georgia."

Braves (NL) 1966—

The Atlanta Braves retained the name of the original Boston franchise when the team moved to Atlanta by way of Milwaukee. *See* Boston Braves (NL).

Chiefs (NASL) 1968-1972

See Atlanta Chiefs (NASL) 1979-1980.

Chiefs (NASL) 1979-1980

The first Chiefs team was formed in 1967 and played in the National Professional Soccer League (NPSL), which merged with the United Soccer Association (USA) to form the NASL. Some of the backers of the Chiefs were owners of the Atlanta Braves, so the name was selected as a tie-in to the Atlanta Braves.

The second Chiefs team picked up the name of the earlier entry in the NASL.

Falcons (NFL) 1966—

A Name the Team contest was held to select the name for the Atlanta entry in the NFL. Rankin Smith, owner of the team, made the announcement in a prerecorded message during the pregame ceremonies at the Baltimore Colts-Pittsburgh Steelers exhibition game (8/28/65) in the new Atlanta Stadium.

The winning entry was submitted by a high school teacher, Julia Elliot, from Griffin, George. Ms. Elliot had picked the name because "the Falcon is proud and dignified, with great courage and fight."

Of the names submitted to the selection committee, Lancers and Thrashers tied for second place in the final vote.

Flames (NHL) 1972/73-1979/80

The announcement of the name for the Atlanta entry in the NHL was made on a hot day in June (6/2/72) by Bill Putnam, president of the new team. Of the 9,414 entries submitted in a Name the Team contest, 198 had picked the name Flames. The winner of the contest was a nineteen-year-old sophomore at DeKalb College. Thrashers, which had been popular in the contest to name to Atlanta Falcons (NFL), was also one of the favorites in the voting.

The team name refers to the burning of Atlanta during the Civil War.

Some of the names that were submitted were listed in the Atlanta *Constitution*. It's doubtful the committee gave much thought to such names as Albatross, Appalationeers, B-72s, Convention City Blue Blades, Diarrheas, Gandy Dancers, Ice Brown Thrashers, Icestronauts, Kudzus, Neanderthals, Pucker Pushers, Piranhas, Peachtree Bumpers, Yucca Pucks, or Y'alls.

Hawks (NBA) 1968/69—

See Buffalo Bisons (NBL) 1946/47.

ATLANTIC CITY (NJ)

Bacharach Giants (ECL) 1923-1928
Bacharach Giants (ANL) 1929
Bacharach Giants (NNL-2) 1934

The Atlantic City team was originally the Duval Giants of Jacksonville, Florida (Jacksonville is in Duval County). Some sources say that the team was brought north in 1916 by two black Atlantic City politicians, Tom Jackson and Henry Tucker, and named after the then-mayor, Henry Bacharach. Other sources indicate that it was Bacharach himself who was impressed with the team and invited them to play as the Atlantic City Bacharach Giants. The truth is probably part of both stories.

See also Cuban Giants.

Sand Snipers (ABL-2) 1936/37

This team played only the first half of the season, dropping out on 12/31/36. The name is confusing. A sandpiper is any of a number of shorebirds, and they are frequently found in the Atlantic City environs. However, this spelling is the one used (Sandsnipers or Sand Snipers). It is a variant spelling of Sandpiper and rarely used. It might be that it was an intentional play on words—a sniper—or that it was an early typographical error that just never got corrected.

Other Atlantic City basketball teams have been called Sandpipers.

BALTIMORE (MD)

Bays (NASL) 1968-1969

Named for the Chesapeake Bay.

Black Sox (ECL) 1923-1928
Black Sox (ANL) 1929
Black Sox (NNL-2) 1933-1934

The Black Sox were founded as an independent team in 1919 by Charles Spedden, a railroad man. There was no connection in the naming of the team with the Chicago "Black Sox" scandal because the problems of the 1919 White Sox did not come to light until the following year.

Blades (WHA) 1974/75

The Blades, an apt name for a hockey team, lasted less than one year. The team started out as the Michigan Stags and moved to Baltimore on 1/23/75.

Blast (MISL) 1980/81—

The Blast were the Houston Summit for two seasons before moving to Baltimore.

Bullets (ABL-2) 1944/45-1946/47
Bullets (BAA) 1947/48-1948/49
Bullets (NBA) 1949/50-1954/55

Announcement of the name for the Baltimore entry in the American Basketball League (ABL-2) was made a scant two weeks before the team played its opening game in the Baltimore Coliseum on 11/16/44. President Stan Behrend made the announcement and the Baltimore *Sun* article hoped the name would be "significant of their explosive talents and speed in humbling the opposition." The choice of the name Bullets may have been for their practice site, which was located near a WW II munitions facility. Some sources have indicated that it was because they played some games in the local armory.

This original Bullets team played in the BAA and NBA before disbanding on 11/27/54 with a 3-11 record for the 1954/55 season.

Bullets (NBA) 1963/64-1972/73

This team moved from Chicago, where they had been known first as the Packers and then as the Zephyrs. (Some early newspaper references were made to them as the Baltimore Zephyrs.) On 6/4/63, the team was renamed the Baltimore Bullets, taking the name of the previous NBA Baltimore entry.

See Capital Bullets (NBA) and Washington Bullets (NBA).

Clippers (ABL-2) 1939/40-1940/41

Named for the great Clipper ships that frequented the Baltimore harbor in the 1800s. The team was also called the Orioles.

Colts (AAFC) 1947-1949
Colts (NFL) 1950

Depending upon the source, there were 1,900 name entries (or 700) that produced 660 suggestions (or 296); however, the list was whittled down to 45 for the selection committee. The winning name of Colts was submitted by Charles Evans of Baltimore. He gave as his reason: "Colts are the youngest entry in the league [the AAFC was in its second year], Maryland is famous for its race-horses, and it is short, easily pronounced, and fits well in newspaper headlines." Although several others suggested Colts, all entries had been dated and timed as to their arrival and the earliest arrival won the contest. The announcement was made 2/7/47.

Colts (NFL) 1953-1983

When Baltimore got its second franchise, the popular name of the earlier team was adopted.

Comets (NASL) 1974-1975

Elites Giants (NNL-2) 1938-1948
Elites Giants (NAL) 1949-1950

See Nashville Elite Giants (NNL-1).

Orioles (AA) 1882-1889

See Baltimore Orioles (AL) 1954—

Orioles (AA) 1890-1891
See Baltimore Orioles (AL) 1954—

Orioles (NL) 1892-1899
See Baltimore Orioles (AL) 1954—

Orioles (AL) 1901-1902
See Baltimore Orioles (AL) 1954—

Orioles (AL) 1954—
Baltimore had a team called the Lord Baltimores in the NA from 1872 to 1874. The team had not done well, and when the city got a chance to get into the AA, a new name, Orioles, which honors the state bird of Maryland, was adopted. One source indicates that the name did not really catch on until the 1890s, although the team played in Oriole Park beginning in 1883. However, Orioles has become synonymous with Baltimore baseball, including its minor-league team in the International League, since that time.

Orioles (ABL-1) 1926/27
Baltimore's first entry in a professional basketball league adopted the name of the baseball team.

Stars (USFL) 1985
See Philadelphia Stars (USFL).

Terrapins (FL) 1914-1915
When Baltimore got a franchise for the Federal League, the nickname Orioles was already in use. (In fact, the Baltimore Orioles of the International League, a minor league, had a young southpaw named George Herman Ruth on its staff.) Perhaps the second most popular nickname in Maryland is Terrapins, and it was an obvious choice for the Baltimore FL team. The terrapin, any of a variety of edible turtles, was plentiful in the state. Terrapins is also the nickname of the University of Maryland athletic teams.

Unions (UA) 1884
This team took the name of the league, the Union Association. Teams in the UA were sometimes called Onions.

(BALTIMORE)

Lord Baltimores (NA) 1872-1874
Lord Baltimore was the title of six members of the Calvert family, the founders or proprietors of the colony of Maryland. In referring to the family, the plural Lords Baltimore identifies George, Cecillus, Charles, Benedict, Charles, and Frederick Calvert.

BIRMINGHAM (AL)

Americans (WFL) 1974
According to an article in the *Birmingham News* (2/18/74), "One of the best kept secrets surrounding the new franchise was un-earthed by the *News* this morning. The well-guarded name came to light quite accidentally. The *Washington Post* was the source."

Although the Birmingham club had not announced the name, it had selected the name Americans and also the colors of red, white, and blue. The Washington franchise had been running a Name the Team contest in which Americans was one of the most frequently submitted names. (The Washington team chose Ambassadors instead. *See* Florida Blazers [WFL] entry.) When the Washington club checked with the league office, they found out that the name had already been chosen by Birmingham. This information was reported in the *Washington Post* where it was read by a *Birmingham News* reporter.

Black Barons (NNL-1) 1924-1925
Black Barons (NNL-2) 1927-1930
Black Barons (NAL) 1937-1938
Black Barons (NAL) 1940-1950
Birmingham's white minor-league team was called the Barons. The black team adopted the name.

Bulls (WHA) 1976/77-1978/79
The *Birmingham News* reported on 5/23/76 that John Bassett was going to move his Toronto Toros to Birmingham. The article referred to the team as the Birmingham Bulls, although the announcement of the move was not made official until 6/30/76.

Toros, a shortened form of Toronto, is also the Spanish word for "bulls." Was the name given to the team by the *Birmingham News*?

Stallions (USFL) 1983-1984

Vulcans (WFL) 1975
If Birmingham had obtained an NFL franchise in 1974, it would have been called the Vulcans. Two local businessmen, Harold Black, Jr., and Frank Thomas, Jr., tried to get the NFL franchise but were unsuccessful. However, in the process they regis-

tered the names Alabama Vulcans and Birmingham Vulcans with the Alabama Secretary of State in July 1974.

When new owners took over the Birmingham Americans franchise, they wanted a different name to show that there was no connection with the 1974 WFL team. Fred Weil, president of the new team, made the announcement on 3/7/75 that the 1975 team would be called the Vulcans, and he thanked Black and Thomas for "having graciously donated their registered name to the new team as a civic gesture."

Coach Jack Gotta was quoted as saying, "The Birmingham Vulcans is everything we could have hoped for in a name for our new team. It personifies strength and civic pride."

Vulcan was the god of fire and metalworking in Roman mythology and an apt name for a Birmingham team. The city was settled because of the discovery of elements needed for steel production, and it is named after the steel-making center of Birmingham, England.

BOSTON (MA)

Beacons (NASL) 1968

An assumption can be made that the team name has a connection to the famous Beacon Hill section of Boston or to the term beacons for the lights in the old North Church that signaled the beginning of Paul Revere's ride.

Beaneaters (NL) 1883-1906

Boston is famous for its baked beans, so it was natural for the team to be called beaneaters.

Bears (AFL-3) 1940

The Bears were owned by Sheldon Fairbanks and played in Fenway Park. The origin of the team name is unknown.

Bees (NL) 1936-1940

When Bob Quinn took over the Boston Braves franchise, he held a contest for a new team name. The contest produced over 10,000 entries and 1,327 different names, including Pilgrims, Beacons, Puritans, Minute Men, and Bunker Hills. According to the *Sporting News* (2/6/36), the vote of the selection committee (made up of 26 sports writers) went as follows: Bees 14; Blue Birds, 4; Beacons, 3; Colonials, 2; and 1 each for Blues, Bulls, and Bulldogs. The

winning name had been sent in by 13 fans, including one from Chicago. The winner, drawn from a hat, was Arthur J. Rockwood of East Weymouth (MA), the father of nine children. He received two season tickets, and the others received two tickets for the opening game. The Chicago fan? He was sent two tickets for the first Boston-Chicago game at Wrigley Field in Chicago.

Braves (NFL) 1932

When George Preston Marshall was awarded a franchise for a Boston team, he named the team Braves because they would be playing in the same ballpark as the Boston Braves of the NL. (If the NL team had been named Bees, as they were in 1936, would Marshall have named them Bees?) The following year (1933), the team had to move to Fenway Park, home of the Boston Red Sox of the AL, so Marshall renamed the team Redskins, thus keeping the Indian motif.

Braves (NL) 1912-1935
Braves (NL) 1941-1952

In 1912, the Boston NL franchise had new owners and a new name. They were called Braves because James Gaffney, the owner, was directly connected to Tammany Hall, the New York City political machine, and its members were known as "braves." (Tammany was a distinguished Indian chief of the Leni-Lenape confederacy.)

Breakers (USFL) 1983

Bruins (NHL) 1924/25

Boston had the honor of being the first American city in the NHL. Charles F. Adams, a millionaire owner of a grocery store chain, was an avid hockey fan and believed that Boston could support a team. He was able to obtain a franchise, and he named his team Bruins.

Bulldogs (AFL-1) 1926

Bulldogs (NFL) 1929

The Pottsville Maroons franchise was transferred to Boston, and the team was renamed Bulldogs, a name that had more appeal than Maroons and one that had been used in Boston previously.

Celtics (BAA) 1946/47-1948/49
Celtics (NBA) 1949/50—

Although this team has no connection with the New York Original Celtics, the name was chosen by the owner, Walter Brown, because of its importance in basketball history and because Boston had a very large Irish population.

Doves (NL) 1907-1908

During the time that the Boston team was owned by the Dovey Brothers (George B. and John S. C.), the team was known as the Doves. George was president from 1906 until his death (6/19/09), and then John ran the team until it was bought by William Russell in December of 1910. During the 1909-1911 period, it was primarily known as the Pilgrims, although there are some references to the name Rustlers (for Russell) during 1911. Russell died a year after buying the team.

Minutemen (NASL) 1974-1976

An expansion franchise named for the Minutemen of the American Revolution.

Patriots (AFL-4) 1960-1969
Patriots (NFL) 1970

The name Patriots was chosen by a selection committee of Boston sports writers. Patriots' Day, in Massachusetts, is a state holiday in honor of the anniversary of Paul Revere's famous ride. The team retained the name when they became the New England Patriots of the NFL, in 1971.

Pilgrims (NL) 1909-1911

Pilgrims is a term applied to Massachusetts' teams in honor of the Pilgrims who first landed at Plymouth in 1620.

Puritans (AL) 1905-1906

The Boston AL team had several nicknames during the period between 1901-1907, including Pilgrims. The name Puritans perhaps had greater use just prior to their becoming known as the Red Sox. As with Pilgrims, Puritans reflects the Colonial period of Massachusetts. The Puritans were a Protestant religious group that settled in New England.

Redskins (NFL) 1933-1936

See Boston Braves (NFL).

Reds (PL) 1890
Reds (AA) 1891

The names used by teams in the Players League are not easy to identify. The Boston team probably wore red stockings and was attempting to use a name already identified with Boston teams. This was often the case with teams in an "outlaw" league.

When the Players League collapsed, the Boston team moved to the American Association.

Red Caps (NL) 1876-1882

There is some confusion as to the name of the Boston NL team during the period 1876-1882. The team was actually called the Red Stockings during the early part of this period. Red Stockings had been their name in the National Association (*see* entry). However, at some point, perhaps 1878 or 1879, they were being referred to as the Red Caps. The Cincinnati team was being called Reds, and it may be assumed that the sports writers and fans started to use Red Caps (in reference to the color of their caps) to avoid confusion between the teams.

Red Sox (AL) 1907—

In 1907, the Boston NL club stopped using red stockings. (Although they were not officially known as the Red Stockings, many fans still considered the NL club as owner of the name because of the color of the socks.) The president of the AL club, John Irving Taylor, then adopted the name Red Sox.

Red Stockings (NA) 1871-1875

The Boston Red Stockings got their name from the Cincinnati Red Stockings of 1869-1870, baseball's first professional team. The Cincinnati team won fifty-six straight games before losing. However, the team disbanded in the fall of 1870, and Boston was anxious to duplicate Cincinnati's domination of baseball. The new Boston team included four of the former Cincinnati Red Stockings, including Harry Wright, who became the Boston manager. He promptly adopted the Cincinnati-style uniform, especially the red stockings.

Shamrocks (AFL-2) 1936-1937

The owners selected a name that would appeal to Boston's large Irish population. The name brought luck in 1936, when the Shamrocks won the championship with an 8-3 record, but they fell to 2-5 the following year.

Somersets (AL) 1901-1904

The Boston AL team was owned by Charles W. Somers and thus the nickname.

Trojans (ABL-2) 1934/35

Unions (UA) 1884

This team took the name of the league, the Union Association. Teams in the UA were sometimes called Onions.

Whirlwinds (ABL-1) 1925/26

This team adopted the name of the New York Whirlwinds, a team that had been organized by Tex Rickard and was an outstanding barnstorming team.

Yanks (NFL) 1944-1948

The Boston Yanks were owned by Ted Collins, manager of singer Kate Smith. Collins had tried to get a franchise in New York and specifically in Yankee Stadium. When he got a Boston franchise, he decided to call the team Yanks anyway. Besides, Yanks is an appropriate name for a Boston team.

In 1949, Collins did get a New York franchise, but the rival AAFC had a New York Yankee team. Collins chose Bulldogs as the new name for the Yanks. He selected the name because of its rich gridiron associations.

In 1950, the AAFC was gone, and Collins got his wish of having a New York Yanks football team. The Yanks played two seasons (1950-1951) and then Collins sold his franchise back to the NFL. The franchise was sold to Dallas and became the Texans.

BRIDGETON (NJ)

Bridgeton (EL) 1931/32-1932/33

This team was one of many of the early basketball teams that was known only by its city or town name.

BRONX (NY)

Americans (ABL-2) 1933/34

This team was also known as the St. Martin's. *See* Brooklyn Americans (ML-2) and Bronx Braves (ML-2).

Braves (ML-2) 1932/33

The Braves played only eleven games (5-6) and were sometimes called the Bronx St. Martin's. They were sponsored by the St. Martin of Tours Council 449 of the Knights of Columbus. *See* Brooklyn Americans (ML-2).

Yankees (ABL-2) 1937/38

This team started the season as the Bronx Yankees, a name they adopted from the AL baseball team that played in the Bronx. However, the baseball team is better known as the New York Yankees, so the club decided to change their name from Bronx to New York.

The change was made about halfway through the first half of the season. The team completed the first half as the New York Yankees and then disbanded on 1/11/38.

BROOKLYN (NY)

Americans (NHL) 1941/42

See New York Americans (NHL).

Americans (ML-2) 1932/33 (first half)
Americans (ML-2) 1932/33 (second half)

This is a team that moved around.

They began the 1932/33 season as the Brooklyn Americans (1-10) and then became the Brooklyn Hill House (2-2) for the balance of the first half.

In the second half of the 1932/33 season, they began (again) as the Brooklyn Americans (2-7) before finishing the season as the Bronx Braves (5-6).

The next season (1933/34) they moved to the ABL-2 and played the entire season as the Bronx Americans.

Arcadians (ABL-1) 1925/26-1926/27

This team took its name from the hall (Arcadia) in which it played its home games. In its first season, the team was owned by Harry Heilmann, the Detroit Tigers (AL) batting star and Hall of Fame member.

Atlantics (NA) 1872-1875

The Atlantic Club was first organized in 1856 and was one of the strongest amateur teams in the period before the National Association. It was the Atlantics who ended the winning streak of the Cincinnati Red Stockings at fifty-six games in 1870. The Atlantics home field was on Atlantic Avenue in Brooklyn.

Bridegrooms (AA) 1889
Bridegrooms (NL) 1890-1898

Because the Brooklyn team had so many newly-weds on the club in 1889, they were called the Bridegrooms. (Some sources put the number at four.) However, several other names were used during this period, most associated with the current manager. Thus, they were called Ward's Wonders, for John Ward; Foutz's Fillies, for Dave Foutz; and Barnie's Boys, for Billy Barnie.

The name Trolley Dodgers is also associated with the team during this period. *See* Brooklyn Dodgers (NL).

BrookFeds (FL) 1915

Several of the teams in the short-lived Federal League had nicknames that combined the city (Brook) and the league (Feds).

Brooklyns (AA) 1884-1888

Some sources have indicated that the team was also called Church City Nine (Brooklyn was called the City of Churches) or the Atlantics. There is also a case made that they received the name Trolley Dodgers in the AA.

See Brooklyn Dodgers (NL).

Celtics (ABL-1) 1926/27
Celtics (ABL-2) 1940/41

The Celtics team name can be traced back to the New York Celtics (1914/15-1916/17) and the Original Celtics, which appeared in late 1918, after the end of World War I. However, there were several New York, Brooklyn, and Troy teams that used the name Celtics, including singer Kate Smith's Original Celtics. As far as league competition is concerned, the Brooklyn Celtics of 1926/27 comes closest to the Originals.

The first Celtics team was organized by Frank Mc-Cormack in 1914 as a settlement house team in the predominantly Irish Westside of New York. Thus, the name Celtics.

The term Original Celtics was devised by Jim and Tom Furey. The New York Celtics had disbanded when the United States entered World War I. The Fureys wanted to reorganize them as the New York Celtics but could not get permission from Frank McCormack to use the name. Therefore, the Fureys called the new team the Original Celtics.

As one of the best barnstorming teams in the early 1920s, the Original Celtics team became known as the Celtics to most fans and sports writers. In 1922/23, they played briefly in the Metropolitan League (ML-1) and in the original Eastern League, but it was not until the 1926/27 season that they entered a pro league for a stay of more than a few games.

Dodgers (AAFC) 1946-1948

This team played in Ebbets Field and was owned by Branch Rickey, owner of the Brooklyn Dodgers (NL) baseball team. Rickey named the football team after his baseball team.

Dodgers (ML-1) 1921/22-1922/23

This basketball team adopted the name of the NL baseball team.

Dodgers (NFL) 1930-1943

This team played in Ebbets Field and adopted the name of the baseball Brooklyn Dodgers. In 1944, the team changed its name to Tigers for one year; then in 1945 the team merged with the Boston Yanks.

Dodgers (NL) 1932-1957

The Dodgers trace their origin to 1883, when they were organized by Charles H. Byrne and played in the Interstate League. The team won the league championship and in 1884 joined the American Association (*see* Brooklyns). Some sources claim that the team became known as the Trolley Dodgers in their days in the AA, but the term was most frequently used to describe not just the fans but anyone who lived in Brooklyn. Because the city was a web of trolley lines that crisscrossed one another, Brooklynites seemed to be forever dodging trolleys. The Brooklyn NL team had many nicknames before officially becoming the Dodgers in 1932. In 1933, the word Dodgers made its first appearance on the team uniform.

However, even as late as 1936 some Dodger fans wanted a new nickname. In a letter to the editor of the *New York Times* (11/28/36), one fan suggested a return to Robins, and another suggested that the team be called the Burleighcues for its new manager, Burleigh Grimes.

The *Times* editor responded that "out of respect for the President of the club, Steve McKeever, it has been suggested that the new name of the team be Stevedores."

Eagles (NNL-2) 1935

The Eagles were owned by Abe Manley, but it was his wife, Effa, who pretty much ran the business of the team. The Eagles started in Brooklyn, playing in Ebbets Field, but the next year (1936) they moved to Newark. The origin of the team name is unknown.

Eckfords (NA) 1871-1872

The Eckfords were formed in 1856, one of two clubs for the "working man," the other being the Atlantics. The team was formed by shipwrights and mechanics, who named the club after Henry Eckford, a Brooklyn shipbuilder.

In some early sources there are references to two clubs: Eckford of Brooklyn and Henry Eckford of New York.

The Eckfords replaced the Fort Wayne Kekiongas in August of 1871, when the Fort Wayne team folded. In a post-season convention, the NA struck the Eckford games from the record books on the basis of their late entry into the league. Ironically, the Eckfords had been at the organizing meeting of the National Association but had decided not to enter because they thought the organization too shaky and did not want to risk the ten-dollar admission fee.

If one sports writer had had his way, the Eckfords would have been known as the Yellow Stockings, as the following 1871 news item from the *New York Clipper* shows.

> The new nine of the Eckford club of Brooklyn put in an appearance in a regular match game for the first time in 1871, on Monday April 17th on the Union Grounds, Brooklyn, on which occasion they had the Black Stockings nine of the Tony Pastor club as their opponents. The Eckfords appeared in their new uniform of white flannel shirts and knee breeches and yellow belts and stockings, and henceforth this season they will be known as the "Yellow Stockings" of Brooklyn.

Gladiators (AA) 1890

This team was the Ridgewood Club of Brooklyn and was sometimes called the Ridgewoods. The team played at Ridgewood Park, on the Brooklyn-Queens border, and Ridgewood is actually a section of Queens that abuts the Bushwick section of Brooklyn. The origin of the team name is unknown.

On August 3, 1890, the Gladiators became the Baltimore Orioles (AA) 1890-1891 and then the Baltimore Orioles (NL) 1892-1899.

Hill House (ML-2) 1932/33

This team plaued only four games (2-2) in the first half of the season. *See* Brooklyn Americans (ML-2). The name is associated with the facility in which the team played its home games.

Horsemen (AFL-1) 1926

Harry Stuhldreher and Elmer Layden, two of the famous Four Horsemen of Notre Dame, played for the team. Grantland Rice, the sports writer, gave the Notre Dame backfield the nickname when he covered the Army-Notre Dame game of 1924. His oft-quoted report stated:

> Outlined against the blue-gray October sky, the Four Horsemen rode again. In dramatic lore they were known as famine, pestilence, destruction, and death. These are only aliases. Their real names are Stuhldreher, Miller, Crowley, and Layden.

Indians (ABL-2) 1942/43

See Camden Indians (ABL-2).

Indians (ABL-2) 1943/44

This team was a different franchise from the Indians of 1942/43. The team adopted the name of the previous team when the 1942/43 team moved back to Wilmington as the Blue Bombers.

Infants (NL) 1911-1913

The short-lived Infants name was applied to the Brooklyn NL team because Charles Ebbets, president of the club, had stated that baseball was "in its infancy."

Jewels (ML-2) 1931/32-1932/33
Jewels (ABL-2) 1933/34
Jewels (ABL-2) 1936/37

The Jewels were composed of players who had been members of the famous St. John's University "Wonder Five." As a college team they had an 86-8 record (with four of those losses coming in their freshman year). They stayed together and played first as a touring team and then as a league team. The origin of the nickname is unknown. In 1931/32, they sometimes played as the Bronxville Jewels and in

1932/33 they were sometimes known as the Flushing Jewels. Flushing is in the borough of Queens and Bronxville is in Westchester County.

Jewish Center (ML-2) 1931/32

The team was named for the facility in which they played their home games.

Lions (NFL) 1926

Brooklyn received an NFL franchise on 7/10/26. The origin of the team name is unknown. After the team posted a 3-8 record, the franchise was transferred to C. C. Pyle's New York Yankees (AFL-1) and became the New York Yankees (NFL) for two years (1927-1928).

Pros (ML-1) 1921/22-1922/23

Their full name was the Prospect Big Five. Pros is a shortened form of both Prospect and professional. Prospect is a section (Prospect Park) of Brooklyn.

Robins (NL) 1914-1931

Next to Dodgers, Robins was probably the most popular of the many nicknames that the Brooklyn NL team had. The name was in honor of Wilbert Robinson, manager of the team and then president of the club. Some newspaper sources in the 1920s use all three nicknames (Robins, Superbas, and Dodgers) in the same article.

See Brooklyn Superbas (NL) and Brooklyn Dodgers (NL).

Royal Giants (ECL) 1923-1927

The Royal Giants were sponsored by the Royal Cafe in Brooklyn. *See* Cuban Giants.

Superbas (NL) 1899-1910

The owner and manager of the Brooklyn NL team in 1899 was Ned Hanlon. At the same time, there was a very popular acrobatic show known as the Hanlon Brothers' "Superbas." Brooklyn fans adopted the name.

Tigers (AFL-2) 1936

This team moved to Rochester on 11/13/36 when the Rochester Braves folded and played as the Rochester Braves for the balance of 1936 and all of 1937. Origin of the name Tigers for the Brooklyn team is unknown.

Tigers (NFL) 1944

This team was the Brooklyn Dodgers (NFL) 1930-1943. The name was changed for one year (1944). Reason for the change is unknown. The Tigers merged with the Boston Yanks on 4/10/45.

Tip Tops (FL) 1914

This team was owned by the Ward Brothers, owners of the Ward Baking Company and makers of Tip Top bread.

Visitations (ML-1) 1921/22-1927/28
Visitations (ABL-1) 1927/28-1930/31
Visitations (ML-2) 1931/32-1932/33
Visitations (ABL-2) 1933/34-1938/39

The Brooklyn Visitations took their name from the church in which they were organized. However, especially in their earlier years, they were known as the Visitation Triangles.

Why Triangles?

The most plausible reason seems to be as follows. The Visitation Church was one of three churches located in South Brooklyn that used the name Triangles. The other churches are the Assumption Church (ML-1) and St. James Church.

The churches were close together geographically (even though Assumption was considered to be in West Brooklyn), and they formed a triangle. They worked together on many parish-level projects and were referred to as the Triangles.

The Visitation Triangles played from 1918 until the late 1930s. The names are interchangeable: Visitations, Visitation Triangles, or Triangles. Most old-timers, especially those who played on the teams or lived in South Brooklyn, made references to the Triangles.

To those outside Brooklyn, it's the Brooklyn Visitations. The Visitation uniform shown in early photographs clearly shows the triangle on the jersey.

Both of the other two churches, especially Assumption, had very good local teams, but not in the same class as the Visitations.

Wonders (PL) 1890

John Ward owned the team and named it after his Wonder Bread Company. *See also* Brooklyn Tip Tops (FL).

(BROOKLYN) GREENPOINT

Knights (ML-1) 1921/22-1926/27

The Knights of Columbus at St. Anthony's Church sponsored the team. They were known as the Knights of St. Anthony's.

(BROOKLYN) WEST BROOKLYN

Assumption Triangles (ML-1) 1926/27

The team was sponsored by the Assumption Roman Catholic Church. For information about Triangles. *See* Brooklyn Visitations (ML-1).

BUFFALO (NY)

All-Americans (APFA) 1920-1921
All-Americans (NFL) 1922-1923

The Buffalo team began with six players from Walter Camp's All-American selections and thus received their nickname.

Bills (AAFC) 1947-1949

The Buffalo AAFC team played its first season (1946) as the Bisons, an often-used name for Buffalo teams. The club held a contest to come up with a different name, and the name Bills, because of its connection with Buffalo Bill (William F. Cody), was the winning entry, submitted by Jimmy Dyson.

Bills (AFL-4) 1960-1969
Bills (NFL) 1970—

When Buffalo got its AFL franchise, the fans expressed a strong preference for the name that had been used by the AAFC team. Owner Ralph Wilson decided that happy fans are the best, so he adopted the nickname of the former team.

Bisons (AAFC) 1946

Bisons has often been used as a nickname for Buffalo teams. Although bison and buffalo are used almost interchangeably, there is a difference. The American buffalo is actually a bison. True buffaloes are found only in Asia and Africa. (Thus, Buffalo Bill was actually Bison Bill!)

The Buffalo AAFC team kept the nickname for one year before becoming the Buffalo Bills (AAFC).

Bisons (MBC) 1935/36

See Buffalo Bisons (AAFC).

Bisons (NBL) 1937/38

This team played nine games (3-6) before dropping out of the league. *See* Buffalo Bisons (AAFC).

Bisons (NBL) 1946/47

The Atlanta Hawks of the NBA began as a team sponsored by the Erie County American Legion in the National Basketball League (NBL). As was usual for the legion, when it sponsored a professional team, it formed a separate local organization; in this case, Buffalo Legion Basketball, Inc., with Raymond Ast as chairman and Leo Ferris as general manager. The team played in Memorial Auditorium and was 4-8 when it moved to the tri-cities of Moline and Rock Island, Illinois, and Davenport, Iowa, on 12/27/46. The three towns are adjacent to one another on the Mississippi River.

See Tri-Cities Blackhawks (NBL).

Bisons (NFL) 1924-1925
Bisons (NFL) 1927
Bisons (NFL)1929

In 1924, the Buffalo All-Americans (NFL) changed their name to Bisons, since the name was more appropriate for a Buffalo team and since they no longer had the "All-American" image of the 1920 APFA team. The team forfeited its franchise on 7/12/30.

Bisons (NL) 1879-1885

The Buffalo NL team adopted the name associated with the town. Other teams had used the name even earlier.

See Buffalo Bisons (AAFC).

Bisons (PL) 1890

The team adopted the name used by other Buffalo teams.

See Buffalo Bisons (AAFC).

Blues (FL) 1915

The Buffalo team in the Federal League had been called the BufFeds in 1914 and changed it to Blues for 1915. The reason for the selection of Blues is unknown, but anything was better than BufFeds. Other nicknames used in 1915 included Electrics and that old favorite, Bisons.

Braves (NBA) 1970/71-1977/78

More than 14,000 fans submitted names in a contest to give the Buffalo team a nickname. On

4/28/70, the announcement was made that the team would be called the Braves. The winning entry was submitted by David Lajewski of Dunkirk (NY), who received the first prize of two season tickets for his suggestion.

In 1978, the Buffalo team moved to San Diego, where it was renamed the Clippers. However, the then owner of the team, John Y. Brown, had first tried to relocate his team in Dallas and had named them the Dallas Express in anticipation of the move.

BufFeds (FL) 1914
Several of the teams in the short-lived Federal League had nicknames that combined the city (Buf) and the league (Feds). In 1915, the BufFeds became the Blues.

Germans (ABL-1) 1925/26
The original Buffalo Germans were organized in 1895, just three years after the first basketball game (1892) was played between two different organizations. The Buffalo team was a group of fourteen- and fifteen-year-olds who played at a YMCA on the east side of Buffalo, a neighborhood with a predominantly German population. The team, led by Al Heerdt and Eddie Miller, played together for over two decades and compiled a 792-86 record. At one point they amassed 111 straight wins.

Indians (AFL-3) 1940
The Buffalo team had a 2-8 record in 1940 and changed their name to Tigers for 1941. Neither name helped; their 1941 record was 2-6.

Rangers (NFL) 1926
The Buffalo franchise that started in the APFA as the All-Americans, in 1920, changed its name to Bisons in 1924 and then to Rangers in 1926. This name lasted only one year, and the Buffalo team went back to being called Bisons. The reason for the selection of Rangers as a nickname is unknown.

Sabres (NHL) 1970/71—
Out of more than 13,000 entries received in a Name the Team contest for Buffalo's entry into the NHL, only four suggested the name Sabres. Perhaps that is one reason it was selected. Club officials had set as one of their guidelines that the new name should not be Bisons or some variation on buffaloes. In selecting Sabres, they achieved that goal with a short

name for headlines and a unique one for professional sports teams.

The club announcement stated, "A sabre is reknowned as a clean, sharp, decisive, and penetrating weapon of offense, as well as a strong parrying weapon on defense." A very approriate name for a hockey team.

A drawing was held among the four who submitted the name, and the winner was Robert Sonnelitter, who received a pair of season tickets.

Stallions (MISL) 1979/80-1983/84

Tigers (AFL-3) 1941
See Buffalo Indians (AFL-3).

CALGARY (Alberta)

Boomers (NASL) 1981
Calgary was a "boom" town in the 1970s and early 1980s as a result of the oil industry that sprang up in the area. *See* Alberta Oilers (WHA).

Flames (NHL) 1980/81—
When the team moved from Atlanta to Calgary, it kept its nickname of Flames. *See* Atlanta Flames (NHL).

Stampeders (WHA) 1975/76-1976/77
Calgary is famous for its annual rodeo, the Calgary Stampede, and for its cattle industry, very much similiar to cities in the American West, and the team name is a reflection of this history. The team was also called Cowboys.

CALIFORNIA

See also Southern California, Golden Bay, Golden State.

Angels (AL) 1966—
When the Los Angeles Angels moved to Anaheim, they changed their name to California Angels. *See* Los Angeles Angels (AL).

Golden Seals (NHL) 1970/71-1975/76
See California Seals (NHL).

Seals (NHL) 1967/68
The Seals took their name from the San Francisco Seals of the Western Hockey League. The team had

been purchased by a syndicate headed by Barry van Gerbig, and as soon as they obtained an NHL franchise, the team was relocated across the bay in Oakland. In order to appeal to a larger community, the team name was changed to California Seals. It didn't work, and midway through the 1967/68 season the name was changed to Oakland Seals. Prior to the 1970/71 season, the team name was briefly changed to Bay Area Seals, the back to Oakland Seals, and finally, on 10/15/70, to California Golden Seals.

Surf (NASL) 1978-1981

When the St. Louis Stars moved to California, they could have retained their name, and it would have seemed quite logical. However, the team opted for a new name and chose the very appropriate nickname of Surf. The team was located in Anaheim.

CAMDEN (NJ)

Brewers (ABL-2) 1933/34

This team was briefly sponsored by a brewery, but it was also called Athletics. *See* North Hudson Thourots (ABL-2).

Camden (EL) 1931/32

This team was one of the many early basketball teams that was known only by its town or city name.

Indians (ABL-2) 1942/43

These Indians fell victim to World War II. Because of gas rationing, the franchise was moved on 1/18/43 to Brooklyn. It was felt that the Brooklyn facilities were accessible by mass transit and therefore could draw larger crowds.

CANTON (OH)

Bulldogs (APFA) 1920-1921
Bulldogs (NFL) 1922-1923

The Canton Bulldogs trace their origins back to the Canton Athletic Club of 1905. In 1906, the Bulldogs and the Massillon Tigers were fierce competitors and probably the two best pro teams. Because of a betting scandal that developed when the two teams played that year, Canton discontinued its professional competition. The only teams in Canton were semiprofessional, until 1912, when a new team was organized. It was first called the Canton Professionals because of concern about the memories of the 1906 scandal.

However, in 1913, the name Bulldogs was reintroduced, and it stuck. In 1924, the Bulldogs moved to Cleveland.

Bulldogs (NFL) 1925-1926

This team adopted the name of the previous team, but it was a different franchise. The 1923 Canton franchise had been purchased by the owner of the Cleveland franchise, Sam Deutsch. He then sold the franchise back to the Canton Professional Football Company (but kept the players).

CAPITAL (Washington, DC)

Bullets (NBA) 1973/74

The selection of Bullets is obvious, but the selection of Capital is not as obvious.

The Baltimore Bullets moved to Washington and were renamed the Capital Bullets in April 1973. They moved into their new stadium, the Capital Centre, in Landover, MD, on 12/2/73. The team was called Capital Bullets because of the Capital Centre and because Washington is the nation's capital. On 4/20/74 the team was renamed the Washington Bullets.

However, earlier in the year (1/22/74), the Bullets' owner, Abe Pollin, had selected the name Washington Capitals for his new NHL franchise. Although he was criticized for this choice, Pollin had at least used proper selection of Capital (not Capitol) for the team name. (*Capital* refers to the city; *capitol* refers to the building.)

For a more detailed account of the Capitol/Capital conflict, *see* Washington Capitals (NHL). For Bullet information, *see* Baltimore Bullets (ABL-2) and Baltimore Bullets (NBA) 1963/64-1972/73.

CAROLINA (NC)

Cougars (ABA) 1969/70

When the Houston Mavericks were purchased by Southern Sports, Inc., and moved to North Carolina, Don DeJardin was named general manager. One of his first tasks was to select a new name for the team, and he selected Cougars as the nickname. The Cougars played in Charlotte, Raleigh, and Greensboro.

CATSKILL (NY)

Catskill (ML-1) 1927/28

This team was one of the many early basketball teams that were known only by its town or city name.

CHARLOTTE (NC)

Hornets (NBA) 1988/89

If the name is Hornets, we must be in Charlotte.

The city is proud of its history and the fact that British General Charles Cornwallis was stopped in Charlotte as he tried to push through the Carolinas. In a letter, he is quoted as saying, "There's a rebel behind every bush. It's a veritable nest of hornets."

Hornets became synonymous with Charlotte teams. The Charlotte Hornets were a minor-league baseball team for many years and also the name of the WFL team. If Charlotte had gotten its entry in the USFL, it would probably have been Hornets.

However, the first choice of a name for the NBA team was Spirit, a name selected by a committee from a pool of suggested names. The fans rebelled, and owner George Shinn enlisted the *Charlotte Observer* to help in a second Name the Team contest. The vote was a landslide for Hornets.

Hornets (WFL) 1974-1975

See Charlotte Hornets (NBA).

CHICAGO (IL)

American Gears (NBL) 1944/45-1946/47

This team was owned by Maurice White and sponsored by his American Gear Company. White organized the Professional Basketball League of America (PBLA) for the 1947/48 season. The league included White's team and fifteen other franchises: Grand Rapids Rangers, Kansas City Blues, Louisville Colonels, Omaha Tomahawks, St. Louis Outlaws, St. Paul Saints, Waterloo Pro-Hawks, Atlanta Crackers, Birmingham Skyhawks, Chattanooga Majors, Houston Mavericks, New Orleans Hurricanes, Oklahoma City Drillers, Springfield (MO) Squires, and the Tulsa Ranchers. The league disbanded on 11/13/47.

American Giants (NNL-1) 1920-1931
American Giants (NNL-2) 1937-1950

Rube Foster, a great player and manager in the black leagues, organized the American Giants in 1911. The team was often referred to as Rube Foster's Giants. Foster was also the founder and president of the Negro National League (NNL-1), until his death in 1926.

See (Chicago) Cole's American Giants (NSL-2).

Bears (NFL) 1922—

When George Halas brought the Decatur Staleys to Chicago in 1921, he kept the name Staleys for one year, as he had promised A. E. Staley. During that year (1921), the Staleys played in Wrigley Field. According to *Halas by Halas*, the Papa Bear considered calling the team the Chicago Cubs, out of respect for William Wrigley and William Veeck, Sr., "But I noted football players are bigger than baseball players; so if baseball players are cubs, then certainly football players must be bears!"

It should also be noted that George Halas was a lifelong Chicago Cub fan.

In addition to changing the name of the Staleys to the Bears for the 1922 season, Halas also suggested the change of the league name from American Professional Football Association (APFA) to National Football League (NFL).

See Decatur Staleys (APFA) and Chicago Bruins (ABL-1 and NBL).

Black Hawks (NHL) 1926/27—

The official name of the Chicago NHL team is Black Hawks, but it will be frequently shown as Blackhawks or Hawks. The team was named by its first owner, Major Frederic Mclaughlin, who had led a unit of the 85th (Black Hawk) Division in World War I. The division was named after the great Indian orator and chief, Black Hawk, who led the Sauks during the Black Hawk War of 1832.

Blitz (USFL) 1983

According to club officials, they received 3,351 suggestions and over 20,000 entries in a Name the Team contest. George Allen, coach and part owner, made the announcement of the winning name on 7/23/83. According to the *Chicago Tribune*, Allen stated,

> Blitz is my kind of name. I wanted a short, aggressive, attacking, physical name. The

definition of "blitz" refers to ground attack and air attack. My definition is to hit the enemy with everything you have. A team effort—offense, defense, special teams, coaches, staff, and fans.

The contest winner was Mike Wehrli, of Oak Park (IL), who had the earliest postmark of the entries suggesting Blitz. Wehrli received four season tickets. In 1984, the Blitz and the Arizona Wranglers traded franchises. *See* Arizona Wranglers (USFL) 1984.

Blitz (USFL) 1984
See Arizona Wranglers (USFL) 1983.

Bruins (ABL-1) 1925/26-1930/31
When George Preston Marshall founded the American Basketball League in 1925, George Halas, owner of the Chicago Bears, sponsored a team in the league. Halas asked that Joe Carr, who was then president of the NFL, serve as president of the ABL, and he did.

Halas called his team the Bruins, a variation on the name Bears (NFL), which he had named for the Chicago Cubs (NL).

Bruins (NBL) 1939/40-1941/42
This team was also owned by George Halas, and he adopted the name he had used for his entry in the ABL-1.

Bulls (AFL-1) 1926
The name may have been selected because of the livestock and meat-packing industry of the city.

Bulls (NBA) 1966/67—
The Chicago Bulls moved into town before anyone knew they were there! When the NBA announced that a group headed by Dick Klein had been awarded a franchise, Klein sent telegrams to the media, announcing that he would hold a press conference the next day (1/27/66) to divulge full details of the new team and its ownership. The telegram was signed "the Chicago Bulls." One sports writer, noting Chicago's problems in getting a professional basketball team to survive, suggested that Chicago Optimists might be more appropriate. However, Klein, who had been a college player at nearby Northwestern University and had a brief stint with the Chicago American Gears (NBL) believed Chicago was ready to support a good team.

Cardinals (APFA) 1921
Cardinals (NFL) 1922-1943
Cardinals (NFL) 1945-1959
See (Chicago) Racine Cardinals (APFA).

ChiFeds (FL) 1914
Several of the teams in the short-lived Federal League had nicknames that combined the city (Chi) and the league (Feds). In 1915, the ChiFeds became the Whales.

Colts (NL) 1894-1897
After winning the pennant in 1886, the Chicago (NL) team sold or traded a number of veteran players. Because these "old horses" were gone, the team began to have more younger players, and sports writers started to refer to the team as Colts. In addition, two other events accelerated the change from White Stockings to Colts.

In 1888, the team had a new uniform and no longer wore white stockings. Now the stockings were black. (According to Arthur Ahrens, who has documented the entire spectrum of nicknames for the team, they were the Black Stockings in 1888 and 1889.)

In 1895, the Chicago manager, Adrian "Cap" Anson, appeared in a play entitled *The Runaway Colt*. The play had been written for Anson by Charles Hoyt.

Cougars (WHA) 1972/73-1974/75

Cubs (NL) 1900—
During the time the Chicago NL team was being referred to as Colts and then Orphans, a third name was gaining in popularity. In the newspaper field, a neophyte reporter is often called a cub. Thus, the references to Cubs grew out of the same tradition as the references to the Colts. Sports writers, and then the fans, began to use the name. In 1898 a contest was held by a local newspaper. Cubs was the overwhelming choice, and in 1900 it was made the official name of the team.

Duffy Florals (MBC) 1935/36-1936/37
The team was sponsored by Duffy Florists and was sometimes called the Florals.

Fire (WFL) 1974
When Tom Origer obtained his franchise for a WFL team, he was quoted as saying, "I always wanted to

own a football team, but I'll run it like a business. It's football and it's Chicago. I may call 'em the Bootleggers. I'll think of a catchy name."

Origer named them the Fire. However, the team didn't catch fire and disbanded before the end of the season, with a record of 7-12.

The name, of course, is a reference to Chicago's Great Fire of 1871.

Giants (NNL-1) 1920-1921
The Chicago Giants were formed in the early 1900s (perhaps 1905-1906) and were owned by Joe Green when they joined the NNL-1. *See* Cuban Giants.

Horizon (MISL) 1980/81

Hornets (AAFC) 1949
The Chicago franchise of the AAFC changed its name from Rockets to Hornets in hopes of shaking its losing image. They did have their best record (4-8), but the AAFC folded at the end of the year.

Majors (ABL-3) 1961/62-1962/63
When Abe Saperstein, owner of the Harlem Globetrotters, was rejected in his attempt to get an NBA franchise, he decided to start his own league, the American Basketball League (ABL-3). Saperstein sponsored one of the teams (the Majors) in the league.

Mustangs (NASL) 1968
The name was selected to represent a "spirited" team. One of the owners was John Allyn, of the Chicago White Sox, and the team had played the previous year (1967) in the United Soccer Association (USA).

Orphans (NL) 1898-1899
The Chicago NL team was known as Orphans when Adrian "Cap" Anson was no longer the manager.
See Chicago Colts (NL) and Chicago Cubs (NL).

Packers (NBA) 1961/62
According to the announcement (5/15/61) made by President David Trager, the club had received hundreds of suggestions for a name. The club chose Packers (which may or may not have been one of the suggestions). The name was appropriate, since the new NBA team was scheduled to play the majority of its home games at the Amphitheater in the stockyards, location of many meat-packing companies. Trager was an insurance executive and not the owner of a packing company, as some sources have indicated.

In 1962/63, this team became the Chicago Zephyrs before moving to Baltimore for the 1963/64 season.

Pirates (PL) 1890
Although Chicago had no known nickname in the short-lived Players League, some references were made to them as Pirates. The references could have been applied because the team "pirated" players away from the NL, but that could be said of any of the PL teams.

Rockets (AAFC) 1946-1948
The Chicago franchise chose a nickname that had only recently come into common usage. The German V-2 rockets in World War II, just ended, had been used against Great Britain with great success. To the fans, the Rockets were supposed to represent something new and deadly.
See Chicago Hornets (AAFC).

Stags (BAA) 1946/47-1948/49
Stags (NBA) 1949/50
The Stags was the only team in the new BAA that was not owned by someone who owned an arena. This team was owned by a lawyer, Arthur Morse, and the club president was Judge John Sbarbaro. (Many of the early references to the BAA were to the Arena League.) Judge Sbarbaro announced the team name on 10/17/46, along with the team colors of red, white, and blue.

Staleys (APFA) 1921
See Decatur Staleys (APFA) 1920.

Sting (NASL) 1975-1984
Sting (MISL) 1982/83
Sting (MISL) 1984/85-1987/88
Some references have indicated that the team was named for the movie *The Sting,* which was set in Chicago and starred Paul Newman.

Because the NASL played a summer schedule and the MISL played a winter-spring (indoor) schedule, the Sting were able to play in two leagues in the same year.

Studebakers (NBL) 1942/43

When George Halas decided to fold his Chicago Bruins, after the 1941/42 season, the NBL was able to keep a franchise in Chicago by getting the United Auto Workers at the local Studebaker plant to sponsor a team. Because the plant had been converted to war production, players who worked at the plant were exempt from the draft.

Tigers (APFA) 1920

The Tigers had been a very strong independent team in Chicago in the pre-APFA era; however, the team disbanded at the end of the 1920 season.

Unions (UA) 1884

This team took the name of the league, the Union Association. Teams in the UA were sometimes called Onions.

Whales (FL) 1915

During the 1914 season, the Chicago franchise of the Federal League was called the ChiFeds, a nickname that seemed bland for a team trying to compete for attention in a city with the Cubs and White Sox. A contest was held to select a new name, and a Chicago resident, D. J. Eichoff, was the winner. He said the name Whales appealed to him because the best commercial whales were found in the North, and the ChiFeds played on the North Side of Chicago. Also, *to whale* meant to lash, thrash, or drub, and a whale is anything extraordinary, particularly in size.

After finishing second in 1914 as the ChiFeds, the newly named Whales won the 1915 pennant from the St. Louis Terriers by .001. Although the Federal League and the Whales were gone at the end of the 1915 season, the ballpark that was built for the Whales by owner Charles Weeghman became the home of the Cubs in 1916 and was later renamed Wrigley Field.

White Sox (AL) 1901—

The franchise that became the Chicago AL team began in the Western League that had been organized by Ban Johnson. Johnson was to become president of the American League. In 1894, the Sioux City Huskers won the league championship but were last in attendance. Charles Comiskey was persuaded by Johnson to buy the team, and Comiskey moved them to St. Paul, where they became the Saints.

In 1900, the Saints moved to Chicago, where Comiskey adopted the familiar nickname that had long been associated with the Chicago NL teams. (*See* Chicago Cubs.) Also, in 1900, the Western League became the American League, but it was considered a minor league until the following year.

Two theories exist as to how the name White Stockings was shortened to White Sox. One is that the Chicago NL team raised legal questions about the use of the name; the other, more likely, is that sports writers Carl Green and Irving "Cy" Sanborn of the *Chicago Tribune* shortened it for headlines.

White Stockings (NA) 1871
White Stockings (NA) 1874-1875
White Stockings (NL) 1876-1893

Originally organized in 1870, the White Stockings took their name, as did many early baseball teams, from the color of their stockings.

See Chicago Cubs (NL) and Chicago White Sox (AL).

Wind (WFL) 1975

The Wind was a new team that replaced the Chicago Fire (WFL). It took its nickname from Chicago's reputation as the Windy City. The team folded after five games, with a 1-4 record.

Zephyrs (NBA) 1962/63

After one season as the Packers, the Chicago NBA club moved its home games from the Amphitheater, which was located in the heart of the meat-packing industry. Owner Dave Trager decided the team needed a new name, and this time they solicited names in a Name the Team contest. The contest generated 236 names from over 2,000 entries. The name was selected by a committee of sports writers and announced by General Manager Frank Lane.

The word is derived from *Zephyrus* (Latin) and *Zephyros* (Greek), both of which mean the god of the west wind. It means "a breeze from the west, a soft gentle breeze." Of course, Chicago's nickname is the Windy City.

Although the name Zephyr was suggested by several entrants, the winner, based on his letter of explanation, was Richard L. Jakubauskas, of Chicago. Mr. Jakubauskas won a $500 savings bond. The second-place winner of two season tickets was Andy Boroian.

(CHICAGO)

Cole's American Giants (NSL) 1932
Cole's American Giants (NNL-2) 1933-1935
During this period of time, Robert J. Cole owned the club that originally had been owned by Rube Foster. (Foster died in 1926.)When the team reverted to the name of American Giants (NAL), it was owned by H. G. Hall, one of the leaders in organizing the new league. *See* Cuban Giants.

Racine Cardinals (APFA) 1920
The Cardinals trace their history back to 1899, when Chris O'Brien, a painting and decorating contractor, started the Morgan Athletic Club. The team started to play its games in Normal Field and soon were being called the Normals. The name Cardinal is supposed to have come from the color of some secondhand jerseys that O'Brien got from the University of Chicago. Although the jerseys were actually maroon, he called them cardinal. Some sources say he just didn't like the color maroon.

Because Normal Field was located at Normal Boulevard and Racine Avenue, the team became known as the Racine Cardinals. Although the team had to suspend operations from 1906 to 1912 and again in 1918, they remained the Racine Cardinals until they entered the APFA in 1920. However, by the end of the season, they were known mostly as the Chicago Cardinals.

CHICAGO-PITTSBURGH

Card-Pitt (NFL) 1944
During World War II, the Pittsburgh franchise merged twice. In 1943, they merged with the Philadelphia team; in 1944, they merged with the Chicago Cardinals. It was officially the Chicago-Pittsburgh team, but unofficially (and for the benefit of fans and sports writers) it was the Card-Pitts. *See* Philadelphia-Pittsburgh (NFL).

CINCINNATI (OH)

Bengals (AFL-2) 1937
Bengals (AFL-3) 1940-1941
When the Cleveland Rams (AFL-2) moved to the NFL after the 1936 season, the Cincinnati Bengals, a new franchise, replaced them. The Bengals also played in 1938 as an independent, in 1939 as a member of the minor-league AFL, and in 1940-1941 in AFL-3. The team folded after the 1941 season.

Bengals (AFL-4) 1968-1969
Bengals (NFL) 1970—
This expansion franchise in the AFL-4 was given to a syndicate headed by Paul Brown, who had built a powerhouse team with the Cleveland Browns (AAFC and NFL). Two theories exist concerning the team name. One is that Brown selected the name because of the popularity of the earlier Bengal team (AFL-2 and AFL-3), and the other is that he liked the idea of keeping the same initials (CB) that he had with the Cleveland Browns.

Buckeyes (NAL) 1942
Ohio is the Buckeye State, and the state nickname has been used by many teams in different cities in Ohio. This team played only one year in Cincinnati before moving to Cleveland as the Buckeyes. However, in 1949, it played in Kentucky as the Louisville Buckeyes.

Celts (APFA) 1921
The Celts played only four games in the APFA, posting a 1-3 record. However, several sources indicate that the team had played as an independent team in the early part of the second decade of this century.

Clowns (NAL) 1943
Clowns (NAL) 1945
The Clowns had originally been the Miami Clowns and then the Ethiopian Clowns. To help boost attendance in their barnstorming tours, some black teams had resorted to burlesque skits and clown routines. The Ethiopian Clowns were especially noted for their antics, and their nickname helped promote the team.

Comellos (NBL) 1937/38
The Comellos played as the Richmond (IN) King Clothiers in the first half of the season, before moving to Cincinnati.

Cuban Stars (NNL-1) 1920-1922
This team was owned by Augustin Molina and was primarily a road team, except for 1921, when it played its home games in Cincinnati. It later became known as the Cuban Stars (West), to avoid confusion with the Cuban Stars (East).

Kelly's Killers (AA) 1891

This team was named for the aggressive behavior of the manager, Mike Kelly. The club moved to Milwaukee, as the Brewers, in mid-August.

Kids (MISL) 1978/79

Outlaw Reds (UA) 1884

The Union Association was an "outlaw" league to the NL and AA. Since there was a Cincinnati Reds in the AA, the UA team was the Outlaw Reds.

Redlegs (NL) 1944-1945

The Cincinnati NL club officially changed its name to Redlegs for this two-year period, and the name was used in variant spellings (Red Legs, Redlegs) as late as 1960. However, it was still best known to the fans as the Reds.

Reds (NL) 1876-1880

See Cincinnati Reds (NL) 1946—.

Reds (AA) 1882-1889
Reds (NL) 1890-1943
Reds (NL) 1946—

When Cincinnati entered the NL, they were given the nickname Reds, which was a shortened version of the Red Stockings name that had been used by the famous 1869 championship team. The Boston team of the National Association had taken the name and was using it when the NL was formed. From 1881 to 1889, Cincinnati did not have a team in the NL; but the AA team took the same name, and it later joined the NL.

Reds (NFL) 1933-1934

The team adopted the name of the Cincinnati baseball team. The club folded on 11/5/34 and was replaced by the St. Louis Gunners.

Royals (NBA) 1957/58-1971/72

See Rochester Royals (NBL).

Stingers (WHA) 1975/76-1978/79

Tigers (NAL) 1937

CLEVELAND (OH)

Allmen Transfers (NBL) 1944/45-1945/46

This team was sponsored by the Allmen Transfer Company, a moving and storage company owned by Stan Allmen.

"Babes of the AA" (AA) 1887-1888

When Cleveland joined the American Association (1882-1891), in 1887, they were referred to as the Babes or the Babies of the AA.

Barons (NHL) 1976/77-1977/78

When the California Golden Seals franchise was moved to Cleveland, the team adopted the name of the minor-league (American Hockey League) Cleveland Barons.

Bears (NAL) 1939-1940

Blues (AL) 1902-1904

This nickname for the Cleveland AL team came from the color of their uniform.

Bronchos (AL) 1901

It is not known how the Cleveland AL team acquired the name Bronchos, although some sources indicate that the team chose it themselves. However, it did not catch on and the team became known as the Blues.

Browns (AAFC) 1946-1949
Browns (NFL) 1950—

Cleveland's entry into the AAFC had to make two selections from their Name the Team contest.

The first choice was Panthers, and of the thirty-six entrants who suggested it, a navy man, John J. Harnett, of Lawrence (MA), was selected as the winner. However, there had been a Cleveland Panthers in the first American Football League (1926), and the team had not fared well, dropping out in mid-season with a 3-2 record. Coach Paul Brown vetoed the name for the AAFC team, feeling it would give a losing image.

The second choice was Browns. Some have suggested that the name would honor the coach; others have suggested it in honor of boxing champion Joe Louis, the Brown Bomber. Paul Brown rejected the nickname at first but finally agreed. Cleveland would be the Browns.

The winner for submitting the name Browns was William E. Thompson.

Browns (NNL-1) 1924

Buckeyes (NAL) 1943-1948
Buckeyes (NAL) 1950
See Cincinnati Buckeyes (NAL).

Bulldogs (NFL) 1924-1925
Bulldogs (NFL) 1927
The 1923 Canton Bulldog team moved to Cleveland and brought the famous nickname with them.

Cavaliers (NBA) 1970/71—
The Cleveland *Plain Dealer* ran a Name the Team contest for Cleveland's entry into the NBA. More than 11,000 fans responded, and the judges selected five names: Cavaliers, Jays, Foresters, Towers, and Presidents. These final five were then voted on by the fans, and more than 2,000 of the 6,000 votes chose Cavaliers. Jerry Tomko of Eastlake was the winner of the contest and received two season tickets. His winning entry said, "The name Cleveland Cavaliers represents a group of daring, fearless men, whose life's pact was never surrender, no matter what the odds."

Chase Brass (NBL) 1943/44
This team was sponsored by the Chase Brass Company. The team was also known as the Brassmen.

Crunch (MISL) 1989/90—
The Crunch was an expansion franchise that replaced the Cleveland Force, one of the original members of the MISL.

Crusaders (WHA) 1972/73-1975/76
More than 8,000 suggestions for a team nickname were received in a five-day contest. Cleveland's entry in the WHA was officially named the Crusaders and announced on 7/6/72.

An attempt was made to move the franchise to Hollywood (FL) for the 1976/77 season, but it failed.

Cubs (NNL-1) 1931
From 1930 to 1950, this team, which was owned by Tom Wilson, went by the name Elite Giants. (*See* Nashville Elite Giants.) This one year was the only time it had the name Cubs.

However, there had been a Cleveland Elites team, and it may have been that the Elite Giants wanted to avoid confusion between the names.

Elites (NNL-1) 1926
This team played only the first half of the season.

Force (MISL) 1978/79-1987/88

Forest Citys (NA) 1871/72
Forest Citys (NL) 1879-1884
The name Forest Citys (or sometimes Forest Cities) can be traced to 1868, when it was used by an amateur team in Cleveland. Cleveland was known as the Forest City, and its early teams adopted the city nickname. *See also* Rockford Forest Citys.

Giants (NNL-2) 1933
This team joined the league in August.
See Cuban Giants.

Hornets (NNL-1) 1927

Indians (AL) 1915—
The name Indians was chosen in a contest sponsored by a local newspaper in 1915, and it is generally believed that the name was selected to honor Louis Sockalexis, an American Indian. Sockalexis had played for Cleveland's NL teams of 1897-1899. He was the first full-blooded Indian to play in the majors.

Indians (APFA) 1920-1921
Indians (NFL) 1923
See Cleveland Indians (NFL) 1931.

Indians (NFL) 1931
The 1931 Indians were a different franchise from the earlier team, but they both adopted the name of the Cleveland AL baseball team.

Infants (PL) 1890
Some references indicate that the Cleveland entry in the PL was called Infants, but it is questionable. However, from 1887 to 1888, the Cleveland entry in the AA had been called Babes or Babies of the AA. It would have been logical to call another new team Infants.

Molly McGuires (AL) 1912-1914
James "Deacon" McGuire had been manager of the Cleveland team from 1909 through 1911. The nickname was in his honor.

Naps (AL) 1905-1911
Future Hall of Famer Napoleon "Naps" Lajoie played with Cleveland from 1903 until 1914 and was its manager from 1905 to 1909. His nickname became the team nickname.

Panthers (AFL-1) 1926
The Panthers lasted only five games before dropping out of the league with a 3-2 record.

Pipers (ABL-3) 1961/62
The Pipers were owned by George Steinbrenner, later to become owner of the New York Yankees (AL). The Pipers had played in the National Industrial League, winning two titles.

Rams (AFL-2) 1936
Rams (NFL) 1937-1942
Rams (NFL) 1944-1945
A franchise was awarded to Harold Paddock, Damon "Buzz" Wetzel, and Reuel A. Lang for a Cleveland entry in the AFL-2. However, Wetzel became discouraged about the league's financial situation and decided to disband the team. The franchise was then purchased by a group headed by Homer Marshman, and Wetzel was persuaded to stay on as coach. At a meeting of the owners and sports writers, the question of a name for the new team came up. It was decided that the name should be short—to fit in headlines—and recognizable. They then chose Rams, because one of the best teams at that time was the Fordham Rams, and the name was short.

The following year Marshman had decided that he did not want to continue in the AFL and was going to disband, when he was invited to join the NFL.

Rebels (BAA) 1946/47
The owner of the Cleveland Rebels also owned the minor-league Cleveland hockey team in the American Hockey League. The Rebels dropped out after the first year of the BAA.

Red Sox (NNL-2) 1934

Rosenblums (ABL-1) 1925/26-1930/31
This team was sponsored by Max Rosenblum, who owned a department store in Cleveland. The team was also known as the Rosies.

Spiders (NL) 1889-1899
The nickname Spiders is supposed to have been pinned on the Cleveland team by one of the owners (Colonel House), who thought the players were as skinny and spindly as spiders.

In 1899, most of the good players were sent to St. Louis, since both teams had the same owners. The team that was left over was soon being called Misfits. The 1899 team set the record for the most losses (134) by one team in a season.

Stokers (NASL) 1968
In 1967, Cleveland had been represented in the United Soccer Association (USA) by the Stoke City Potters of Stoke-on-Trent, England. The city is Britain's prime center for the production of porcelain.

Tate Stars (NNL-1) 1922
George Tate was a vice-president of the Negro National League (NNL-1) and an officer of the Cleveland club. Although the team played only one season in organized baseball, it had played in earlier years as an independent club.

White Horses (NBL) 1938/39

COLORADO (CO)

Caribous (NASL) 1978

Rockies (NHL) 1976/77-1981/82
The team was named for the famous mountain chain. In 1982/83 the team became the New Jersey Devils (NHL).

COLUMBUS (OH)

Athletic Supplys (MBC) 1936/37
Athletic Supplys (NBL) 1937/38
The team was sponsored by the Columbus Athletic Supply Company.

Blue Birds (NNL-2) 1933
The team dropped out of the league in midseason.

Buckeyes (AA) 1883-1884
See Columbus Buckeyes (NNL-1).

Buckeyes (AA) 1889-1891
See Columbus Buckeyes (NNL-1).

Buckeyes (NNL-1) 1921
These teams adopted the state nickname (especially appropriate since Columbus is the state capital).

Bullies (AFL-3) 1940-1941
The Bullies were definitely the toughest team in the AFL-3. They won the championship in both years. However, it is not known how they originally got the name.

Elite Giants (NNL-2) 1935
See Nashville Elite Giants (NNL-1).

Panhandles (APFA) 1920-1921
Panhandles (NFL) 1922-1924
The Panhandles were organized in 1907 by Joe Carr, who would later become president of the NFL and the ABL-1. The team was composed of employees of the Panhandle Division of the Pennsylvania Railroad. The club changed its name to Tigers for 1925-1926, because the players were no longer primarily railroad employees.

When the team was predominantly composed of railroad workers, they were able to keep travel expenses at a minimum. Since the workers rode free, they would schedule as many teams as possible from towns along the railroad lines.

Tigers (NFL) 1925-1926
See Columbus Panhandles (APFA).

Turfs (NSL) 1932
The team played the second half of the season only.

CONNECTICUT (CT)

Bicentennials (NASL) 1977
See Hartford Bicentennials (NASL).

CUBAN

Cuban Giants
The Cuban Giants are listed in this book, even though they played at the turn of the century and never played in one of the black leagues, because they had a major impact on the naming of black baseball clubs.

The original Cuban Giants were formed in the summer of 1895 by Frank P. Thompson, headwaiter at the prestigious Argyle Hotel, in Babylon, on Long Island's South Shore. Originally Thompson called his team the Athletics. After playing at the hotel for the benefit of the guests, the team went on the road in the fall, under the management of John F. Lang.

Within a year, the club was under the management of a Trenton businessman, Walter Cook, and was making Trenton its home base.

Because of racial prejudice (and also class prejudice; they were mere waiters), the players tried to pass themselves off as Cubans, even to speaking in a Spanish-sounding gibberish while on the field. The most respected professional baseball team at the turn of the century was John McGraw's New York Giants. Thus, the name of the team became Cuban Giants. By 1900, the name had been changed to Genuine Cuban Giants.

Between 1890 and 1920, the vast majority of black baseball teams used the nickname Giants in some combination, while a few others used Cubans in combination.

Cuban Stars (East) (ECL) 1923-1928
Cuban Stars (East) (ANL) 1929
See Cuban Giants.

Cuban Stars (West) (NNL-1) 1923-1930
See (Cincinnati) Cuban Stars (NNL-1) and Cuban Giants.

DALLAS (TX)

Chaparrals (ABA) 1967/68-1969/70
Chaparrals (ABA) 1971/72-1972/73
According to Terry Pluto's history of the ABA, *Loose Balls*, the Dallas team was given its name by one of the team investors. At one of the meetings held in the Chaparral Room in the Dallas Sheraton, one of the investors was looking at a napkin with the

chaparral on it and suggested that Chaparrals would be a good name for the team.

A chaparral is a roadrunner—a large terrestrial bird of the cuckoo family that is a speedy runner and ranges from California to Texas. (It is perhaps best known as a famous cartoon character!)

Cowboys (NFL) 1960—
The Dallas NFL entry was originally going to be called the Rangers, in honor of the famous Texas Rangers, the state police force. However, it was decided that there might be confusion with the local minor-league baseball team, also known as the Rangers.

The team owners decided to rename the team, and in March 1960 they announced that the team would be the Cowboys, a name that was symbolic of the West and Texas.

Mavericks (NBA) 1980/81—
Radio station WBAP held a Name the Team contest for the Dallas NBA club and received over 4,600 entries. A five-person committee narrowed the choices to Mavericks, Wranglers, and Express, and finally recommended Mavericks as their choice to owner Donald Carter. The winning name had been submitted by forty-one people, each of whom received two tickets to the opening game. The first prize of a pair of season tickets was awarded to Carla Springer.

Sidekicks (MISL) 1984/85—
This team borrowed its name from soccer terminology: a side kick.

Texans (AFL-4) 1960-1962
Lamar Hunt was the owner of the Dallas franchise in the AFL-4 and also the driving force behind the organization of the league. Hunt had tried to get an NFL franchise for Dallas but had been told that, because a team had failed in 1952 in Dallas, the NFL would not be interested in moving to or starting a team in Dallas.

Hunt then decided to start a rival league, and he asked Ken "Bud" Adams, another Texas millionaire, to join with him in starting the American Football League (AFL-4).

It was hunt who chose the name Texans for his Dallas franchise, and while the name is quite appropriate for a Texas team, it should be noted that the team that had failed in 1952 in the NFL had been

named the Dallas Texans. Perhaps Hunt was telling the NFL they were wrong. The NFL must have realized that Dallas could support a team, since they quickly established the Cowboys to compete with the Texans.

Dallas could support pro football but not two teams, and in 1963 Hunt moved his team to Kansas City and renamed them the Chiefs.

Texans (NFL) 1952
A franchise was awarded to Dallas, and the club purchased the assets of the New York Yanks, which owner Ted Collins had sold back to the NFL. The Dallas team was named the Texans, in honor of the state, but had a disastrous season. The team failed in midseason, and the NFL operated it as a road team for the last five games. It ended the season with a 1-11 record.

Tornado (NASL) 1968-1981
Tornados, violent and destructive windstorms, are common in Texas, and the team picked the name hoping to be just as much trouble to their opposition.

DARBY (PA)

See Hilldale.

DAYTON (OH)

London Bobbys (MBC) 1936/37
The team was sponsored by the brewers of London Bobby Beer.

Marcos (NNL-1) 1920
Marcos (NNL-1) 1926
Owned by John Matthews, this club was one of the original members of the NNL-1.

Metros (MBC) 1935/36
Metros (NBL) 1937/38
Team was officially the Metropolitans but were called by the shortened version of Metros.

Rens (NBL) 1948/49
Although this team bore the name of the famous Renaissance teams of New York, it was no longer the great team of the past. The Renaissance Big Five was organized in 1922 by Bob Douglas and played it first game on 11/30/23. Most of their home games were

played at the Renaissance Casino in New York City's Harlem.

Rens is a shortened form of Renaissance and one that was almost immediately given them as a nickname.

In their first twelve seasons they posted a 1373-204 record, primarily as a barnstorming team that took on all comers. Although the Rens, like the Celtics and the Buffalo Germans, continued to play for many years after their founding, it is the earlier teams that are the reason for their enshrinement in the Basketball Hall of Fame.

Triangles (APFA) 1920-1921
Triangles (NFL) 1922-1929

The Triangles can be traced back to a team called the St. Mary's Cadets of 1913 and 1914. In this period, the Cadets won the Dayton city championship and then beat the Cincinnati Celts for the Southern Ohio championship. In 1915, the Cadets became the Dayton Gym Cadets.

The following year (1916) the team gained new sponsorship and its new name. The Triangles were now sponsored by an industrial "triangle" of plants in the downtown section of the city. The sponsors were DELCO (Dayton Engineering Laboratories Company), DMP (Dayton Metal Products), and DECO (Domestic Engineering Company, which later became DELCO Light).

These companies were owned by Edward Deeds and Charles Keating. Later, Dayton Wright Airplanes also became a sponsor.

DECATUR (IL)

Staleys (APFA) 1920

The team that was later to become the Chicago Staleys (1921) and then the Chicago Bears was originally sponsored by the A. E. Staley Manufacturing Company, a maker of corn products, primarily starch. The company was founded in 1912 by A. E. Staley and had sponsored company teams in baseball and football before hiring George Halas to coach and manage the football team. Halas was able to recruit standout players who were then given full-time jobs with the company.

The cost of underwriting the team proved to be too much for Staley, and he suggested to Halas that he take the team to Chicago, where it would have a greater fan potential. Staley gave Halas $5,000 to pay

costs and asked only that the team be called the Staleys for one more season.

(Although it is easy to trace the Staley connection, no sources the author has seen indicate what the initials A. E. stand for. Even George Halas always referred to A. E. Staley as Mr. Staley.)

DENVER (CO)

Avalanche (MISL) 1980/81-1981/82

The Avalanche played two seasons in Denver before moving to Tacoma to become the Stars.

Broncos (AFL-4) 1960-1969
Broncos (NFL) 1970—

When Denver joined the new American Football League (AFL-4), it held a Name the Team contest for its entry. The contest required a written statement of twenty-five words or less and produced 162 different names in 500 entries.

The judges of the contest (John Harcourt, president of the Visitors and Convention Bureau; Ted Johnson, a past president of the local President's Round Table; Cal Pond, executive secretary of the Retail Merchants Assn.; and John Davis III, president of the Chamber of Commerce) chose the entry submitted by Ward M. Vining, of Lakewood. Vining was one of seven people to submit the name Broncos.

Denver had had a previous Broncos team—its 1921 entry in the Midwest Baseball League.

Dynamo (NASL) 1974-1975

The Denver team took the name of the famous Soviet sports club Dynamo, and in particular, Moscow Dynamo, a soccer team that holds a special place in soccer history.

Gold (USFL) 1983-1985

The USFL team name reflects, as does the name of the Denver Nuggets, the gold-mining industry of Colorado.

Nuggets (NBL) 1948/49
Nuggets (NBA) 1949/50

Basketball has a long tradition in Denver, a city that often referred to itself as the "Basketball Capital." Between 1931 and 1947 Denver produced powerhouse teams in the Amateur Athletic Union (AAU) competition, and the city hosted the annual AAU tournament (except for 1949) from 1935 through 1968.

Denver's original AAU entry was organized by William N. Haraway, an official of the Safeway and Piggly Wiggly Stores. Although popularly called the Pigs, the team was properly known as the Denver Safeways and won the National AAU title in 1937. In 1938, they finished second.

In 1939, Safeway dropped its sponsorship, but the team stayed intact and was sponsored by local civic groups. The name was then changed to Nuggets, a reflection of the gold-mining industry of Colorado.

That year Denver beat the Phillips 66ers for the National AAU championship, and in 1940 the 66ers beat the Nuggets. During the next few years the same team played as the Denver Legion, Denver Ambrose Jellymakers, or Denver Nuggets, depending on the sponsor.

In 1948, the Nuggets and the Phillips 66ers met again for the championship, with the 66ers winning their sixth consecutive title. The Nuggets then joined the National Basketball League (NBL) for the 1948/49 season.

Nuggets (ABA) 1974/75-1975/76
Nuggets (NBA) 1976/77—

Denver's entry in the ABA was originally known as the Rockets (1967/68-1973/74); however, when it looked as if a merger with the NBA would be imminent, the team name was changed to Nuggets. Denver changed the name because the NBA already had a team named Rockets (Houston) and Nuggets had long been a favorite name in Denver. *See* Denver Nuggets (NBL).

Rockets (ABA) 1967/67-1973/74

Denver's ABA entry was originally called the Larks, but this name was changed to Rockets before the team began the 1967/68 season. The owner of the team, Bill Ringsby, owned the Rocket Truck Lines. *See* Denver Nuggets (ABA).

Spurs (WHA) 1975/76

The Spurs began the season in Denver but ran into financial problems and moved to Ottawa on 1/2/76, despite efforts by city officials to save the franchise. Denver owner Ivan Mullenix said he lad lost $2 million in the operation of the team.

DETROIT (MI)

Altes Lagers (MBC) 1936/37

The team was sponsored by a local brewery.

Cardinals (ABL-1) 1927/28

The Detroit Cardinals were owned by the owners of the Detroit Cougars (NHL) team. The team lasted until 1/3/28, when it disbanded with a 5-13 record.

Cougars (NASL) 1968

The Cougars were members of the United Soccer Association (USA) in 1967 and played one season in the NASL.

Cougars (NHL) 1926/27-1929/30

When Detroit got its NHL franchise, it needed a team, so the new owners bought the Victoria Cougars of the Western Hockey League and brought the players and the nickname to Detroit. The Victoria team had been the last non-NHL team to win the Stanley Cup.

Eagles (NBL) 1939/40-1940/41

The Eagles were the best basketball team in Detroit until the Detroit Pistons came to town. The 1940/41 team won the World's Professional Basketball Tournament, sponsored by the Chicago *Herald-American*. In 1941/42, the Eagles dropped out of the NBL and played as a barnstorming team, again making it to the World Tournament. This time they lost by 43-41 to the Oshkosh All-Stars.

Express (NASL) 1978-1980

Falcons (BAA) 1946/47

The Detroit BAA franchise was supposed to go to Indianapolis, but in August 1946 it was moved to Detroit. The move was supposedly made because of the lack of materials to make hasty changes in the Indianapolis arena surface from hockey to basketball. Both the Indianapolis and Detroit stadiums were owned by the same corporation.

Falcons (NHL) 1930/31-1932/33

Detroit fans did not like the name Cougars that the NHL club had adopted when it entered the league in 1926/27. Most of them complained that there were no cougars in Detroit! The team decided to change its name to Falcons. In 1933/34, the team became the Red Wings. *See* Detroit Red Wings (NHL).

Gems (NBL) 1946/47
The team was owned by Maurice Winston, a Dearborn jeweler and sponsor of several local basketball and baseball clubs.

Hed-Aids (MBC) 1935/36
This team was sponsored by a local company, possibly a drugstore chain. In 1936/37, the team became the Detroit Altes Lagers (MBC).

Heralds (APFA) 1920
The Heralds disbanded at the end of the 1920 season. However, it was one of the pre-APFA teams that played in the 1910s.

Lightning (MISL) 1979/80
The team played one season, then moved to San Francisco as the Fog (1980/81), and finally settled in Kansas City as the Comets (1981/82—).

Lions (NFL) 1934—
The Portsmouth (OH) Spartans franchise was purchased by G. A. "Dick" Richards, owner of Detroit radio station WJR, for $21,500. Richards ran a Name the Team contest on his radio station. It is assumed that the name Lions was one of those that were submitted, but it is known that Richards selected the name. The selection was a logical choice to tie in with the Detroit Tigers (AL) baseball team. Also, lions are the kings of the jungle and hopefully would do better than the previous Detroit NFL team, the Panthers.

Panthers (NFL) 1925-1926
League president Joe Carr got Jimmy Conzelman to start a franchise in Detroit. Conzelman was owner, coach, and player. All the backers of the new team were from the Chicago area, including Henry Horner, a future governor of Illinois.

Pistons (NBA) 1957/58—
See Fort Wayne Zollner Pistons (NBL).

Pulaski Post Five (ABL-1) 1925/26-1926/27
The team was sponsored by Pulaski Post No. 270, which received its permanent charter on June 29, 1921. The Pulaski Post team played the full 1925/26 season, but there is some confusion about the 1926/27 season.

The team did play six games in 1926/27, losing all six and disbanding on 12/24/26. At the end of the season, Joe Carr, president of the ABL, nullified the games and dropped Detroit from the record books. (Carr also dropped teams from the NFL records in the early 1920s, when they did not play enough games to qualify as a league franchise. Carr was also president of the NFL.)

Some sources indicate that the 1926/27 team had changed sponsorship and was called the Detroit Lions. The team did have most of the Pulaski Post players.

Red Wings (NHL) 1933/34—
The Detroit NHL team received its third and final name when it was purchased in 1933 by James D. Norris, Sr. As a youth, Norris had played on a team in Montreal called the Winged Wheelers. The Wheelers insignia was a wheel with red wings. Norris felt the insignia was appropriate for the Motor City and took the name Red Wings from it.

Stars (NNL-1) 1920-1931
Stars (NNL-1) 1933
Stars (NAL) 1937
The Stars were formed in 1919, when Rube Foster (owner of the Chicago American Giants) set up J. T. "Tenny" Blount as a baseball promoter in Detroit.

Tigers (AL) 1901—
Early references had given credit for the naming of the Tigers to manager George Stallings, partially because Stallings had himself taken the credit. However, later research indicates that the Detroit team was called Tigers by the fans and sports writers and not by Stallings.

The nickname was due to the striped black and yellowish color of their stockings. Stallings did make this change in his first year (1896). However, he didn't call them Tigers. The team retained the name Wolverines (after Michigan's state animal, from 1896 until 1899, when the Tiger nickname became the more popular team name. Philip J. Reid, a Detroit city editor, is credited with being the first to call the team the Tigers in print, sometime in 1896.

Stallings was the manager in 1896 and again from 1899 to 1901.

Tigers (APFA) 1921
The team adopted the name of the Detroit AL baseball team.

Vagabond Kings (NBL) 1948/49
The Vagabond Kings were owned by King Boring and played from 11/1/48 until 12/17/48 before disbanding with a 2-17 record. The team had no home arena, thus the name Vagabonds combined with the owner's name.

Wheels (WFL) 1974
The Detroit WFL team picked its nickname on 1/28/74 in recognition of Detroit's nickname as the Motor City. The team disbanded before the end of the season with a 1-13 record.

Wolverines (NFL) 1928
Wolverines is the nickname of the University of Michigan, and it is also the state animal. Some sources have suggested that the franchise owners picked the name in hopes of getting Bernie Friedman to join the team. Friedman had been a great backfield star at Michigan. While Friedman did play with the Wolverines in 1928, it is unlikely that he did so because of the team name.

Wolverines (NL) 1881-1888
This team adopted the name of the state animal. The team was also know as the Detroits.

DULUTH (MN)

Eskimos (NFL) 1926-1927
When owner Oluf Haugsrud signed Ernie Nevers to a contract, he may have saved the NFL. Nevers was a player who could be compared to the great Red Grange, who had signed with the rival AFL-1. In order to take full advantage of the drawing power of Nevers, the NFL scheduled the Eskimos to play twenty-nine games (league and exhibition) with only one of them at Duluth.

Why Eskimos? A local clothier gave the team mackinaws with the lettering ERNIE NEVERS ESKIMOS on the back. Haugsrud was not about to look a gift horse in the mouth and changed the team name from Kelleys to Eskimos.

Kelleys (NFL) 1923-1925
The team was originally known as the Kelley-Duluths and was sponsored by the Kelley Duluth Hard-

ware Store. The team had been an excellent independent team, and when it decided to join the NFL the name was shortened to Kelleys.

In 1926, the team became the Duluth Eskimos (NFL).

EDMONTON (Alberta)

Drillers (NASL) 1979-1982
The oil industry dominates the Calgary and Edmonton region.
See Alberta Oilers (WHA).

Oilers (WHA) 1972/73-1978/79
Oilers (NHL) 1979/80—
When Edmonton got a WHA franchise, the team held a Name the Team contest. The winning suggestion was Oilers, a name that was well received by the fans and owners. Bill Hunter, owner of the franchise, also owned the Edmonton Oil Kings, a great junior hockey team.

Although the team started its initial season as the Alberta Oilers, the name was soon changed from the province to the city.
See Alberta Oilers (WHA).

ELIZABETH (NJ)

Elizabeth (ML-1) 1922/23
This team was one of many of the early basketball teams that were known only by their town or city name.

Resolutes (NA) 1873
This nickname is something of a puzzle. Most often, the name Resolutes can be traced to a local firehouse or fire company, since many of the early companies went by such names as Resolutes, Alerts, Mutual, Exempts, Minnie HaHa, etc. However, the Elizabeth name did not come from a local fire company. There never was a Resolute fire company in the city.

In the first city directory for Elizabeth, published in 1869, the Resolute Base Ball Club is listed with the following officers: James Gale, President; S. B. Amory, Vice-President; J. Aug. Ritter, Secretary; and Thomas Forsyth, Treasurer. Ritter was also listed as Captain of the 1st Nine.

It is known that the Resolutes played in Elizabeth for quite a few years before and after their one-year appearance in the National Association. Nearby Jersey City also had a team called Resolutes, and there was another one in Brooklyn.

EVANSVILLE (IN)

Crimson Giants (APFA) 1921
Crimson Giants (NFL) 1922
The Crimson Giants were granted a franchise for the APFA on 8/27/21, but because they did not play a minimum of six league games, Evansville was dropped from the final standings. The team played a full league schedule in 1922 but disbanded at the end of the season.

FLINT (MI)

Dow A. C. (NBL) 1947/48
See Midland Dow A. C. (NBL).

FLORIDA (FL)

Blazers (WFL) 1974
Before this franchise settled in as the Blazers, it was scheduled to be the Washington Ambassadors. (Actually it was originally the Baltimore-Washington franchise; then it was going to move to Norfolk. The club was unable to obtain a suitable stadium in either city and therefore relocated the franchise to Florida before the start of the 1974 season.)

The name Ambassadors was selected by E. Joseph Wheeler, team owner, and announced on 2/25/74. Wheeler made the selection from 1,500 suggestions in a Name the Team contest that attracted 16,000 entries. Seven people suggested the name, and a drawing was held to select the winner of the $1,000 first prize. The winners were Mr. and Mrs. Richard S. Berardino of Laurel (MD). Berardino, a Department of Defense employee who had recently moved to Washington from the Boston area, said that "at heart I'm a Patriots fan." His first choice for the Washington team would have been Spartans.

Floridians (ABA) 1970/71-1971/72
See Miami Floridians (ABA).

FORT LAUDERDALE (FL)

Strikers (NASL) 1977-1983
The term *striker* is used to indicate a forward or goal scorer. In the 1940s and 1950s the forward line usu-ally consisted of a left and right wing, a left and right inside forward, and a center. Just as football positions have changed over the years, so have soccer positions. The offense now consists of strikers and wings in various combinations.

Fort Lauderdale chose the nickname because it stresses action.

FORT WAYNE (IN)

Caseys (ABL-1) 1925/26
The team was sponsored by the local Knights of Columbus (K.C.s). In 1926, the team adopted the nickname Hoosiers.

Firemen (NPBL) 1932/33
It is assumed that this team may have been sponsored by a local Texaco station or chain of stations, since the team was also called the Fire Chief and Chiefs. One of Texaco's brands of gasoline was Fire Chief.

General Electrics (MBC) 1936/37
General Electrics (NBL) 1937/38
These teams were sponsored by the General Electric plant in Fort Wayne.

Hoosiers (ABL-1) 1926/27-1930/31
The former Caseys (1925/26) adopted a new nickname and chose the state nickname: Hoosier.

Kekiongas (NA) 1871
The Miami Indians had a name for the tribal village where Fort Wayne is now located. The name was Kekionga. It was a name that had been used by several Fort Wayne amateur baseball teams, so it was logical for Fort Wayne's entry into professional baseball to take the same nickname.

But the team that called itself the Fort Wayne Kekiongas in 1871 was actually the Maryland Base Ball Club of Baltimore. The Baltimore team made a tour in 1870, and when it got to Fort Wayne, a group of local businessmen convinced the team to turn professional and represent Fort Wayne in the National Association.

The Fort Wayne franchise folded in August 1871 and was replaced by the Brooklyn Eckfords, a team that had been at the organizing meeting of the National Association but didn't want to risk the ten-dollar admission fee.

Pistons (BAA) 1948/49
Pistons (NBA) 1949/50-1956/57
See Fort Wayne Zollner Pistons (NBL).

Zollner Pistons (NBL) 1941/42-1947/48
Fred Zollner was the owner of the Zollner machine works on the outskirts of Fort Wayne. The company produced pistons for the major automobile manufacturers. A rugged individualist, he treated both players and workers as if they were part of a big family. New employees received a $500 trust fund the day they were hired, and additional amounts were added each year. Workers (and players who were on the payroll) received very liberal vacation and sick benefits.

Zollner was an avid sports fan and supported several local teams, including a world championship softball nine.

When the team moved from the NBL to the BAA (and then to the NBA), it dropped the Zollner name and became the Pistons. In 1957, the Pistons moved to Detroit, a city where many of the pistons from the Zollner plant had been going for years.

FRANKFORD (PA)

Yellow Jackets (NFL) 1924-1931
Just after World War I, the Frankford Athletic Association was organized with the help and support of the local American Legion Post. The association was a strong community-backed operation, and its purpose was to provide Frankford, then a suburb of Philadelphia and home of the famous U.S. arsenal, with top-flight sports and recreational facilities.

Teams named Yellow Jackets had played football at the site of a local trotting racetrack as early as 1913. The association built a new facility for all sports, including the trotters, and for its football team of the early 1920s. When the team entered the NFL in 1924, it was still known as the Yellow Jackets.

GOLDEN BAY

Earthquakes (NASL) 1983-1984
Earthquakes (MISL) 1982/83
See San Jose Earthquakes (NASL).

GOLDEN STATE

Warriors (NBA) 1971/72

See Philadelphia Warriors (BAA) and Philadelphia Phillies (ABL-1).

GREEN BAY (WI)

Packers (APFA) 1921
Packers (NFL) 1922—
Earl "Curly" Lambeau formed the Green Bay team on 8/11/19 and was able to get financial support from the company he worked for, the Indian Packing Company. The packing company had just moved to Green Bay from Providence, RI, and they gave Lambeau $500 for sweaters and stockings, with the proviso that he put Indian Packing Co. on the sweaters. The company felt it would be good advertising and goodwill.

The 1919 and 1920 teams were strong, independent clubs. When the Green Bay team joined the APFA on 8/27/21, the franchise was granted to John and Emmett Clair, of the Acme Packing Company. The Acme Company had bought out the Indian Packing Company, and the team sweaters now read Acme Packers. However, from the beginning the team had been referred to as the Packers.

Because of a rules violation (using ineligible players), Green Bay's franchise was revoked by league president Joe Carr, who was using the Packers as an example. Lambeau was able to get some Green Bay businessmen to get another franchise, and the team became a community-owned club. When the packing company folded, Lambeau tried to change the name of the team. Some sources indicate that he wanted to call the team the Blues; others say the name Big Bay Blues was used by the local paper. However, the Milwaukee and Chicago papers still referred to the team as the Packers, and the name stuck.

HAMILTON (Ontario)

Tigers (NHL) 1920/21-1924/25
The Quebec Bulldogs moved to Hamilton and renamed their team Tigers, hoping the move would bring more fans.

In 1924/25, after winning the NHL championship, the players refused to play in the Stanley Cup playoffs, demanding extra pay for these additional games. The league then canceled the Tigers' championship and revoked their franchise. The players were then transferred to the New York Americans, an expansion franchise.

HAMMOND (IN)

Calumet Buccaneers (NBL) 1948/49
Although this entry in the NBL was from Hammond, the Calumet Buccaneers were more of a regional franchise. The team was owned by 200 fans residing in the Indiana cities of Hammond, Whiting, and East Chicago, and Calumet City, IL. The industrial area known as Calumet consisted of these towns and Gary, Indiana, and Lansing, Illinois. It was an area in which there were many independent basketball teams, some of which, such as Hammond and Whiting, made the professional ranks.

Ciesar All-Americans (NBL) 1938/39-1940/41
See Whiting Ciesar All-Americans (MBC).

Pros (APFA) 1920-1921
Pros (NFL) 1922-1926
The team took its name from a shortened version of *professional*. The Pros were an independent team before joining the APFA for the 1920 season.

HARRISBURG (PA)

Giants (ECL) 1924-1927
See Cuban Giants.

Senators (ABL-2) 1942/43
Harrisburg is the state capital of Pennsylvania and thus the team was appropriately called Senators for the state senate. (Washington, DC, also had a Senators team, but it is doubtful that any team was ever called Congressmen, Legislators, or Representatives.)

HARRISBURG-ST. LOUIS

Stars (NNL-2) 1943
The team played part of the first half of the season, then was suspended when they withdrew to go on a barnstorming tour with a team headed by Dizzy Dean. *See* St. Louis Stars (NNL-1).

HARTFORD (CT)

Bicentennials (NASL) 1975-1976
The team was named for the American Bicentennial celebrations that were in process when Hartford got its NASL franchise. The team changed its name to Connecticut Bicentennials in 1977.

Blues (NFL) 1926

Blues (NL) 1876-1877
The Hartford NL team was named Blues for the color of their uniforms. Although they played all their 1877 home games in Brooklyn, they were still called the Hartford Blues.

Hartfords (NA) 1874-1875
The Hartford NA team was known simply by the name of the city.

Hellions (MISL) 1979/80-1980/81

Whalers (NHL) 1979/80—
See New England Whalers (WHA).

HAWAII

See also **Hawaiians and Team Hawaii.**

Chiefs (ABL-3) 1961-1963
The ABL team chose its name in honor of the leaders (chiefs) of the many tribes that inhabited the Hawaiian Islands.

HAWAIIANS

Hawaiians (WFL) 1974-1975
The team took its name from the state name. Hawaii is also the name of the largest of the islands that make up the state.

HILLDALE

Hilldale (ECL) 1923-1927
Hilldale (ANL) 1929
Hilldale is not a location, but few ever referred to the team by any other name. There are some references to the Darby Daisies (the team was from Darby, PA) and here Daisies is from the slang expression of the day meaning "an excellent or first-rate person or thing."

Hilldale was originally formed as a boys' team around 1910, but it soon became a very strong professional team that played most of its games in the Philadelphia area.

HOBOKEN (NJ)

Lisas (ML-2) 1931/32-1932/33
The team was owned by "Doc" Lisa, and they adopted the owner's name.
See North Hudson Thourots (ABL-2).

HOMESTEAD (PA)

Grays (ANL) 1929
Grays (NNL-2) 1935-1948
Everything in Homestead was gray. The town was near the giant steel mills of the U. S. Steel Corporation (then the Carnegie Steel Corporation), and the community was laden with soot and smoke from the mills. Around the turn of the century, black steelworkers organized a team called the Homestead Blue Ribbon nine, which later became known as the Murdock Grays.

The Murdock team, although mostly black, was an integrated team, and in 1912 it became the Homestead Grays. About the same time (1911), Cumberland "Cum" Posey joined the team, and the Grays became one of the dominant teams on the East Coast.

The Grays played in Homestead and later in Pittsburgh. In the late 1930s, the Grays began to play games in Washington, DC, as the Washington Homestead Grays. In 1940, although still referred to by most as the Homestead Grays, they were playing home games in both Pittsburgh and Washington and were often billed as the Washington Homestead Grays.

HOUSTON (TX)

Aeros (WHA) 1972/73-1977/78
Named for Houston's association with the aerospace industry.

Astros (NL) 1965—
Houston's Astrodome was the world's first indoor ballpark. When the Houston Colts moved to the Astrodome (in 1965), they changed their name to Astros in honor of their new home.
See Houston Colt .45s (NL).

Colt .45s (NL) 1962-1964
The Houston NL expansion team announced its team name on 3/7/61, when it picked Colts as the name and a .45 revolver as its emblem. Although the name selected was Colts, the Houston Sports Association, which owned the franchise was selecting the revolver, not a horse, as the name.

More than 12,000 entries were received, with the winner receiving a trip for two to the World Series.

Eagles (NAL) 1949-1950
See Brooklyn Eagles (NNL-2).

Gamblers (USFL) 1984-1985
The Gamblers received their name from Jerry Argovitz, one of the owners of the Houston entry in the USFL. His selection didn't sit well with the TV network that was going to broadcast USFL games, but Argovitz contended that "the name symbolized the bold, imaginative, gambling style" of the team.

Hurricane (NASL) 1979-1980
The Houston NASL team held a Name the Team contest, receiving over 9,000 entries. According to general manager Hans von Mende, Hurricane was by far the most popular. Other frequently mentioned names included Kickers and Stars. In addition, a number of names associated with the aerospace or space theme and the oil business were received.

The winner, selected from the Hurricane entries, received an expense-paid trip with the team to any one of its road games.

Mavericks (ABA) 1967/68
The name Maverick, a reference to an independent individual who refuses to conform, fits the image that Texans like to project. (Samuel Maverick, a Texan who fought for Texas independence, did not brand his calves, and thus they were called mavericks.)

The Houston ABA team used the name for the one short season that it was in the league. It would later be adopted by the Dallas team of the NBA.

Oilers (AFL-4) 1960-1969
Oilers (NFL) 1970—
The Oilers were named by owner Kenneth "Bud" Adams on 10/31/59. Adams, a wealthy oilman and cofounder of the AFL, chose the name that reflected his business and also reflected the major industry of Houston.

Rockets (NBA) 1971/72—

Some teams move from one location to another and do not change their names. When the Jazz moved from New Orlean to Utah, the name Utah Jazz didn't seem to make much sense. However, when the San Diego Rockets moved to Houston and retained their name, it was more than appropriate.

In fact, Houston, home of the NASA Space Center and an active part of the rocket industry, was a natural home for a team called the Rockets.

See San Diego Rockets (NBA).

Stars (NASL) 1968

Summit (MISL) 1978/79-1979/80

The Houston team played in the Houston Summit arena, thus they adopted the name of the arena.

Texans (WFL) 1974

The Houston team took the name of several previous Texas professional football teams, none of which had been successful. Before the season was complete, the team moved to Shreveport (LA) and changed its name to Steamer.

HUDSON (NY)

Hudson (ML-1) 1927/28

This was one of many of the early basketball teams that was known only by its town or city name.

INDIANAPOLIS (IN)

ABC's (NNL-1) 1920-1926
ABC's (NNL-1) 1931
ABC's (NSL) 1932
ABC's (NAL) 1938-1939

In 1904, Charles I. Taylor took over the Birmingham Giants as manager, and in 1914 he moved the team to West Baden (or West Baden Springs, IN, sources are not unanimous) and changed its name to the West Baden Sprudels. In 1915, he moved the club to Indianapolis where he obtained the financial support of the American Brewing Company; thus the name ABC's.

Athletics (NAL) 1937

Clowns (NAL) 1946-1950

See Cincinnati Clowns (NAL).

Colts (NFL) 1984—

See Baltimore Colts (AAFC).

Crawfords (NAL) 1940

See Pittsburgh Crawfords (NNL-2).

Hoosiers (NL) 1878

See Indianapolis Hoosiers (FL).

Hoosiers (AA) 1884

See Indianapolis Hoosiers (FL).

Hoosiers (NL) 1887-1889

See Indianapolis Hoosiers (FL).

Hoosiers (FL) 1914

Many Indianapolis teams adopted the state nickname (Hoosier) for their name.

Jets (BAA) 1948/49

When the Indianapolis Kautskys of the NBL joined the BAA, they had to change their name, because the BAA did not want teams to have commerical sponsors. (*See* Indianapolis Kautskys.)

Kautskys (NPBL) 1932/33
Kautskys (MBC) 1935/36-1936/37
Kautskys (NBL) 1937/38-1939/40
Kautskys (NBL) 1941/42
Kautskys (NBL) 1945/46-1947/48

Frank Kautsky was born and raised in Indianapolis. He farmed until he was twenty-nine, then started a grocery business. In 1928, he started an amateur team that won the state independent title. The next year the team turned professional, and the Kautskys were on their way.

Although Kautsky never played basketball, he had been a semipro baseball player and sponsored a team until World War II.

When the NBL was formed in 1937, it was Kautsky who wanted it to be called the National Basketball League, not the Central League, as most owners preferred.

When his team made the move to the BAA, his name had to be dropped, and the team was called the Jets.

Olympians (NBA) 1949/50-1952/53

The University of Kentucky Wildcats had been the NCAA champions in 1948 and 1949. The entire team (Alex Groza, Ralph Beard, Cliff Barker, Wah Wah

Jones, and Joe Holland) had played as part of the 1948 U. S. Olympic team. They wanted to continue to play together, and the NBL gave them their own franchise when they graduated in the spring of 1949.

The natural name for this group of Olympians was Olympians.

However, the NBL and the BAA agreed to merge before the 1949/50 season began. There were now two teams from Indianapolis: the Jets (*nee* Kautskys), who had played in 1948/49, and the Olympians, who had not played as yet.

The Jets dropped out, and the Olympians played their first season in the new NBA.

Racers (WHA) 1974/75-1978/79

Indianapolis is well-known for the Speedway and the auto races held there.

U. S. Tires (MBC) 1935/36-1936/37

The team was sponsored by the U. S. Tire and Rubber Company.

INDIANAPOLIS-CINCINNATI

Clowns (NAL) 1944

See Cincinnati Clowns (NAL).

INDIANA (IN)

Pacers (ABA) 1967/68-1975/76
Pacers (NBA) 1976/77—

When a group of Indianapolis businessmen formed Indiana Professional Sports, Inc., and got an ABA franchise, they decided to use the state name rather than the city name.

Then on 6/8/67, general manager Mike Storen announced that the team would be called Pacers because:

> (1) We feel we will set the pace in the ABA, (2) we will be playing at the Fairgrounds Coliseum across the street from where the pacers race at the fair, and (3) the pace in auto racing is set in Indianapolis each May.

JACKSONVILLE (FL)

Bulls (USFL) 1984-1985

The Bulls announced their name during the July Fourth fireworks display over the St. John's River. The name was selected in a Name the Team contest.

Express (WFL) 1975

Red Caps (NAL) 1938
Red Caps (NAL) 1941-1942

The Red Caps were so named because most of their players had jobs as red caps at the train station, and this was an inducement to get players to sign with the team.

Sharks (WFL) 1974

The Sharks disbanded before the end of the season with a 4-10 record.

Tea Men (NASL) 1981-1982

See New England Tea Men (NASL).

JERSEY CITY (NJ)

Diamonds (ML-2) 1932/33

The team played the second half of the season only and was also known as the Palace Diamonds.

JERSEY (NJ)

Knights (WHA) 1973/74

The New York Golden Blades were in financial trouble in the early part of the 1973/74 season, and the league moved the team out of Madison Square Garden and into the less-expensive Cherry Hill Arena in Cherry Hill, NJ. At the same time, the league gave the franchise a new name: Knights.

Reds (ABL-2) 1934/35-1939/40

The team disbanded 1/24/40.
See Union City Reds (ML-2).

KANKAKEE (IL)

Gallagher Trojans (NBL) 1937/38

Because most of the players were from the Gallagher Business School, in Kankakee, the team took the school name and nickname.

KANSAS CITY (MO)

Athletics (AL) 1955-1967
See Philadelphia Athletics (AL).

Blues (NFL) 1924
Kansas City entered the NFL on 1/26/24 and played the first season under the name Blues, which had been used when the team was an independent. In 1925 the team changed its name to Cowboys, a reflection of the Western tradition of the state, and then disbanded at the end of the 1926 season. Some sources continued to refer to the Cowboys as the Blues.

Chiefs (AFL-4) 1963-1969
Chiefs (NFL) 1970—
When H. L. Hunt decided to move his Dallas Texans to Kansas City, he renamed the team Chiefs in honor of H. Roe Bartle, the mayor of Kansas City. Bartle, whose nickname was "the Chief," had been instrumental in getting the Texans to move by promising to enlarge the stadium and guaranteeing three times as many season tickets sales as Hunt had in Dallas.

Comets (MISL) 1981/82—
The team played as the Detroit Lightning (1979/80) and San Francisco Fog (1980/81) before becoming the Comets.

Cowboys (NL) 1886
See Kansas City Cowboys (AA).

Cowboys (AA) 1888-1889
Kansas City was very much a part of the Western frontier in the 1880s, and teams then, as later, took nicknames that reflected the Western tradition and the cattle industry.

Cowboys (NFL) 1925-1926
See Kansas City Blues (NFL).

Kings (NBA) 1975/76-1984/85
When the Royals moved to the Kansas City area (they first played as the Kansas City-Omaha team), they decided that a new name was needed. The owners did not want to cause confusion with the Kansas City Royals (AL) baseball team.

A Name the Team contest was held, and among the suggestions were names that reflected the history of the city (Scouts, Plainsmen, River Kings, etc.) and names that continued the Royals tradition (Barons, Crowns, Kings, Regals). Kings was selected in the fan balloting.

Monarchs (NNL-1) 1920-1927
Monarchs (NNL-1) 1929-1930
Monarchs (NAL) 1937-1950
The Monarchs were organized by J. L. Wilkinson, the only white man in the Negro National League, in 1920. Wilkinson had been involved in baseball since organizing the interracial All-Nations team in Des Moines (IA). In 1915, he moved the team to Kansas City, and it disbanded in 1918 because of World War I.

When Wilkinson formed the 1920 team for the NNL, he took the core of his All-Nations team and added a considerable number of players from a former army team (the 25th Infantry Wreakers) that had been stationed at Fort Huachuca, Arizona. Because of the number of players from the 25th, the early Monarchs were sometimes referred to as the "army" team.

The name Monarchs, however, came from a previous team that had played in Kansas City at the turn of the century. The team played into the early 1910s before disbanding.

At first, most of the players on the Wilkinson team wanted to name it the Kansas City Browns, but it was pitcher John Donaldson who suggested Monarchs, and the team became a legend in baseball.

Packers (FL) 1914-1915
Kansas City is famous for its stockyards and meatpacking industry, and the name Packers, along with Cowboys and Steers, reflects this heritage.

Royals (AL) 1969—
Although Kansas City selected the name of their AL expansion team in a Name the Team contest, there had been a previous Royals team. As early as 1940, a team called the Kansas City Royals was organized by Chet Brewer, a great pitcher for the Kansas City Monarchs. These Royals played in the integrated California State Winter League, a nonofficial league comprised of barnstorming teams. For Brewer's team, Royals was a natural variation of the Monarchs name.

When the AL team held its contest, they received more than 17,000 entries. Club officials selected Royals, and the winner, based on his letter of explanation, was Sanford Porte, of Overland Park, Kansas. Some of the other names suggested included Blues (for the Kansas City minor-league team) and numerous nicknames (Steers, Cowpokes, etc.) reflecting the stockyards and Western heritage.

Scouts (NHL) 1974/75-1975/76
Named after the scouts who worked for the U. S. Army and for wagon trains going westward from Kansas City.

Spurs (NASL) 1968-1970
Considering the range of Western-related names (Cowboys, Scouts, etc.) that Kansas City teams used, Spurs seems a natural. Spurs are worn by cowboys.
However, this Kansas City team got its name in 1967, when it was the Chicago franchise in the National Professional Soccer League (NPSL). When the club moved to Kansas City, it just kept the name.
Steers (ABL-3) 1961/62-1962/63
See Kansas City Packers (FL).

Unions (UA) 1884
When the Altoona team dropped out of the UA, Kansas City was given its franchise. The Kansas City team took the name of the league, as did most UA clubs, for their team name.

KANSAS CITY-OMAHA

Kings (NBA) 1972/73-1974/75
See Kansas City Kings (NBA).

KENOSHA (WI)

Maroons (NFL) 1924
See Toledo Maroons (NFL).

KENTUCKY

Colonels (ABA) 1967/68-1975/76
When the team announced its name Colonels, it was sometimes referred to as the Louisville Colonels; however, the team owners used the more regional state name to attract a larger fan base.
The nickname Colonels has long been used by teams in the state, especially in Louisville.

KEOKUK (IA)

Westerns (NA) 1875
The Keokuk team was incorporated on June 13, 1872, as the Western Base Ball Association of Keokuk. Despite the fact that it was a relatively small town (11,000 population), Keokuk got a chance to play in the NA during the league's final season.
Keokuk played only thirteen games, winning only one, but it had its brief moment of glory. In later years, Keokuk would be represented in the Western League by the Keokuk Kernels.

KINGSTON (NY)

Colonials (ML-1) 1924/25
Colonials (ML-1) 1926/27-1927/28
See Kingston Colonials (ABL-2).

Colonials (ABL-2) 1935/36-1939/40
Kingston had a rich history in Colonial America, and it is possible that the earlier teams in the Metropolitan League were named to reflect this heritage. However, the American Basketball League team was definitely sponsored by a local Colonial Cities Services gas station. It is unclear if the earlier teams had the same sponsor. Teams named Colonials played in Kingston prior to the 1924/25 season.
The ABL team disbanded on 12/19/39.

KOKOMO (IN)

Kelts (NPBL) 1932/33
The Kelts were owned and operated by George Von der Ahe, who, as far as we know, was not related to the St. Louis baseball team owner. George Von der Ahe owned the local Phillips 66 gas station, and the team was sometimes referred to as the Phillips 66ers, but there was definitely no connection to the great Oklahoma AAU team of the same name.
Kelts is a variant spelling of Celts, and the original word may have meant "warrior." The Celts were primarily the peoples of Scotland, Ireland, Wales, and Brittany.

LAS VEGAS (NV)

Americans (MISL) 1984/85
See Memphis Americans (MISL).

Quicksilver (NASL) 1977

Quicksilver is another name for mercury, which is silver-white in color. Although there is no documentation to support the theory, the name may have been chosen as a play on words, since Mercury is also the Roman speedster (and soccer is a fast sport) and quicksilver relates indirectly to Las Vegas's casinos and the desire for "quick silver."

LINCOLN GIANTS

See (New York) Lincoln Giants.

LONG BEACH (CA)

Chiefs (ABL-3) 1962/63
See Hawaii Chiefs (ABL-3).

LONG ISLAND (NY)

Pros (ML-2) 1931/32-1932/33

This team's full name was Pro-Imps but they were called the Pros by everyone. The Pros dropped out of the league at the end of the first half of the 1932/33 season.

LORAIN (OH)

Fisher Foods (NBPL) 1932/33

The team was sponsored by the Fisher Foods Company.

LOS ANGELES (CA)

Angels (AL) 1961-1965

The AL expansion team owned by Gene Autry took its name primarily from the farm club of the NL Chicago Cubs. In fact, the AL team played its first season in Wrigley Field, the home of the minor-league team.

The original Angels had played in the Pacific Coast League (PCL) from 1919 until 1957, when the Dodgers brought major-league baseball to Los Angeles. The PCL Angels (and the AL team) took the name Angels because Los Angeles is known as the City of Angels.

Aztecs (NASL) 1974-1981

The team was named for the great Mexican civilization and the fact that Los Angeles has a large Mexican-American population who are avid soccer fans.

Buccaneers (NFL) 1926

The Buccaneers were the first Los Angeles team in the NFL, but they were primarily a road team and although they posted a 6-3-1 record, the traveling costs proved too much. The team received permission to suspend league operations for 1927, but on 8/12/28 withdrew from the league.

Bulldogs (AFL-2) 1937

The Bulldogs were an independent team, newly organized in 1936 and sponsored by Professional Sports, Inc., a subsidiary of the local American Legion. The powerful West Coast team beat the Pittsburgh Pirates of the NFL 27-7 in an exhibition game, and the Pirates were 6-5 at the time.

The 1936 team was granted a "probationary franchise" by the NFL, but despite the team's stong showing on the field and in attendance, the NFL felt that costs for West Coast travel would be prohibitive.

In 1937, the NFL opted to bring in the Cleveland Rams (AFL-2), instead of the Bulldogs. The Bulldogs then joined the AFL, replacing the Rams.

In 1946, the Cleveland Rams became the Los Angeles Rams.

The Bulldogs won the AFL title in 1937, with a 9-0 record, posted at 10-2-2 record in 1938 (with a 28-7 win over the Rams), and were 7-1 in 1939.

Chargers (AFL-4) 1960

The Los Angeles entry in the AFL held a Name the Team contest to pick the club's nickname, and the final selection of the name was made by Barron Hilton, the team's owner. He selected the name Chargers for three reasons, although some sources believe it was more for the last reason. The first reason was that it reflected an electrical charge (such as the lighning bolt shown on their helmets and pants); the second was that the San Diego club stationery had a symbol of a horse charging; and the last was that the Hilton hotel chain had just launched the Carte Blanche charge card.

Gerald Courtney of Hollywood was selected as the contest winner and received an all-expense-paid trip to Mexico.

Clippers (NBA) 1984/85
See San Diego Clippers (NBA).

Dodgers (NL) 1958—
See Brooklyn Dodgers (NL).

Dons (AAFC) 1946-1949
A don is a Spanish nobleman or gentleman, and its choice as a nickname was a reflection of the Spanish heritage of Los Angeles. Also, it was a reflection of the owner's name, actor Don Ameche.

Express (USFL) 1983-1985

Jets (ABL-3) 1961/62
The team folded midway through the second half of the season.

Kings (NHL) 1967/68—
Although the Kings held a Name the Team contest to select the team name, the final choice was made by owner Jack Kent Cooke.

Lakers (NBA) 1960/61—
See Minneapolis Lakers (NBL).

Lazers (MISL) 1984/85

Raiders (NFL) 1982—
See Oakland Raiders (AFL-4).

Rams (NFL) 1946—
See Cleveland Rams (AFL-2).

Sharks (WHA) 1972/73-1973/74

Stars (ABA) 1968/69-1969/70
Although many teams use the nickname Stars, it is most appropriate for Los Angeles, the city of the movie industry. (There had been a Hollywood Stars team in baseball's PCL for many years.)
When the Los Angeles team moved to Utah (Salt Lake City) it retained the Stars nickname.

Wildcats (AFL-1) 1926
The Los Angeles Wildcats went by several different names. It was an independent team, organized by George Wilson, a former standout player at the University of Washington. It played both before and after its one-year membership in the AFL-1.

The team was called Wilson's Wildcats, the West Coast Wildcats, and really had no home base, except the West Coast.

Wolves (NASL) 1968
In 1967, Los Angeles was represented in the United Soccer Association (USA) by the famous English club, the Wolverhampton Wanderers (also called the Wolves). When Los Angeles got an NASL franchise for 1968, the team adopted the nickname of the Wolverhampton club.

LOUISVILLE (KY)

Black Caps (NSL) 1932
The Black Caps played the first half of the season only.

Brecks (APFA) 1921
Brecks (NFL) 1922-1923
Although a rather unusual name for a football team, it may have been a family name (possibly a shortened form of Breckenridge) and thus a sponsored team. The team began around 1907 or 1908 as a boys' neighborhood team, the Floyd and Brecks.

Buckeyes (NAL) 1949
Buckeyes is not a Kentucky nickname, but when the Cleveland (OH) team played in Louisville for one year, they retained their nickname.
See Cleveland Buckeyes (NAL).

Colonels (NL) 1876-1877
See Kentucky Colonels (ABA).

Colonels (AA) 1884-1891
Colonels (NL) 1892-1899
See Kentucky Colonels (ABA).

Colonels (NFL) 1926
This club was a road team that operated out of Chicago. It posted an 0-4 record and dropped out of the league.
See Kentucky Colonels (ABA).

Eclipse (AA) 1882-1883
Louisville's entry in the AA was initially called Eclipse in honor of American Eclipse, a famous race-horse that had been retired to stud in Kentucky. He died at the age of thirty-three.

In 1884, the Louisville team became known as the Colonels.

White Sox (NNL-1) 1931

MEMPHIS (TN)

Americans (MISL) 1981/82-1983/84

From Hellions to Americans is a rather interesting change, but that's what happened when the Hartford Hellions moved to Memphis. The reason for the nicknames is unknown.

Pros (ABA) 1970/71-1971/72

In an interview with sports editor John Bibb (10/20/70) in the *Nashville Tennessean*, coach Babe McCarthy explained how he named the former New Orleans Buccaneers the Pros.

It was a matter of economics. McCarthy said:

> As you probably know, until eight weeks ago, the franchise was in New Orleans where we were called the Buccaneers. Before moving to Memphis we had invested approximately $1,000 in uniforms for 1970/71. Across the front of each jersey was the word Bucs.

McCarthy wanted to change the name when the franchise moved but he didn't want to toss out $1,000 worth of basketball uniforms.

> I was hard-pressed to come up with a nickname from which I might be able to salvage a letter or two on our new uniforms without altering the style of the jersey. I thought about calling the team the Elks, but that might have been confusing. Finally I cut off the first three letters on a jersey and decided until we came up with new uniforms to add the word Pro to the remaining "s" and that's how it happened.

Although McCarthy indicated that the franchise would have a new name for the following year, the name Pros stuck with the team until it was bought by Charlie Finley and renamed the Tams. (Did you wonder if Mr. Finley used the same jerseys and cut out the first three letters? He didn't.)

Red Sox (NNL-1) 1924-1925
Red Sox (NNL-1) 1927
Red Sox (NNL-1) 1929-1930
Red Sox (NSL) 1932
Red Sox (NAL) 1937-1941
Red Sox (NAL) 1943-1950

Although the Memphis Red Sox played for nearly thirty years, very little is known about the team or its history.

Rogues (NASL) 1978-1980

Showboats (USFL) 1984-1985

The team was named for the Mississippi River showboats that make Memphis their main port of call.

Sounds (ABA) 1974/75

When Charles Finley sold the Memphis Tams, one of the new owners was Isaac Hayes, who also owned Stax Records. The team name was changed to Sounds, even though Hayes did not continue as an owner.

In August 1975, the team was moved to Baltimore and hastily renamed the Hustlers. The new name set off a wave of complaints from the city. David Cohan, president of the club, was quoted as saying, "We didn't mean to offend anyone. We picked the name because we needed one in a hurry and 'hustler' to us has always meant hustling ballplayers." Cohan was alluding to the nickname's association with prostitution. The team's arena was situated just down the street from the honky-tonk section of East Baltimore Street.

Cohan held a Name the Team contest, and the new choice was Claws, which is associated with Maryland's seafood industry. The state is famous for crabs.

However, neither name was ever used. The Baltimore franchise was canceled by the ABA just four days before the season was scheduled to begin.

Southmen (WFL) 1974-1975

The Memphis Southmen were going to be the Toronto Northmen, but owner John Bassett was blocked by restrictions imposed by the Canadian government.

When he moved his franchise to Memphis, the name Northmen was quite inappropriate, so he changed it to Southmen.

Tams (ABA) 1972/73-1973/74
When Charles Finley purchased the Memphis Pros franchise of the ABA, he held a contest to rename the team. Finley announced the winner of the $2,500 first prize on 7/15/72.

According to Finley, more than 20,000 entries were submitted during the two-week contest, and the winner was Bill Barrett of West Point (MS). Barrett suggested the name Tams, using the initials for Tennessee, Arkansas, and Mississippi. Because the Memphis (TN) city limits adjoin the Mississippi and Arkansas state lines, Barrett felt the name would give a regional recognition for the team.

MIAMI (FL)

Dolphins (AFL-4) 1966-1969
Dolphins (NFL) 1970—
The Miami AFL franchise held a Name the Team contest and received more than 20,000 entries. Some of the names included Mariners, Missiles, Sharks, and Marauders.

The dolphin is very popular in Florida and was quickly accepted not only as the nickname but also as the team mascot. The contest winner, Mrs. Robert Swanson, of West Miami, received two lifetime passes to Dolphin games.

Floridians (ABA) 1968/69-1969/70
The ABA team initially took the state name as its nickname and played its games in Miami; however, it became a regional team in 1970/71 by calling itself the Floridians and playing home games in Miami, Tampa, and Jacksonville.

Gatos (NASL) 1972
Gatos is the Spanish word for "cat," and soccer players are supposed to be as fast and agile as cats.

Heat (NBA) 1988/89—
Miami was quite confident of getting an NBA franchise, because they held their Name the Team contest before they were awarded the franchise. Basketball, Inc., the franchise owner, enlisted the support of the local Burger Kings for convenience in balloting. More than 20,000 entries were received, and they were narrowed first to 900 and then the top 20 by a panel of sports writers. The top three choices were Heat, Flamingos, and Waves.

When the final selection was announced, record high temperatures and the hottest October on record made the final selection of Heat seem the only obvious choice. According to one of the owners, Zev Bufman,

> There's something about Heat. It's hot, it really works. It's easy to remember and something that graphically can be turned into something very exciting, with colors like reds, yellows, and oranges.

The contest winner was Stephanie Freed, who was one of 126 who submitted the name Heat. Her name was picked in a drawing, and she received two season tickets and two tickets to see Julio Iglesias in concert (Iglesias was one of the owners!).

The names that didn't make it? Try Bagels, Vice, Hookers, Sand Dribblers, Beachballs, Frosts, Vipers, Muggers, and Maniacs, just for a start.

Seahawks (AAFC) 1946
The Seahawks were owned by Harvey Hester, of Atlanta. After the season, the team folded, and the franchise was replaced by the Baltimore Colts.

Toros (NASL) 1973-1976
In 1972, the Miami team was called Gatos, "cats," but they changed it to Toros, "bulls." Perhaps they wanted to project a more powerful image.

MICHIGAN

Panthers (USFL) 1983-1984
Although the team was called the Michigan Panthers, it was really the Detroit Panthers, since that was where they played their home games. Like several other USFL teams, the Panthers had selected a team name that bore some resemblance to the NFL team in their city. For the Panthers, the competition was the Lions. (For the Oakland Invaders, it was the NFL Oakland Raiders.)

Also, there had been an earlier NFL Detroit Panther team.

Stags (WHA) 1974/75
The Stags moved to Baltimore on 1/23/75 and became the Blades. As a result of the move, the Baltimore Clippers of the minor American Hockey League disbanded.

MIDDLETOWN (CT)

Mansfield (NA) 1872
The Mansfields were the champions of Connecticut in 1870 and a highly regarded team in the New England region. According to a letter to the editor of the *Hartford Courant* (5/22/1871), the team was anxious to take on all challengers and their uniforms were "white with blue trimmings, blue stockings and white hat with blue band around same." The team was named after General Joseph Mansfield, a Union general who was killed in the Civil War at the Battle of Antietam at Sharpsburg, Maryland.

MIDLAND (MI)

Dow A. C. (NBL) 1947/48
For many years, a very successful independent team had been sponsored by the Dow Chemical Company. It was called the Dow Chemicals, although the official name was the Dow A. C. (Athletic Club).

As an expansion franchise in the NBL, the team started to play in Midland but the league felt the gymnasium in Midland was inadequate. The league moved the franchise to Flint (MI) in the early part of the 1947/48 season.

MILWAUKEE (WI)

Badgers (NFL) 1922-1926
The badger is the state animal of Wisconsin, and the team adopted it for its nickname.

Bears (NNL-1) 1923
The Bears dropped out with a 14-32 record before the end of the season.

Braves (NL) 1953-1965
See Boston Braves (NL).

Brewers (NL) 1878
See Milwaukee Brewers (AL) 1970—.

Brewers (AA) 1891
See Milwaukee Brewers (AL) 1970—.

Brewers (AL) 1901
See Milwaukee Brewers (AL) 1970—.

Brewers (AL) 1970—
Milwaukee and Brewers go together. The city has long been known for its many breweries and has been called the Beer Capital of the World. Several other baseball teams, notably the American Association (AA) minor-league club, have carried the Brewer nickname.

The 1891 AA team was originally a team in Cincinnati (Kelly's Killers) that moved to Milwaukee in mid-August.

The 1901 AL team moved to St. Louis and became the Browns in 1902. The 1970 AL team had been the Seattle Pilots in 1969.

Bucks (NBA) 1968/69—
When the Milwaukee NBA team sponsored a Name the Team contest, they drew over 14,000 entries in a competition to win the first prize of a Javelin automobile.

The winner of the contest, R. D. Trebilcox, of Whitefish Bay, was one of forty-five entrants who suggested the name Bucks; Mrs. Clara Sery was the runner-up. Team general manager John Erickson said that the name reflected what he called "the wildlife atmosphere of Wisconsin."

The contest had a rather interesting structure. The contestants had to select five reasons for their choice from a list supplied by the sponsor. Then they had to provide a sixth reason of their own.

Trebilcox, Mrs. Sery, and five others who picked Bucks also picked the following five reasons in the same order as the contest sponsors (the Coca-Cola Co. and the Milwaukee NBA club).

The reasons were: 1) the name fits the Wisconsin image; 2) it fits the sport of basketball; 3) it adapts to promotional use; 4) it is not similar to other names used by professional teams; and 5) it is modern and up-to-date.

Trebilcox's sixth reason was that "Bucks are spirited, good jumpers, fast and agile. These are good qualities for basketball players."

Most of the names suggested for the new team were those of animals or insects, such as, Badgers, Beavers, Skunks, Stags, Stallions, Hornets, and Ponies. Additional suggestions included Packers, Braves, and names of various Indian tribes.

Chiefs (AFL-3) 1940-1941
The Chiefs were owned by George Harris, president of the Milwaukee Football Club, but Harris ran into financial problems. The league then turned the

franchise over to be administered by the local American Legion.

Hawks (NBA) 1951/52-1954/55
See Buffalo Bisons (NBL) 1946/47.

Unions (UA) 1884
Milwaukee dropped out of the league with an 8-4 record. This team took the name of the league, the Union Association. Teams in the UA were sometimes called Onions.

MINNEAPOLIS (MN)

Lakers (NBL) 1947/48
Lakers (BAA) 1948/49
Lakers (NBA) 1949/50—
When Minneapolis joined the NBL for the 1947/48 season, it adopted the nickname Lakers because the state was known as the Land of 10,000 Lakes. This slogan has even appeared on the state auto license plates.

Marines (APRA) 1921
Marines (NFL) 1922-1924

Red Jackets (NFL) 1929-1930
Red Jacket was an American Indian chief who got his name when he was given a red jacket by a British officer. (His Indian name was Sagoyewatha.)

Many early football teams used Indian or Indian-related names for their teams. It is possible that the Minneapolis team got its name in that way.

Also, many of the early fire companies used Indian names to identify their company. Red Jacket was also used in this manner on several occasions.

We may not know how Minneapolis got the name Red Jackets, but we do know how Red Jacket got his name.

MINNESOTA

Fighting Saints (WHA) 1972/73-1975/76
The team was based in St. Paul, and many professional teams, especially baseball teams, from the city have been called Saints. Since this was a hockey team, Fighting Saints may have seemed more appropriate, but is somewhat a contradiction in terms.

Kicks (NASL) 1976-1981
The Denver Dynamos transferred to Minnesota in November 1975, and a Name the Team contest was held to select a new nickname. The winning name was Kicks, which was thought to be most appropriate for a soccer team.

Muskies (ABA) 1967/68
Muskies is itself a nickname. It is a lot easier to say than Muskellunge, the correct name for these sixty- to eighty-pound pike that are considered excellent sport fish.

Muskies abound in the lakes of Minnesota.

North Stars (NHL) 1967/68
Minnesota is known as the North Star State, and its state motto is *L'Etoile du Nord* (The Star of the North). Thus when the new NHL team held its Name the Team contest, it was no wonder that North Stars was the most frequently submitted name, with fifty-two entries.

Then followed, in order, Norsemen, Voyageurs, Blades, Mustangs, Muskies, Lumberjacks, Miners, Mallards, Pioneers, Polars, and Marauders.

The winners of a $100 savings bond and two season tickets were Mr. and Mrs. William R. Swanson of Shoreview, a suburb of St. Paul. Their joint entry was drawn by Minnesota Governor Karl Rolvaag.

Both of the Swansons were high school physical education teachers. Mr. Swanson, a 1960 graduate of the University of Minnesota, had earned three letters in hockey while in college and was still active in the Minnesota Hockey League.

Club president Walter L. Bush, Jr., said the board of directors selected the name North Stars after:

> careful deliberation and study of all submitted entries and some which were not submitted. We wanted a name which is synonymous primarily with the State of Minnesota but which also would be acceptable to surrounding areas from which we will draw our fans.

The contest drew 1,536 entries and 608 different nicknames.

Pipers (ABA) 1968/69
See Pittsburgh Pipers (ABA).

Strikers (NASL) 1984
Strikers (MISL) 1984/85-1987/88
See Fort Lauderdale Strikers (NASL).

Timberwolves (NBA) 1989/90—

The owners of the new NBA franchise in Minneapolis wanted to have everyone in Minnesota feel this was their team. Their first act was to make it the Minnesota team, not the Minneapolis team. Then, when they got down to the final two choices (Timberwolves or Polars), it was left up to the 842 city councils around the state to make the decision. That choice was Timberwolves.

The club held a Name the Team contest four months before the NBA granted Minnesota a franchise. The fans submitted 6,076 entries with 1,284 different nicknames. The winning name of Timberwolves was submitted by seventeen people, and a drawing produced the winner. Tim Pope of Brooklyn Center (MN) received a trip to the 1987 NBA All-Star weekend in Seattle.

According to club officials, the entries ran through a number of different categories, including animals, fish, political interests, outer space, already-existing team names, some names that had to be researched in a dictionary, and a group that couldn't be categorized. A few of the names the judges looked at include Purple Cows, Ice Breakers, Snowballs, Big Dippers, Fat Cats, Whalers, Killer Karps, and Zips—none of which was high on the list!

Twins (AL) 1961—

When the AL agreed to expansion, Calvin Griffith, president of the Washington Senators, expressed the desire to transfer his team to the Twin Cities of Minneapolis and St. Paul. Both cities had a long history of supporting minor-league baseball.

Griffith was allowed to make the move and originally decided to call his new team the Twin Cities (although some sources indicate it was Twin Cities Twins). However, he soon decided that the name of the state (Minnesota) combined with Twins (for the Twin Cities) made an excellent name that appealed to the entire state.

Vikings (NFL) 1961—

The Minnesota franchise almost became an AFL-4 team. The city of Minneapolis had been granted a franchise in the new league but received an offer to join the NFL (which it had been trying to do without success). The NFL franchise was granted on 1/28/60 for a 1961 starting date.

The selection of the team name fell to Bert Rose, the general manager of the team. He selected Vikings because of the rich Nordic heritage of Minnesota and also because the Vikings were fearless warriors.

MONROE (LA)

Monarchs (NSL) 1932

The Monroe Monarchs were owned by J. C. Stovall, a white businessman who owned a drilling company. He not only built very strong teams in the 1920s and 1930s, but he also built an excellent ball park with a swimming pool and dance hall for the black community of Monroe. For visiting black teams, this was probably the best place to play in the South because of the royal treatment Stovall extended to the ball players.

MONTGOMERY (AL)

Grey Sox (NSL) 1932

The Grey Sox played in the 1920s and 1930s, but most of their years were either as a barnstorming team or as a member of the NSL when it was a minor league.

MONTREAL (Quebec)

Canadiens (NHL) 1917/18—

The Montreal team began in 1909 as a member of the National Hockey Association (NHA) and represented the French community in Quebec. In fact, originally this team, know as *Les Canadiens* and as *Les Habitantes* (the inhabitants), could only sign French players, while other teams in the league were not allowed to sign French skaters.

The nickname Canadiens is the French spelling of Canadians. The team has often been referred to as the Habs, and their jersey shows both the letter C (for Canadiens) and H (for Habitantes).

Although the Montreal team carries its French heritage with great pride (often called the Frenchmen), the ban against a team signing only English or French players has long since been dropped by the NHL.

Expos (NL) 1969—

The Montreal franchise was awarded right after the city had been host to the very successful 1967 Montreal World's Fair, known as Expo '67. Club owners decided that Expos would be a perfect name for the new team.

The team played the first two years in Autostate Stadium, which had been built expressly for Expo '67 and financed by the Canadian automobile manufacturers.

Manic (NASL) 1981-1983

The team was named for the Manicouagan River in northern Quebec, where a massive hydroelectric project had just been completed.

Maroons (NHL) 1924/25-1937/38

The Maroons were formed by James Strachan and Donat Raymond, who felt that Montreal needed to have a club for Montreal's English-speaking minority. Strachan and Raymond were head of the organization that had built the Montreal Forum, for the Canadiens.

The Forum opened on 11/29/24. A second team, especially one that had a natural rivalry with the first team (the Canadiens), would increase gate receipts and use of the Forum.

Although the Maroons had won the Stanley Cup in 1934/35, it became evident in the mid 1930s that the Forum and Montreal could only support one team. Since the Forum management now owned both teams, the choice in the predominately French city had to be to keep the Canadiens. The Maroons dropped out of the NHL at the end of the 1937/38 season.

Their nickname reflected to the color of their jerseys.

Olympique (NASL) 1971-1973

Just as Montreal named its NL baseball team for a World's Fair, they decided to name a soccer team for the then-forthcoming 1976 Olympics, which the city hoped to host.

Because Montreal is a predominantly French-speaking city, the spelling of the nickname is the French spelling of Olympics.

Wanderers (NHL) 1917/18

The Wanderers played in the National Hockey Association (NHA) from 1909/10 through the 1916/17 season, when they became one of the four original teams in the NHL.

Prior to playing in the NHA, the Wanderers had played in the Eastern Canada Hockey Association and in the Federal League; perhaps that is how they got their nickname.

Although the Wanderers played in the NHL's first season, they were forced to drop out before the second season was barely underway.

The Wanderers had been playing their games in the Montreal Arena, but the arena burned down, and the Wanderers were homeless.

MUNCIE (IN)

Flyers (APFA) 1920-1921

The Muncie team dropped out of the league after two games in the 1921 season.

Whys (NPBL) 1932/33

The Whys joined the league in mid season to replace the Kokomo Kelts. The team was called the Whys because they played their games at the local Y (YMCA).

NASHVILLE (TN)

Elite Giants (NNL-1) 1930
Elite Giants (NSL) 1932
Elite Giants (NNL-2) 1933-1934

The Elite Giants were started in 1918 as the Standard Giants of Nashville by Thomas T. Wilson.

In 1921, they became the Elite Giants. Wilson owned the team until his death in 1947.

From 1930 until 1950, the Elite Giants played in a league every year, representing Nashville, Columbus (OH), Cleveland, Baltimore, or Washington.

They were always the Elite Giants, except for one year (1931), when they were known as the Cleveland Cubs.

Although his team moved around, Wilson lived in Nashville, where he was the owner of the Paradise Club. He served as president of the NNL-2 from 1938 until 1946 and was president of the NSL.

See Cleveland Cubs (NNL-1) and Cuban Giants.

NEWARK (NJ)

Bears (AFL-1) 1926
This team was owned by George Halas, who also owned the Chicago Bears. There was no connection to the Newark Bears baseball team of the International League.

Bears (ML-1) 1925/26
It is possible that this basketball team may have adopted the name of the popular baseball team of the International League, but further research is necessary.

Dodgers (NNL-2) 1934/35

Eagles (NNL-2) 1936-1948
See Brooklyn Eagles (NNL-2).

Joe Fays (ABL-2) 1933/34
There are some references to this team as the Bears. The source of the nickname Joe Fays is unknown. The Joe Fays became the Newark Mules for the 1934/35 season, but on 1/18/35 the Newark team moved to New Britain (CT) and became the New Britain Mules. There was a team in New Britain called the Jackaways, but they disbanded on 1/18/35. The nickname Mules was used by several Newark teams. Again, the reason is unknown.

Mules (ABL-2) 1934/35
See Newark Joe Fays (ABL-2).

Peppers (FL) 1915
The Indiana Hoosiers of 1914 moved to Newark and became the Peppers. Although called the Newark Peppers, the team actually played their games in nearby Harrison (NJ).

Stars (ECL) 1926
The Stars disbanded in mid season with a 1-10 record.

Tornadoes (NFL) 1930
See Orange Tornadoes (NFL).

NEW BRITAIN (CT)

Jackaways (ABL-2) 1934/35
See North Hudson Thourots (ABL-2).

Mules (ABL-2) 1934/35
See Newark Joe Fays (ABL-2).

Palace (ABL-2) 1933/34
See North Hudson Thourots (ABL-2).

NEW ENGLAND

Patriots (NFL) 1971—
When the Boston Patriots moved to their new stadium in Foxboro (MA), they changed their name to New England Patriots. *See* Boston Patriots (AFL-4).

Tea Men (NASL) 1978-1980
The Tea Men were owned by the Lipton Tea Company. When the team moved to Jacksonville (FL), they retained the name.

Whalers (WHA) 1972/73-1978/79
The WHA franchise for New England started in Boston and moved to Hartford on 4/2/74. In both cities and while it was in the WHA the team was called the New England Whalers. However, when the team moved to the NHL, the name was changed to Hartford to avoid conflict with another New England team, the Boston Bruins.

Team officials selected the nickname Whalers. The whale has played an important part in the history of New England. New Bedford (MA) was the whaling capital of the United States, most of the seaports in Massachusetts were involved in the whaling industry, and the whale is the state animal of Connecticut. Also, the three first letters of Whalers are the initials of the WHA.

NEW HAVEN (CT)

Jewels (ABL-2) 1937/38
The team moved to New York City on 11/30/37 with a 4-2 record.
See Brooklyn Jewels (ML-2).

New Havens (NA) 1875
This was one of the early baseball teams that went by the name of the city (or town).

NEW JERSEY (NJ)

See also **Jersey.**

Americans (ABA) 1967/68

When Arthur J. Brown bought a franchise in the new ABA, he wanted to put it in New York City. Brown originally named the team the New York Freighters, because he owned the ABC Freight Forwarding Company. The team was going to play in New York's 69th Regimental Armory, but to avoid a direct confrontation with the New York Knicks of the NBA and because of a lack of a suitable court, the team was moved to New Jersey.

The team played its games in the Armory in Teaneck (NJ), and the name was changed to Americans, adopting the name from the league name.

One year later (1968/69), the team was moved to Commack, Long Island, and became the New York Nets.

See New York Nets (ABA).

Devils (NHL) 1982/83—

The story of the Jersey Devil is a popular part of New Jersey folklore. The legend concerns a Mrs. Leeds, whose thirteenth child (or in this case, a half-man, half-animal) was the cause of all the trouble. He's been running amok in the pine barrens for the past 250 years.

The name has been popular in the state, and it was the name of a minor-league team (the Jersey Devils) that played in the Eastern Hockey League.

The minor-league team had played in Cherry Hill (NJ), which is closer to Philadelphia and the South Jersey pine barrens, the home of the Jersey Devil.

When the Colorado Rockies franchise came to New Jersey, a new name was in order, so the owners held a Name the Team contest. More than 10,000 votes were cast, and Devils was the popular choice.

Other names among the final eleven were Americans, Blades, Colonials, Lightning, Meadowlarks, Meadowlanders, Coastals, Generals, Gulls, Jaguars, and Patriots.

John McMullen, the team's principal owner, said they rejected Jersey Devils as a name for the team because of possible religious objections. However, they felt that New Jersey Devils would be acceptable.

Generals (USFL) 1983-1985

One of the stipulations that the Meadowlands Sports Complex made to the new USFL franchise was that if they used the Sports Complex, the team's name would have to have some reference to New Jersey or to the Garden State.

The club owners chose to combine the state name and the word General to indicate the regional nature of the franchise.

"It's no use trying to hide your location," said Jim Valek, the club's general manager. "We didn't think that around the country a name like Metros or the Metropolitans would have the proper identification."

Nets (NBA) 1977/78

See New York Nets (ABA).

Rockets (MISL) 1981/82

Ed Tepper, owner of the New Jersey MISL team, chose the name Rockets for the team. He announced the selection on 8/29/81.

NEW ORLEANS (LA)

Breakers (USFL) 1984

Buccaneers (ABA) 1967/68-1969/70

Jazz (NBA) 1974/75-1978/79

In announcing that the New Orleans NBA team would be called Jazz, Fred Rosenfeld, president of the club, said:

> Jazz is one of those things for which New Orleans is nationally famous and locally proud. It is a great art form which belongs to New Orleans and its rich history. Jazz can be defined as collective improvisation, and that would also be an appropriate description of NBA basketball at its best.

The New Orleans club had held a Name the Team contest, and the names that were among the finalists included Jazz, Dukes, Pilots, Cajuns, Crescents, Deltas, and Knights. Dukes and Jazz were the most popular. Over 6,500 entries were received.

When the name was selected, the winning entry was pulled from three entries that had been received on the first day of the contest. Steve Brown, a twenty-seven-year-old stockbroker, was credited with the first prize of a season pass and ticket to the NBA All-Star game. Brown was a transplanted New Yorker who had been an avid Knicks fan.

Brown's reason for choosing Jazz: "The name should be something indigenous to the city. Everyone identifies Jazz with the city."

Saints (NFL) 1967—

Saints is synonymous with New Orleans. The song "When the Saints Go Marching In" could be the city's theme song. The selection of the nickname was made by the club officials, and one of the reasons given was that the franchise had been awarded to New Orleans on All Saints' Day, 11/1/66.

However, the song was probably the most compelling reason for the nickname, since it became the team's fight song.

NEW ORLEANS-ST. LOUIS

Stars (NAL) 1941
See St. Louis Stars (NNL-1).

NEW YORK (NY)

See also **Brooklyn, Bronx, Staten Island, Jamaica, and Long Island.**

Americans (ABL-2) 1943/44

The Americans had been the Jewels but realized that the original members of the team were gone and the name had little significance to the current fans. The team first changed their name to Americans, adopting the league name, and then changed in 1944/45 to the Gothams, a name that is synonymous with New York City. *See* Brooklyn Jewels (ML-2).

Americans (AFL-3) 1941

When William D. Cox took over the New York franchise from Douglas Hertz, he renamed the team because Hertz retained the rights to the name Yankees. Cox adopted the league name for the 1941 team.

Americans (NHL) 1925/26-1940/41

A New York sports writer, William McBeth, who was born in Canada, is credited with convincing bootlegger William "Big Bill" Dwyer to back a hockey team in New York. Because of the early success of the Americans, frequently referred to as the Amerks, in the newly built Madison Square Garden (then located at Eighth Avenue and Forty-ninth Street), the Garden management, led by Tex Rickard, launched the New York Rangers in 1926/27.

Because of a player dispute at Hamilton, the New York team was given permission to sign their players, and the Hamilton franchise was canceled. In essence, the Hamilton Tigers became the New York Americans.

Although there is no documentation to support this theory, the New York team may have taken its name Americans because there was a team in Canada called the Canadiens (Montreal).

The Americans were never the financial success that the Rangers were, and in 1941/42 the Americans moved to Brooklyn for one season before folding.

Arrows (MISL) 1978/79-1983/84

Black Yankees (NNL-2) 1936-1948

The New York Black Yankees were incorporated 5/1/33 by James Semler, but they trace their history to a team called the Harlem Stars. In 1930, Morty Forkins and Bill Robinson conceived the idea of a club that would play in both the Polo Grounds and at Yankee Stadium.

They wanted to call the team the Black Yankees but decided it would be inappropriate for a team that would be playing some of its games in the home (Polo Grounds) of the New York Giants. They then settled on the name Harlem Stars.

In either late 1931 or early 1932, the club was reorganized with new owners (Oscar Barnes and M. E. Goodson), and the name was changed to Black Yankees. In 1933, Semler took over the club.

The Black Yankees purchased the old uniforms of the New York Yankees, but they did not always play in New York. In 1934, for example, their home field was Hinchcliff Stadium, in Paterson (NJ).

Bulldogs (NFL) 1949

When owner Ted Collins was finally able to get his long-desired New York franchise, he had to come up with a new nickname. The team had been the Boston Yanks, and there was a New York Yankees team playing in the AAFC. Also, the name Yanks wouldn't suit a team that was going to share the Polo Grounds with the New York Giants.

Collins selected the name Bulldogs because of the history of the name (Canton Bulldogs, Yale University Bulldogs, etc.) in the early years of football.

Collins was able to change his Bulldogs to Yanks for the 1950 season when the AAFC and the New York Yankees went out of business.

See Boston Yanks (NFL).

Celtics (ABL-1) 1927/28
Celtics (ABL-1) 1929/30
The 1929/30 team dropped out of the league on 12/10/29 with a 5-5 record. All games were stricken from the record books.
See Brooklyn Celtics (ABL-1).

Celtics (ML-1) 1922/23
The Celtics dropped out of the Metropolitan League on 10/17/22 despite a 12-0 record. They joined the original Eastern League (1909/10-1922/23) to become the Atlantic City Celtics.
At the end of the first half of the 1922/23 season, the Celtics dropped out of the Eastern League, and the league folded shortly after the start of the second half of the season.

Cosmos (NASL) 1971-1984
Cosmos (MISL) 1984/85
The Cosmos received their name as the result of a Name the Team contest. The name means "an orderly, harmonious, systematic universe," and the reference here is to a well-organized, smooth-running team.

Cubans (NNL-2) 1935-1936
Cubans (NNL-2) 1939-1948
Cubans (NAL) 1949-1950
See Cuban Giants.

Express (MISL) 1986/87
The team folded on 2/17/87 with a 3-23 record.

Generals (NASL) 1968
The Generals had played in the NPSL in 1967 under the partial sponsorship of RKO-General, thus the name Generals. Although this sponsorship did not continue when the team joined the NASL, the new owners decided to retain the name.

Giants (APFA) 1921
It is not known at what specific date New York became a league member, but the team did compete against league members. The franchise also fielded a team in 1922, but it did not pay any league fees and therefore was not considered a league member for 1922. Its franchise was canceled in 1923.
Since the modern-day Giants of Mara did not join the NFL until 1925, it must be assumed that these earlier Giants adopted (as did Mara's Giants) the name of the New York NL baseball team.

Giants (NFL) 1925—
Owner Tim Mara named his NFL team after the New York NL baseball team, since they would be sharing the same field, the Polo Grounds.

Giants (NL) 1885-1957
The New York NL team was known as the Gothams, and that name continued for some time before it was replaced by Giants. There are conflicting stories as to who first called the New York team Giants.
The early credit was given to Manager James Mutrie, who was quoted as saying, "My boys are not only giants in stature but in baseball ability."
According to many sources, including Horace Stoneham, who served as Giant president, this comment was made when the Giants returned from a successful road trip, and a group of fans told Mutrie that his boys had "played like Giants."
Some sources indicate the road trip was in 1883 (which seems unlikely), while others said 1885. However, research at the Hall of Fame indicates that the quote was in 1888. If so, then Mutrie may have been speaking "after the fact."
P. J. Donohue, a writer, was probably the earliest (1885) to refer to the team as Giants, according to the most recent research.

Giants (PL) 1890
The New York entry in the Players League adopted the name of their National League rivals.

Golden Blades (WHA) 1973/74
See Jersey Knights (WHA).

Gothams (ABL-2) 1944/45-1945/46
See New York Americans (ABL-2) and Brooklyn Jewels (ABL-2).

Gothams (NL) 1883-1884
Gotham is the nickname for New York City.

Hakoahs (ABL-1) 1928/29
This club was a Jewish team organized by ex-Celtic players Nat Holman and Davey Banks. The name may have been adopted from the Hakoah team, a great professional soccer club that toured the United States in 1926, to record crowds.

Highlanders (AL) 1903-1912

Before they became the Yankees, the New York AL team was called the Highlanders, because their playing field (Hilltop Park) was located in Washington Heights, the highest spot in Manhattan.

Also, sources state that because their first president was James Gordon, people drew an association with the famous Scottish regiment, the Gordon Highlanders. During this time the team was also known as the Hilltoppers, because of their playing field.

When the team moved from Hilltop Park to the Polo Grounds (where they played from 1913 through 1922), neither nickname was appropriate, and a new name emerged.

See New York Yankees (AL).

Islanders (NHL) 1972/73—

Owner Roy Boe selected the name for the NHL team on Long Island. Although Brooklyn and Queens, parts of New York City, are on Long Island, it is Nassau and Suffolk countries that most people consider "the Island." The Islanders, sometimes referred to as the Isles, have their home arena in Nassau County.

Jets (AFL-4) 1963-1969
Jets (NFL) 1970—

When the New York Titans looked as if they were going to go out of business, Sonny Werblin brought together a syndicate that bought the franchise for $1 million. Werblin, who came to the team from the Music Corporation of America, began to make changes, and one of the first was to select a new name. Werblin chose Jets, a name that was not as grandiose as Wismer's Titans, because it reflected the jet age, provided a close identification with the colorful Mets, and was easy for headline writers.

Jewels (ABL-2) 1934/35-1935/36
Jewels (ABL-2) 1937/38-1941/42
Jewels (ABL-2) 1942/43

See Brooklyn Jewels (ML-2).

Knickerbockers (BAA) 1946/47-1948/49
Knickerbockers (NBA) 1949/50—

The team is rarely referred to as the Knickerbockers today. Over the years since Ned Irish announced the original name, on 7/24/46, the team has become known as the Knicks.

Irish, like most of the team owners in the BAA, did not announce the reason for the name selection.

However, he was choosing a name that had a long association with New York City. The term refers to a descendant of the early Dutch settlers of New York or a native or resident of the city or state of New York. There are many references to Father Knickerbocker in the media, when it is used to mean New York City.

In an article that appeared in a basketball program of 1921, Jim Furey, the founder of the Original Celtics, is quoted as saying: "Father Knickerbocker deserves a world's championship basketball team as well as a world's champion baseball outfit."

When Irish announced the name, he also said that the team would be wearing the city's official colors, orange and blue.

McDowell Lyceum (ML-1) 1921/22-1922/23

The team played at the McDowell Lyceum, and it was sometimes referred to as the Macs.

Metropolitans (AA) 1883-1887

The Metropolitans played as an independent team beginning in 1880, before joining the AA in 1883. They were known as the Metropolitans or as the Mets, the former reflecting the metropolis of New York.

Mets (NL) 1962—

When club owner Joan Payson announced the name of the New York NL club, it was somewhat anticlimactic. For months before the announcement, New York sports writers (Dan Daniel of the *New York World Telegram* had been first) had been referring to the team as the Mets. The official franchise name was Metropolitan Baseball Club, Inc., and Mets was a lot simpler to use in a news story.

A committee of sports writers had narrowed the list of suggested nicknames to ten: Continentals, Skyliners, Mets, Jets, Burros (as a play on the word *borough*; there are five boroughs in New York City), Meadowlarks, Skyscrapers, Rebels, NYBs, and Avengers.

The fans were then asked to vote, and over 1,000 letters were received. Mets was the winner, with Skyliners a close second.

Mrs. Payson, whose own favorite was Meadowlarks, said the name was one that best met five basic criteria: 1) it met public and press acceptance; 2) it was closely related to the corporate name; 3) it was descriptive of the metropolitan area; 4) it was brief;

and 5) it had historical significance (the Metropolitans of the AA).

Mutuals (NA) 1871-1875
Mutuals (NL) 1876

The Mutuals were organized in 1857 in the firehouse of the Mutual Hook and Ladder Company No. 1. Thus the nickname came from the fire company.

They were also referred to as the Green Stockings in some sources, during their NA years, but upon entering the NL they appeared in red stockings and were sometimes called Red Stockings or Reds.

Also, because the team played its home games in Brooklyn, there are references to the team as the Brooklyn Mutuals.

Nets (ABA) 1968/69-1975/76
Nets (NBA) 1976/77

The New Jersey Americans (ABA) moved to Commack, Long Island, and changed their name to the New York Nets, taking their unique nickname from basketball nets, an integral part of the game's equipment. The name also tied in to other New York teams: the Jets (NFL) and the Mets (NL).

In 1977/78, the Nets returned to their roots in New Jersey and retained the nickname of Nets.

See New Jersey Americans (ABA).

Original Celtics (ABL-2) 1936/37-1937/38

This team, as sports columnist Red Smith pointed out, was neither original nor Celtic. In fact, the team was sometimes called Kate Smith's Original Celtics, and it was owned by her manager, Ted Collins. The team played for about three years before disbanding.

See Brooklyn Celtics (ABL-1).

Pros (ML-1) 1925/26

The team nickname was a shortened version of *professional*. The club dropped out before the end of the first half of the season.

Raiders (WHA) 1972/73

The Raiders lasted one season and then changed their name to the New York Golden Blades for the 1973/74 season. The season had barely started when they moved to Cherry Hill (NJ).

See Jersey Knights (WHA).

Rangers (NHL) 1926/27—

The Rangers were named in honor of George "Tex" Rickard, a native Texan and the person who was instrumental in the building of the "new" Madison Square Garden (then located at Eighth Avenue and Forty-ninth Street). Rickard was a sports promoter and president of the Garden, and he had noticed the excellent crowds that the New York Americans (NHL) had been able to attract in their first year (1925/26) in the Garden.

The team was at first referred to as Tex's Rangers (a play on the name of the famous Texas police force, the Texas Rangers), but was soon shortened to Rangers.

Stars (WFL) 1974

A franchise was awarded to Boston for the WFL, and the team was scheduled to be called the Boston Bulldogs, but in less than twelve hours, Howard Baldwin, the club president, decided to call the team the Bulls.

Neither name was ever used. The franchise was shifted to New York, and a new name was needed.

According to Herb Gluck's book *While the Gettin's Good*, the credit for the name New York Stars goes to Babe Parilli, the coach of the yet-to-be-named team. On the flight from Boston to New York, Parilli told Dusty Rhodes (Baldwin's assistant), "I finally feel like a star . . ." and she said, "Yeah, a New York Star . . ." and he said, "That's it!"

Before the season was over, the New York Stars were moved to Charlotte and became the Hornets.

Tapers (ABL-3) 1961/62

The Tapers began the season as the Washington Capitols but moved to New York in midseason. The New York team was owned by Technical Tape Corporation of New Rochelle (NY), makers of Tuck Tape.

Titans (AFL-4) 1960-1962

The Titans were owned by Harry Wismer, a very flamboyant radio announcer who had once worked for George Richards. Richards was the man who bought the Portsmouth (OH) Spartans and made them into the Detroit Lions (NFL). Wismer had also broadcast the Washington Redskins (NFL) games.

Wismer named his team Titans because he was competing with the NFL's New York Giants. He was quoted as saying Titans are bigger than Giants.

Westchesters (ABL-2) 1944/45

This is the Brooklyn Jewel team that changed its name several times in the mid 1940s. Westchester is the county directly north of New York City, and the team played its games in White Plains. On 1/20/45, the team moved to Brooklyn and changed its name to the New York Gothams.

See New York Americans (ABL-2) and Brooklyn Jewels (ML-2).

Yankees (AAFC) 1946-1949

The AAFC Yankees were owned by Dan Topping, owner of the New York Yankees AL baseball team.

Yankees (ABL-2) 1937/38

See Bronx Yankees (ABL-2).

Yankees (AFL-1) 1926
Yankees (NFL) 1927-1928

This New York Yankee team was the brainchild of C. C. Pyle, who had signed the great Red Grange to a personal contract. Pyle tried to get an NFL franchise for New York but was turned down. So he started his own league.

Pyle, whose nickname was "Cash and Carry," obtained a lease for Yankee Stadium and therefore called his team the Yankees. After one year the league folded, but Pyle was allowed to bring his New York Yankees into the NFL.

Yankees (AL) 1913—

There is still some uncertainty as to who first called the New York AL baseball team the Yankees. The team had been known as the Highlanders (and Hilltoppers), but their move to the Polo Grounds in 1913 dictated a new name.

Research by the Hall of Fame indicates that the name Yankee may have been used as early as 1905. Several sources have cited the need for a shorter name for headlines, and various claims have been made as to who used it. Both Mark Roth and Sam Crane are cited. It is certain that the name was used before the move to the Polo Grounds, and that, with the move, the other names lost all their significance.

Yanks (AFL-2) 1936-1937

This team has also been referred to as the Yankees. Since they played most of their first season in Yankee Stadium, the name Yankees may be correct. Either name was obviously adopted from the New York Yankee AL baseball team.

Yanks (AFL-3) 1940

As with the New York AFL-2 team, this team also played its games in Yankee Stadium and has also been referred to by some sources as the Yankees.

Yanks (NFL) 1950-1951

See New York Bulldogs (NFL).

(NEW YORK) JAMAICA

St. Monicas (ML-2) 1931/32-1932/33

The team played at St. Monica Catholic Church in Jamaica. The St. Monicas dropped out at the end of the first half of the 1932/33 season.

(NEW YORK)

Lincoln Giants (ECL) 1923-1926
Lincoln Giants (ECL) 1928
Lincoln Giants (ANL) 1929

The first Lincoln team was formed in Lincoln, Nebraska, in 1890, but the team that was to become one of the best black teams was formed in New York City in 1911 by Jess McMahon, a white boxing promoter, and his brother. The New York team adopted the names of the Nebraska team.

See Cuban Giants.

NORTH HUDSON (NJ)

Thourots (ABL-2) 1933/34

The Hoboken Lisas (ML-2) became the North Hudson Thourots at the beginning of the 1933/34 season. (Hudson is a county in New Jersey.) Thourot is a relatively common family name in the North Hudson area, and it may be assumed that the team was sponsored by someone named Thourot.

However, the team played only two games (0-2) in Hoboken as the Thourots and on 11/23/33 shifted to Camden (NJ), where it was sponsored by a local brewer. The Brewers posted a 2-8 record and then on 1/8/34 they moved to New Britain (CT) as the New Britain Palace.

The following year (1934/35) the team began the season as the New Britain Jackaways before disbanding on 1/18/35.

See Hoboken Lisas (ML-2).

OAKLAND (CA)

Athletics (AL) 1968—
See Philadelphia Athletics (AL).

Clippers (NASL) 1968
The Oakland-San Francisco Bay area was a home port for many of the great clipper ships of the Pacific. Several West Coast teams have adopted the name of these slick, fast, sailing ships.

Invaders (USFL) 1983-1985
The Invaders was one of the USFL team names that was selected because it bore a resemblance to a rival NFL team name. In this case, Oakland had the USFL Invaders and the NFL Raiders.

Oaks (ABA) 1967/68-1968/69
Pat Boone, owner of the ABA Oakland franchise, wanted to honor author Jack London, who made Oakland his home and twice ran for mayor. Boone was going to call the team the Jacks. However, most sports writers lobbied for Oaks, which had been associated with the Oakland Pacific Coast League baseball team as early as 1904.

The name also had a basketball tradition as the name of the Oakland team in the short-lived ABL-3.

Oaks (ABL-3) 1962/63
The ABL-3 team adopted the name of the Oakland Oaks baseball team of the Pacific Coast League.

Raiders (AFL-4) 1960-1969
Raiders (NFL) 1970-1981
Oakland received an AFL-4 franchise when Minneapolis decided to return its franchise and accept the offer of the NFL that they could have a franchise if they waited one year.

The Oakland club held a Name the Team contest, and the winning entry was Senors, with Dons another favorite. However, club officials vetoed the choice and decided to come up with the name themselves. They chose Raiders.

For the first year of operation, the Oakland Raiders had to play their home games in San Francisco's Kezar Stadium, home of the NFL 49ers.

Seals (NHL) 1967/68-1969/70
See California Seals (NHL).

Stompers (NASL) 1978
Some sources have indicated that the name is related to California's grape or wine industry.

OKLAHOMA

Outlaws (USFL) 1984
The Oklahoma franchise was originally scheduled for San Diego, but the owners, William Tatham, Senior and Junior, couldn't get permission to use Jack Murphy Stadium.

The Tathams moved the franchise to Oklahoma, and they chose the team nickname. According to Gil Swalls, head of media relations:

> They picked it because they wanted an aggressive name. They thought it was in line with what other (USFL) teams were calling themselves. Bandits, Gamblers, Wranglers, and Invaders. The majority of our fans have taken to the name, but a few have objected, saying it was a slam on the state's history. But we explain, with tongue in cheek, that the team is starting as a renegade.

OORANG

Indians (NFL) 1922-1923
There is no city, town, or community named Oorang.

Oorang was the name of a kennel in LaRue (OH) that was owned by Walter Lingo. He specialized in raising Airedales, and his primary avocation was Indian lore. He is supposed to have been able to speak several Indian languages.

While on a hunting trip with Jim Thorpe, Longo got the idea that an all-Indian football team would be a great way to publicize his kennels and to sell Airedales. Thorpe would run the team.

Lingo applied for an NFL franchise (they cost $100, and his Airedales sold for $150) and was granted one on 6/24/22. Because LaRue (which is a small community about fifty miles north of Columbus) had no football field, Marion, a city fifteen miles away, was made the home field.

During their short two-year stint in the NFL, Oorang had a great variety of Indian tribes represented on the team.

ORANGE (NJ)

Tornadoes (NFL) 1929
As early as 1903, the Orange Athletic Club of Newark (NJ) was playing as an independent. It is believed that the athletic club was located in Orange (NJ), which leads to some confusion.

It is known that the team played in Newark as the Newark Tornadoes in 1930.

The origin of the nickname is unknown.

ORLANDO (FL)

Magic (NBA) 1989/90—
The Orlando franchise sponsored a Name the Team contest with the help of the *Orlando Sentinel*. The top two names in the contest (Magic and Juice) were then sent to a panel of local business and community leaders.

The choice was Magic. According to the team's general manager, Pat Williams, "Magic is synonymous with this area. We have the Magic Kingdom and Disney World. The tourism slogan is 'Come to the Magic.'"

Renegades (USFL) 1985
The Renegades were the Washington Federals of 1983-1984.

OSHKOSH (WI)

All-Stars (NBL) 1937/38-1948/49
The Oshkosh All-Stars were organized in 1929, and with the exception of two years during the Depression, they played as an independent team until they joined the NBL. The club was one of the consistently strong Midwest teams.

OTTAWA (Ontario)

Civics (WHA) 1975/76
The Denver Spurs moved to Ottawa on 1/2/76 and played their home games in the Ottawa Civic Center, thus the change of name to Civics. The team disbanded before the end of the season with a 14-26-1 record.

Nationals (WHA) 1972/73
Although it probably was not intentional, the selection of Nationals for the capital city of Canada is similar to the use of Nationals by teams in Washington, DC.

Senators (NHL) 1917/18-1930/31
Senators (NHL) 1932/33-1933/34
Ottawa is the capital of Canada, and Senators is an appropriate nickname. The Senators trace their history back to at least the 1909/10 season.

PASSAIC (NJ)

Bengal Tigers (ABL-2) 1941/42
There were quite a few teams, both league and independent, in the northern New Jersey and Trenton (NJ) areas that used the nickname Tigers, Bengals, or Bengal Tigers. The association may have come from the Trenton area, close to Princeton and the Princeton Tigers. However, there is no documentation to support this theory.

The Passaic Bengal Tigers moved to Trenton in the early part of the 1941/42 season and became the Trenton Tigers.

Passaic (ML-1) 1923/24-1924/25
This was one of many of the early basketball teams that was known only by its town or city name.

Mets (ML-1) 1925/26
See Perth Amboy Mets (ML-1).

Reds (ABL-2) 1935/36
Reds is a shortened form of Red Devils, another name that was used by the team.

PATERSON (NJ)

Continentals (ML-2) 1932/33
The team played the first half of the season only.

Crescents (ML-1) 1926/27
See Paterson Crescents (ABL-2).

Crescents (ABL-1) 1929/30-1930/31
See Paterson Crescents (ABL-2).

Crescents (ABL-2) 1944/45-1945/46
Crescents may have been a social or fraternal organization. While the club produced many excellent basketball teams in Paterson (which sometimes was called the Crescent City), there were also other Crescent teams in other cities. One of the more notable

was the Brooklyn Crescents, who produced some excellent football teams.

Legionnaires (ML-1) 1922/23-1925/26
This team was sponsored by the local American Legion.

Panthers (ABL-2) 1935/36
The Panthers moved to Trenton on 12/13/35.

Pats (ML-1) 1927/28
The Pats played only two games before dropping out of the league. Pats is a shortened form of Paterson.

Powers Brothers Five (ML-1) 1921/22
Three Powers brothers (Artie, Ralph, and Charles) played for the team.

Visitations (ABL-2) 1936/37
The Brooklyn Visitations started the 1936/37 season as the Paterson Visitations, played one game, and returned to Brooklyn.
See Brooklyn Visitations (ML-1).

Whirlwinds (ABL-1) 1928/29
See Boston Whirlwinds (ABL-1).

PERTH AMBOY (NJ)

Mets (ML-1) 1925/26
The Perth Amboy team took their name from the league name. Mets is a shortened form of *Metropolitan*.

In late January 1926, the Mets moved to Passaic (NJ).

PHILADELPHIA (PA)

See also **Frankford** and **Hilldale**.

Athletics (NA) 1871-1875
Athletics (NL) 1876
See Philadelphia Athletics (AL).

Athletics (AA) 1882-1891
See Philadelphia Athletics (AL).

Athletics (AL) 1901-1954

The Athletics trace their name back to 1859, when a social organization, the prestigious Philadelphia Athletic Club, composed of lawyers and merchants, formed a team to play baseball. The team took the club's name.

Atoms (NASL) 1973-1976
The NASL club held a Name the Team contest and received over 3,000 entries. The team name, Atoms, was announced by club owner Tom McCloskey.

The winner of the contest was Sarah Fletcher, of Lakewood (NJ), and she received a trip for two to London for the English soccer Cup Final.

Bell (WFL) 1974-1975
The Philadelphia WFL franchise was awarded to city councilman Jack Kelly on 3/12/74, and he immediately announced that the team would be called the Bell.

He said the name had been one of three considered.

Bells was the suggestion of one of the investors, but Kelly said, "I told them it would have to be singular, or else people might put an 'es' on the end. Then there might be some question as to the virility of the boys."

A second choice (and Kelly's suggestion) had been to call the team the Yellow Jackets in honor of the Frankford Yellow Jackets, one of the pioneering teams of the NFL. Frankford is a suburb of Philadelphia.

A third consideration, but not a serious one, was to call the team the Philadelphia Sneakers. Also suggested but not considered was Pythons.

Blazers (WHA) 1972/73

Blue Jays (NL) 1944-1945
Say Blue Jays and most people think of the Toronto AL team; however, for two short years it was the official name of the Philadelphia NL team. Although it was official, it was rarely used; sports writers and fans continued to call the team the Phillies.

The Philadelphia team had been purchased by the Carpenter family from William D. Cox, who had been banned from baseball by Commissioner Landis for betting on the Phillies games. Robert Carpenter, at twenty-eight years of age, was made president of the club and decided that a new name might help a team that had finished last in five of the previous six years.

A Name the Team contest was held, and 635 names were suggested in 5,064 letters. Mrs. John L. Crooks of Philadelphia submitted the winning entry and received a $100 "war" bond (now called savings bonds) and a season pass.

Mrs. Crooks chose the name Blue Jays "because it reflects a new team spirit. The Blue Jay is colorful in personality and plumage. His plumage is a brilliant blue, a color the Phillies could use decoratively and psychologically."

The Philadelphia Blue Jays have something else in common with the Toronto Blue Jays. On January 5, 1944, at the baseball winter meeting, Robert Carpenter went against the prevailing "Go West" movement of his colleagues by urging that the major leagues should go North and include Toronto and Montreal as major-league cities.

Centennials (NA) 1875
The team was named in honor of the American Centennial (1775-1875).

Eagles (NFL) 1933-1942
Eagles (NFL) 1944—
When the Frankford Yellow Jackets franchise folded, Bert Bell and Lud Wray bought the team and changed the name to the Philadelphia Eagles.

Bell, who would later become NFL commissioner, named the team after the eagle that was on the emblem of the National Recovery Administration.

Fever (MISL) 1978/79-1981/82

Flyers (NHL) 1967/68—
Although the Philadelphia NHL club held a Name the Team contest, very little information is available about the names and number of entries submitted.

According to the club, there was no special significance to the selection of the name Flyers, other than that the owners happened to like the name more than others that were submitted.

Fury (NASL) 1978-1980

Hebrews (ABL-2) 1933/34-1936/37
See Philadelphia Sphas (EL).

Jasper Jewels (EL) 1931/32-1932/33
A team called the Jasper A. C. played in the Philadelphia League (1903/04-1905/06) and represented the Kensington section of Philadelphia. It later

played in the original Eastern League (1909/10-1922/23), which was centered in Philadelphia, South Jersey, Reading (PA), and Scranton (PA). The team played first as the Jaspers and then in 1922/23 as the Philadelphia Jasper Jewels.

Keystones (UA) 1884
The Philadelphia entry in the Union Association took the state nickname (the Keystone State) as its name.

The Keystones dropped out of the UA before the end of the season and were replaced by the Wilmington Quicksteps.

Moose (EL) 1931/32-1932/33
This team was sponsored by the local lodge of the Loyal Order of Moose, a fraternal order.

Philadelphias (NA) 1873-1875
This team adopted the name of the city.

Phillies (ABL-1) 1926/27
When Philadelphia joined the one-year-old ABL-1, it had several of the players from the Philadelphia Sphas.

However, because the league was attempting to show a more national image, the Jules Aronson team had been originally called the Phillies, a popular name for Philadelphia teams; and there were a few references to the team as the Quakers.

Aronson wanted a different name, and he asked Gordon Mackay of the Philadelphia *Inquirer* if he had any ideas for a new name. Mackay said he didn't. A few days later, in an article headlined "Greet the Warriors," which appeared in the *Inquirer* on 1/20/27, Mackay recounts the selection of the name Warriors for the Philadelphia team.

> "I got the name for our gang," he [Aronson] shouted jubilantly. "I saw a picture of Hannibal last night, and the name popped right into my head. Warriors, that's the name for our bunch. And that's the name we will take."
> So tonight watch the Warriors.

Although Warriors was first used in the *Inquirer* on 1/26/27, the name Phillies continued to be used in the newspaper ads for the team's games until the end of the season.

Phillies (NL) 1883-1943
Phillies (NL) 1946—
When the Worcester team was purchased by A. J. Reach and moved to Philadelphia, it almost immediately became known as the Phillies. The name was a natural nickname for a Philadelphia team.

Some sources have indicated that it was Reach who named the team, while others say it was spontaneous.

Quakers (PL) 1890
See Philadelphia Quakers (NHL).

Quakers (AFL-1) 1926
See Philadelphia Quakers (NHL).

Quakers (NHL) 1930/31
Philadelphia, the City of Brotherly Love, was laid out by William Penn and settled primarily by the Quakers. Many amateur and professional teams in the city have been called Quakers.

76ers (NBA) 1963/64—
When the Syracuse franchise was moved to Philadelphia, a Name the Team contest drew over 4,000 entries. A three-man board of judges selected 76ers, which had been submitted by nine contestants.

The winner of the contest, based on his accompanying reason for his choice, was Walter Stalberg, a longtime pro basketball fan from West Callingswood (NJ). His prize was a three-day trip to San Francisco.

Stalberg had written:

> No athletic team has ever paid tribute to the gallant men who forged this country's independence, and certainly Philadelphia, shrine of liberty, should do so.

Club president Irv Kosloff stated:

> The Nats [Syracuse Nationals] were loaded with spirit as anyone can attest who had ever seen them play. We look for a hustling club again this year and the new nickname is certainly appropriate.

Stalberg's daughter was a sophomore at Syracuse University, and he and his wife timed their visits to their daughter so he could see a Syracuse Nationals home game.

Sphas (EL) 1931/32-1932/33
Sphas (ABL-2) 1937/38-1945/46
The Sphas were organized by Eddie Gottlieb, Harry Passon, and Hughie Black in 1918, when the three recent high-school graduates convinced the board of directors of the South Philadelphia Hebrew Association (S.P.H.A.) to sponsor a team. The nickname Sphas is credited to Bill Scheffer, a sports writer for the Philadelphia *Inquirer.*

During its long history, the Sphas were also referred to as the Hebrews, and for one period of time (1933/34-1936/37) it was their official name.

From its inception in 1918 until it disbanded in the 1950s, it was Eddie Gottlieb's team. Gottlieb was involved in many other sports enterprises, but the Sphas were always the team closest to him.

See Philadelphia Warriors (ABL-1) and Philadelphia Phillies (ABL-1).

Stars (NNL-2) 1934-1948
Stars (NAL) 1949-1950
Eddie Gottlieb, owner of the Sphas, was a part owner of the Stars.

Stars (USFL) 1983-1984
The Stars and the Pittsburgh Maulers merged at the end of the 1984 season and became the Baltimore Stars.

Tapers (ABL-3) 1962/63
See New York Tapers (ABL-3).

Tigers (ECL) 1928

Warriors (ABL-1) 1927/28
In 1925/26 the first effort was made to make professional basketball a national sport with the formation of the American Basketball League. The following year, Eddie Gottlieb and Jules Aronson secured a franchise for Philadelphia, and the team was first called the Phillies. *See* Philadelphia Phillies (ABL-1) 1926/27. Interest in the league, which was ahead of its time, began to wane, and the Warriors disbanded after the 1927/28 season. It was still the era of the barnstorming team, and Gottlieb reorganized his Sphas.

Warriors (BAA) 1946/47-1948/49
Warriors (NBA) 1949/50-1961/62
When the BAA was formed, a franchise was given to Pete Tyrrell, the general manager of the Philadelphia Arena. Tyrrell hired Eddie Gottlieb as coach and manager of the new team, and they revived the name of the earlier ABL team: the Warriors.

See Philadelphia Warriors (ABL-1) and Philadelphia Phillies (ABL-1).

WPEN A. C. (EL) 1932/33
Because the team was sponsored by radio station WPEN, it was sometimes called the Broadcasters.

PHILADELPHIA-PITTSBURGH (PA)

Steagles (NFL) 1943
During World War II, the Pittsburgh franchise combined with the Philadelphia franchise for one year. Their nickname was a combination of their individual nicknames: Steelers and Eagles. Thus, the unlikely name Steagles.

PHOENIX (AZ)

Cardinals (NFL) 1988—
See (Chicago) Racine Cardinals (APFA).

Inferno (MISL) 1980/81-1982/83

Pride (MISL) 1983/84
When the Phoenix Inferno folded, the Phoenix community leaders tried to get a new team, a team that would be the pride of Phoenix.

Roadrunners (WHA) 1974/75-1976/77
The roadrunner is well known from cartoon shows. It is basically a land bird that is an extremely fast runner and is found in the Southwest. The Phoenix team is named after the bird.

The Roadrunners were in the minor Western Hockey League before they joined the WHA, and they continued as a minor-league team after dropping out of the WHA.

Suns (NBA) 1968/69—
A Name the Team contest was held for the Phoenix entry in the NBA, and over 28,000 entries were received. The contest was cosponsored by the team and the *Arizona Republic*.

The winning name, Suns, was submitted by 377 entrants. The contest winner was Mrs. Selinda King, whose name was picked from a hat by the Phoenix mayor. She received $1,000 and two season tickets.

Mrs. King, a clerical supervisor for the state health department, had been a fan of the Philadelphia 76ers. Names that didn't make it (and for good reason!) included Box Cars, Baby Staters, Cactossers, Light Footers, Jumping Beans, Dominators, Tipineers, Claimjumpers, and Area Zoners.

PITTSBURGH (PA)

Alleghenys (AA) 1882-1886
Alleghenys (NL) 1887-1889
The team was located in the Allegheny section of Pittsburgh and was called Alleghenys or Alleghenies. The first spelling is more likely to be found in reference before 1900. Later sources tend to use the second spelling.

Americans (AFL-2) 1936-1937
The Pittsburgh team took its name from the league name (American Football League).

Burghers (PL) 1890
A burgher is an inhabitant or resident of a city or town. It can also be called a short form of Pittsburgh.

Condors (ABA) 1970/71-1971/72
Sometimes a Name the Team contest causes more problems than it solves.

The Pittsburgh ABA franchise had been called the Pipers and decided to run a contest for a new name. On 6/25/70, the club announced the results and said the team would now be called the Pioneers. The winning entry was submitted by Donald E. Seymour, a law student, of Pittsburgh, and he received $500 and two lifetime tickets to Pioneer home games. Others (146 had picked Pioneers) who submitted the same name received a basketball and two tickets to the season opener.

However, the choice was quickly attacked on two fronts. First, Point Park College, a small liberal arts college in Pittsburgh, had been calling its teams Pioneers. The school felt there was no need for the Pipers to become the Pioneers. They even threatened an injunction.

The second problem was that an injunction had already been filed against the Pioneers (*nee* Pipers) by Mrs. Angela B. Weaver of Wexford. Mrs. Weaver had also picked the name Pioneers, but she had done so in "25 words or less," as required by the contest rules. The winner, Donald Seymour, had used 57 words.

The name problem was the first that incoming president and general manager Marty Blake had to face. His initial choice (7/10/70) was Condors, but he said his research on these large, nearly extinct birds (actually vultures) made him wonder if the name was appropriate for a basketball team. However, on 7/23/70, at a news conference on the campus of Point Park College, Blake announced that Condors would be the team name. "I like the sound of it. No other team we know of uses the name."

Crawfords (NNL-2) 1933-1938

The Crawfords were organized by Jim Dorsey, the director of the Crawford Recreation Center, as a semipro independent team called the Crawford Colored Giants.

In 1931, the team, or at least the name, was taken over by W. A. "Gus" Greenlee. Greenlee was a tavern owner and numbers king in Pittsburgh's black Hill District. Greenlee started the NNL-2.

Innocents (NL) 1890

In 1890, many of the best players in the NL jumped to the Players League. Pittsburgh was particularly hard hit. It also lost fan support because the local support went over to the Players League. The nickname most likely was due to the fact that fifty players, old and young, mostly inexperienced, wore the Pittsburgh uniform that year. A bunch of innocents.

Ironmen (BAA) 1946/47

The team name was a reference to the steel industry of Pittsburgh.

Keystones (NNL-1) 1922

Pennsylvania is the Keystone State.

Maulers (USFL) 1984

The nickname was picked as a tribute to Pittsburgh's steelworkers.

Penguins (NHL) 1967/68—

The Pittsburgh NHL expansion team, like Philadelphia, solicited suggestions from the fans for the team

name but gave very little information on the results. The name picked was Penguins, and the club stated that there was no specific reason behind the selection, just that it was thought to be a good nickname.

Pipers (ABA) 1967/68
Pipers (ABA) 1969/70

Gene Rubin, owner of the ABA team, chose the name Pipers for the team and gave the following reasons for his choice. He liked the alliteration of Pittsburgh Pipers and he felt that the name was associated with bagpipes and the Scotch-Irish people who settled the area.

Pirates (NHL) 1925/26-1929/30
See Pittsburgh Pirates (NBL).

Pirates (NFL) 1933-1938
See Pittsburgh Pirates (NBL).

Pirates (NBL) 1937/38-1938/39

Numerous Pittsburgh teams adopted the name of the Pittsburgh NL baseball team. The NFL team did so because they played in the same ballpark.

Pirates (NL) 1891—

In 1890 there had been three leagues: the Players League, National League, and American Association. The American Association and the National League had lost players to the Players League. When the PL folded, it was generally expected that all players in that league would return to the team they had played for in the NL or the AA.

Somehow the Philadelphia Athletics of the AA did not get around to re-signing Louis Biebauer, and Biebauer signed with the Pittsburgh team (then called the Innocents). The Athletics asked the Pittsburgh team for the return of their player. Pittsburgh said no, and the Athletics (along with the rest of the American Association) screamed "Pirates."

The Pirates kept Biebauer and the nickname.

Raiders (NBL) 1944/45

The Raiders may have taken their name as a variation of the Pittsburgh Pirates name.

Rebels (FL) 1914-1915

The Pittsburgh team started in 1914, being called PittsFeds, but a change in managers gave them a better nickname. "Rebel" Oakes replaced Doc

Gessler as manager after the first month of the season.

Rens (ABL-3) 1961/62-1962/63
See Dayton Rens (NBL).

Spirit (MISL) 1978/79-1979/80
Spirit (MISL) 1981/82-1985/86

Steelers (NFL) 1939-1942
Steelers (NFL) 1945—
   The Pittsburgh team decided to change its name and solicited suggestions in a Name the Team contest. (The contest was not a widely promoted one, relying mostly on suggestions from employees and sports writers.) The winning suggestion was Steelers, and it is credited, depending on the source, to the wife or girlfriend of the Pittsburgh ticket manager.

Unions (UA) 1884
   This team took the name of the league, the Union Association.

YMHA (MBC) 1935/36-1936/37
   This team was sponsored by the local Young Men's Hebrew Association (YMHA).

PORTLAND (OR)

Breakers (USFL) 1985
See Boston Breakers (USFL).

Storm (WFL) 1974
   Although the reason for the nickname is not known, the following year the team called itself Thunder.

Thunder (WFL) 1975
See Portland Storm (WFL).

Timbers (NASL) 1975-1982
   The Portland NASL team selected its name in recognition of the West Coast forest industry.

Trail Blazers (NBA) 1970/71
   The Portland entry in the NBA, like all new teams, was looking for a name that had not been used by someone else. They held a Name the Team contest and drew almost 10,000 entries. The selection committee then reviewed the top choices and decided on Trail Blazers, which had been submitted by 172 contestants.
   The announcement was made on 3/13/70, during ceremonies at a game between the New York Knicks and the Seattle Supersonics, in Portland's Memorial Coliseum.

PORTSMOUTH (OH)

Spartans (NFL) 1930-1933
   Portsmouth was granted an NFL franchise on 7/12/30 and played four years before its franchise was sold to Detroit and became the Lions.
   The origin of the team name is unknown.

POTTSVILLE (PA)

Maroons (NFL) 1925-1928
   The Pottsville team took its nickname from the color of its jerseys.

PROVIDENCE (RI)

Grays (NL) 1873-1885
   This team took its nickname from the color of its uniforms.

Steam Roller (NFL) 1925-1931
   The original team was founded in 1916 by Pierce Johnson; Charles Coppen, sporting editor of the *Providence Journal*; and Edward Whelan, assistant sporting editor of the *Providence Journal*.
   The naming of the team, as recounted by Pierce Johnson, gives credit to Charles Coppen. When Providence played its first game, it had no name and was just called Providence.
   During half-time of the game that was going to become a 52-0 rout, Coppen overheard a spectator in the stands say, "Gee, they're steamrolling them."
   Coppen, a former English instructor at Brown University, named the team Steam Roller because he didn't believe in a plural team name. Coppen reasoned that you only play one team (Steam Roller), not several (Steam Rollers). The nickname, always two words, has become synonymous with Providence football teams ever since.

Steamrollers (BAA) 1946/47-1948/49
The Providence franchise in the BAA adopted the nickname of the football team but did not make it singular, nor did it keep it as a two-word nickname.

QUEBEC (Quebec)

Bulldogs (NHL) 1919/20
The Quebec Bulldogs played in the National Hockey Association and as an independent before entering the NHL. In 1920/21, the Quebec team moved to Hamilton as the Hamilton Tigers.

In 1911/12 and 1912/13, the Bulldogs won the Stanley Cup.

Nordiques (WHA) 1972/73-1978/79
Nordiques (NHL) 1979/80—
The name of the Quebec team was chosen following a contest organized by a sportsmen's club, *Les Sportifs du Quebec*. The selection committee chose *Les Nordiques*, basically because the team is one of the most northern professional teams in hockey.

RACINE (WI)

Legion (NFL) 1922-1924
The team was sponsored by an American Legion post in Racine.

Tornadoes (NFL) 1926
The Tornadoes disbanded at the end of the season.

RICHMOND (IN)

King Clothiers (NBL) 1937/38
The team was sponsored by King Clothiers, but moved to Cincinnati before the end of the season and became the Comellos.

RICHMOND (VA)

Virginias (AA) 1884
The Washington (DC) franchise was transferred to Richmond and became the Virginias, taking the name of the state. The Washington team had a 12-51 record when it moved.

ROCHESTER (NY)

Braves (AFL-2) 1936
The Rochester Braves played only one game (and lost). On 11/5/36 the team folded because of financial difficulties.
See Syracuse Braves (AFL-2).

Centrals (ABL-1) 1925/26-1930/31
The Centrals began as a group of Jewish boys who attended public schools in the Central Avenue area of Rochester, around 1905 or 1906. From a boys' team they grew into a very strong semipro team and finally turned professional. In 1924, they beat the world-champion New York Celtics.

Jeffersons (APFA) 1920-1921
Jeffersons (NFL) 1922-1925
The Jeffersons began as a neighborhood team in Rochester as early as 1911.

Lancers (NASL) 1970-1980

Rochesters (AA) 1890
With the coming of the Players League in 1890, there were three major leagues, and the American Association needed replacement franchises. The AA turned to some of the smaller cities such as Rochester.

Although the Rochester entry had no official name, it was drawn primarily from the Rochester Hop Bitters, a minor-league team. The Hop Bitters were owned by a man who sold Hop Bitters, a patent medicine that was supposed to cure all sorts of ailments.

Royals (NBL) 1945/46-1947/48
Royals (BAA) 1948/49
Royals (NBA) 1949/50-1956/57
In November 1945, a contest was held to pick a name for the team that Les Harrison was going to enter in the NBL. The previous year Harrison had called his team the Rochester Pros.

The winner of the contest was fifteen-year-old Richard Paeth. His entry stated that Royal is defined by Webster as "pertaining to a king or crown, befitting or like a King, majestic."

Tigers (AFL-2) 1936-1937

This club began the 1936 season as the Brooklyn Tigers. On 11/5/36, the Rochester Braves folded, and the Tigers moved to Rochester on 11/13/36.

The Tiger record was 0-4-1 in Brooklyn and 0-2-0 in Rochester for the 1936 season.

ROCKFORD (IL)

Forest Citys (NA) 1871

The Forest City Base Ball Club of Rockford, IL, was organized in August 1865. Both Rockford and Cleveland were known as the Forest City and had teams that bore the name Forest City or Forest Citys.

ROCK ISLAND (IL)

See also **Tri-Cities.**

Independents (APFA) 1920-1921
Independents (NFL) 1922-1925
Independents (AFL-1) 1926

The Independents were a strong team in the days prior to the formation of the APFA. In 1926, the team jumped to the new AFL-1.

SACRAMENTO (CA)

Kings (NBA) 1985/86—
See Kansas City Kings (NBA).

ST. LOUIS (MO)

All-Stars (NFL) 1923

Blues (NHL) 1967/68—

The selection of the team name was made by St. Louis owner Sid Salomon, Jr.

> The name of the team just has to be the Blues. It's part of the city where W. C. Handy composed his famed song while thinking of his girl one morning.
> No matter where you go in town there's singing, that's the spirit of St. Louis.

A number of names were suggested to Salomon, but Blues was the only one that reflected the St. Louis music heritage.

Bombers (BAA) 1946/47-1948/49
Bombers (NBA) 1949/50

The Bombers were owned by Emory Jones, who owned the St. Louis Arena and the St. Louis Flyers in the American Hockey League.

Browns (NL) 1876-1877
See St. Louis Browns (NL) 1892-1897.

Browns (AA) 1882-1891
Browns (NL) 1892-1897

The first St. Louis NL team (1876-1877) was called the Browns because of the color of its socks. The name stuck with the pre-1900 St. Louis teams, but at the beginning of the turn of the century, uniform changes led to a change in the team's nickname.

Browns (AL) 1902-1953

When the Milwaukee Brewers of 1901 moved to St. Louis, the new club adopted the nickname Browns, which had been a part of St. Louis baseball history.

Cardinals (NFL) 1960-1987
See (Chicago) Racine Cardinals (APFA).

Cardinals (NL) 1900—

In 1899, the St. Louis NL team had a new owner (Frank D. Robinson) and new uniforms. The traditional brown socks and trim were replaced with cardinal red. A sports writer for the *St. Louis Republic*, William McHale, is credited with being the first to refer to the team as the Cardinal in 1899. By 1900, the team was being referred to as the Cardinals.

Eagles (NHL) 1934/35

The Ottawa Senators moved to St. Louis and became the Eagles for one season.

Giants (NNL-1) 1920-1921

The St. Louis club was a strong, independent team in the 1910s, and was one of the organizing teams of the NNL-1. *See* Cuban Giants.

Gunners (NFL) 1934

The St. Louis Gunners was an independent club that purchased the Cincinnati Reds (NFL) franchise on 11/6/34, when the Reds defaulted on salary payments. The club was formed in 1931, when the National Guard's 126th Field Artillery decided to sponsor a team, which quickly became known as the Battery A Gunners.

When the National Guard dropped its sponsorship, the team was renamed the St. Louis Gunners. The Gunners dropped out at the end of the 1934 season but continued to play in the minor football leagues before folding in 1940.

Hawks (NBA) 1955/56-1967/68
See Buffalo Bisons (NBL) and Tri-Cities Blackhawks (NBL).

Maroons (UA) 1884
Maroons (NL) 1885-1886
The St. Louis UA team was called Maroons because of their uniform color. When the team moved into the NL, they retained their colors and nickname.

Perfectos (NL) 1898-1899
For a brief time, the St. Louis NL team was referred to as the Perfectos. The origin of this nickname is unknown.

Reds (NA) 1875
The St. Louis NA team probably took its name from the color of its uniform trim or socks.

SlouFeds (FL) 1914
Several of the teams in the short-lived Federal League had nicknames that combined elements of the city name and the league.

St. Louis (NA) 1875
This team just went by the city name, without a nickname.

Stars (NNL-1) 1922-1931
Stars (NAL) 1937
Stars (NAL) 1939
The St. Louis Stars became the better of the two black teams in St. Louis. The Giants was the other team. In 1921, the Giants dropped out of the NNL-1, and the Stars replaced them in the league.

Stars (NASL) 1968-1977

Steamers (MISL) 1979/80-1987/88
It is assumed that the Steamer nickname is related to the steamboats that ply the Mississippi. However, no documentation is available.

Storm (MISL) 1989/90—
The name of one of the newest teams in the MISL was chosen from more than 1,000 that were submitted by the fans. The final list was narrowed to Storm, Spirit, Dynamos, and Lightning. "We are happy with the name," owner Milan Mandaric said. "It gives us a new, fresh name. It should be something people identify with. Storm is a good name. We'll be scary. I hope we'll be scary for our opponents." Originally the team management had wanted to use the name of the previous MISL team in St. Louis, the Steamers. But they decided against it because of negative feelings about the team's final season.

Terriers (FL) 1915

(ST. LOUIS)

Spirits of St. Louis (ABA) 1974/75
The St. Louis team was usually referred to as Spirits. Although the initial reaction is that the nickname had something to do with the Charles Lindbergh plane, there is no connection. (His plane was the *Spirit of St. Louis*.)

ST. PAUL (MN)

Saints (UA) 1884
The St. Paul team was one of the few in the UA that was not called Unions. However, Saints has a long history of being the nickname for St. Paul teams.
Some references were made to the team as the Apostles.

SAN ANTONIO (TX)

Gunslingers (USFL) 1984-1985
The San Antonio team received several thousand suggestions from fans for the team name. A selection committee reduced the list to about a dozen. The final choice was made by Clinton Manges, the majority stockholder.
Some of the names that were seriously considered were Stampede, Defenders, and Texans. However, he finally settled on Gunslingers because he thought it was appropriate to the atmosphere of San Antonio.
Roger Gill, the San Antonio general manager, stated, "We wanted to get away from typical animal names and be unique. Gunslingers seemed appropriate to our territory."

Spurs (ABA) 1973/74-1975/76
Spurs (NBA) 1976/77—
When the Dallas Chaparrals relocated to San Antonio, the club decided that a new name, one more fitting to San Antonio, should be picked. Suggestions were solicited from the fans, and Spurs became the choice. It was short, and it reflected the Western tradition and heritage of San Antonio.

Thunder (NASL) 1975-1976
Thunder was picked in a Name the Team contest.

Wings (WFL) 1975

SAN DIEGO (CA)

Chargers (AFL-4) 1961-1969
Chargers (NFL) 1970—
See Los Angeles Chargers (AFL-4).

Clippers (NBA) 1978/79-1983/84
Although San Diego selected their team nickname in a Name the Team contest, it is not unusual for West or East Coast port cities to select this name. The name has been used in Baltimore, Los Angeles, Oakland, and San Diego, to mention a few.
Clippers were sleek, fast ships that were a major part of the shipping industry during the 1800s.

Conquistadors (ABA) 1972/73-1974/75
The nickname for the San Diego ABA team was announced by Leonard Bloom, owner of the franchise. He indicated that the name—Spanish for "conquerors"—was selected from almost 10,000 suggestions submitted in the club's Name the Team contest. Bloom also announced that a figure of Spanish explorer Cabrillo would be the team's emblem.

Jaws (NASL) 1976

Mariners (WHA) 1974/75-1976/77
The nickname for the WHA team reflects the maritime heritage of San Diego.

Padres (NL) 1969—
San Diego was the site of the first Spanish mission in California in 1769. From that base, missions were built by the Spanish, up the California coast. San Diego's team in the Pacific Coast League has always been called Padres, so it was only natural to call the new NL team from San Diego by the same name.

Rockets (NBA) 1967/68-1970/71
This San Diego club held a Name the Team contest when it was granted a franchise in the NBA. The contest winner was C. W. Lacey.
The contest provided more than 1,000 different names and approximately 10,000 entries. The selection committee picked Rockets because it kept with the city's theme of a "City in Motion," while reflecting the tremendous growth of the space-age industries in San Diego.

Sails (ABA) 1975/76
This team, the former San Diego Conquistadors, changed its name to reflect the maritime heritage of San Diego. The team folded after eleven games, with a 3-8 record.

Sockers (NASL) 1978-1984
Sockers (MISL) 1982/83
Sockers (MISL) 1984/85—
Sockers is a variation of the word *soccer*, and it also provides the feeling of action.

Toros (NASL) 1968
The Toros played in the National Professional Soccer League (NPSL) during the 1967 season as the Los Angeles Toros. Toros means "bull" in Spanish.

SAN FRANCISCO (CA)

Fog (MISL) 1980/81
Fog is a common occurrence in San Francisco, so this team nickname would seem quite appropriate. The name was announced on 5/29/80 by owner David Schoenstadt, who had purchased the Detroit Lightning franchise and moved it to San Francisco.

49ers (AAFC) 1946-1949
49ers (NFL) 1950—
Tony Marabito had always wanted to own a pro football team and had tried to bring the NFL to San Francisco. A native of the city, he was involved in the trucking and lumber industries.
When he got an AAFC franchise, there were numerous suggestions as to what to name the team. Some of the early suggestions used names that revolved around one of the most famous periods in San Francisco history, the gold rush of 1849.
At some point, the name "Forty-niner" was proposed either by A. E. Sorrell or E. J. Turre, both of whom were part owners. Marabito liked the nick-

name, and it was adopted in the spelled-out version. Later, the nickname evolved to 49ers.

Giants (NL) 1958—

See New York Giants (NL).

Saints (ABL-3) 1961/62

The Saints moved across the bay and became the Oakland Oaks in 1962/63.

Warriors (NBA) 1962/63-1970/71

See Philadelphia Warriors (BAA) and Philadelphia Phillies (ABL-1).

SAN JOSE (CA)

Earthquakes (NASL) 1974-1982

Because the team played their home games not far from the San Andreas Fault, the team took the nickname Earthquakes.

Sharks (NHL) 1991/92—

The newest NHL franchise chose the name Sharks from more than 2,300 entries received in a Name the Team contest. Although the club had said that names that were either earthquake-related or gang-related (such as Blades) would not be considered, the first choice of the fans was Blades. The announcement was made on 9/7/90.

According to Matt Levine, executive vice-president of business operations, Sharks (the second most popular entry) was selected because it is easy to remember, it sounds good, it is regional, and it has good marketing potential. Among the fifteen finalists were such names as Rubber Puckies, Screaming Squids, and Salty Dogs.

Sharks are abundant in the local waters and they are "relentless, determined, swift, agile, bright, and fearless. We wanted a name that communicated the characteristics we want in a hockey team," Levine said.

Although the team will be called the San Jose Sharks, it will play its first season at the Cow Palace in Daly City while a new arena is being built.

Some other names suggested were Cansecos (for the Oakland A's baseball slugger and local hero), Rambos, Faults, Fog Horns, and Piranhas.

SEATTLE (WA)

Mariners (AL) 1977—

The Seattle AL baseball team selected its nickname in a Name the Team contest that resulted in over 15,000 entries. Mariners was chosen from over 600 different names that were submitted.

Roger Szmodis of Bellevue (WA) was selected as the winner, on the basis of his reason for choosing Mariners. "I've selected Mariners because of the natural association between the sea and Seattle and her people, who have been challenged and rewarded by it."

Pilots (AL) 1969

The nickname for Seattle's first major-league baseball team was selected in a contest.

The winner had suggested Pilots because it was indicative of Seattle's leadership in both marine and air activities. Aircraft plants and naval and shipping operations are a vital part of the Seattle-area economy.

In 1970, the Pilots moved to Milwaukee and became the Brewers.

Seahawks (NFL) 1976—

Seattle got an NFL franchise on 6/4/74 and held a Name the Team contest for its nickname. Over 20,000 entries were received, with 151 suggesting the eventual winner: Seahawks.

Many of the suggestions were names that related to the maritime, fishing, wildlife, or the lumber industry of the Northwest.

One suggestion, Mariners, was later picked in the contest for a name for Seattle's new AL baseball team.

Sounders (NASL) 1974-1983

In December 1973 the owners of the Seattle entry in the NASL announced the winner of the Name the Team contest. Sounders had been selected, in part because of Puget Sound. Seattle is located on the sound.

Supersonics (NBA) 1967/68—

Although Supersonics was the name that was picked as the winner in its Name the Team contest, club management immediately confirmed that only Sonics would appear on the Seattle uniforms.

The winning entry was submitted by Howard E. Schmidt and his ten-year-old son, Brent, who sent in a joint entry. Schmidt was a high-school economics and history teacher. The Schmidt entry was declared the winner because it had been the first to be received with the Supersonics name.

General Manager Don Richman said, "We think the name best expresses Seattle's people and its present and future."

According to Richman, 162 other persons had entered Supersonics, and 278 entries listed either Supers or Sonics. Schmidt received a weekend trip to Palm Springs (CA) and two season tickets.

SHEBOYGAN (WI)

Red Skins (NBL) 1938/39-1948/49
Red Skins (NBA) 1949/50
The Red Skins was organized in 1938 by 120 businessmen and professionals. It was operated as a civic venture, and all eleven directors served without pay.

The team name was officially two words but was often seen in the one-word form. Several teams in the early 1910s and 1920s in Wisconsin were named Red Skins, and it is assumed that the selection by Sheboygan was a continuation of the tradition.

SHREVEPORT (LA)

Steamer (WFL) 1974-1975
The Steamer began the 1974 season as the Texans in Houston.

SOUTH BEND (IN)

Guardsmen (NPBL) 1932/33
The team played its home games in a National Guard Armory.

SOUTHERN CALIFORNIA

Sun (WFL) 1974-1975
The Southern California Sun were located in Anaheim (CA). The team management held a Name the Team contest that resulted in the selection of the singular Sun being picked as a nickname.

What it didn't result in was the selection of the following names: Vipers, Orange Peelers, Barracudas, Godzillas, Orangutans, or Eurekas.

STATEN ISLAND (NY)

Staples (NFL) 1931-1932
See Staten Island Stapletons (NFL).

Stapletons (NFL) 1929-1930
Stapleton is one of the towns (neighborhoods, since Staten Island is a borough of New York City) on Staten Island. The town was established on 7/4/1836 by William J. Staples.

The Stapletons played as an independent team, perhaps as early as the mid 1910s, before joining the NFL.

The team shortened its name to Staples for the 1931/32 season.

SYRACUSE (NY)

All-Americans (ABL-1) 1929/30
The All-Americans played most of the first half of the season but dropped out on 1/6/30. Their record was 4-16 at the time, and with forfeits of the remaining games, it became 4-20.

Braves (AFL-2) 1936
The Braves lost five straight games, and on 10/20/36 arrangements were completed to shift the team to Rochester. The Braves then beat the unbeaten Boston Shamrocks and moved to Rochester. They played one game in Rochester as the Rochester Braves and then folded on 11/5/36.

Nationals (NBL) 1946/47-1948/49
Nationals (NBA) 1949/50-1962/63
The Syracuse Professional Basketball Club, Inc., was formed by co-owners Dan Biasone and George Mingin to bring a NBL franchise to Syracuse. The club took the name of the league and were officially the Nationals. However, they were most frequently referred to as the Nats.

Stars (NL) 1879
See Syracuse Stars (AA).

Stars (AA) 1890
The Star Base Ball Club of Syracuse was formed in 1868, and the nickname Star was used by the NL club of 1879. The AA club of 1890 does not seem to have an official name but was referred to as Stars on at least one occasion.

TACOMA (WA)

Stars (MISL) 1983/84—

TAMPA BAY (FL)

Bandits (USFL) 1983-1985
As did other USFL teams, the owners chose a name that bore a resemblance to the NFL team (Buccaneers) in the same city.

Buccaneers (NFL) 1976—
A Name the Team contest was held by a Tampa Bay radio station (WFLA). More than 400 nicknames were then submitted to an advisory board, and the unanimous verdict was Buccaneers.

Hugh Culverhouse, the Tampa Bay owner, said the new name "catches the spirit. We want our football team to be as aggressive, high-spirited, and colorful as were the old buccaneers."

Richard Molloy of Tampa was selected as the winner of the contest, and he won a television set and a pair of season tickets.

Rowdies (NASL) 1975-1984
The team nickname for Tampa Bay's entry in the NASL was picked in a Name the Team contest.

Rowdyism is a term often used to describe unruly, troublesome, or rough behavior, especially by soccer fans or players.

TEAM HAWAII

Team Hawaii (NASL) 1977
This team took its name from the state name.

TEXAS

Chaparrals (ABA) 1970/71
See Dallas Chaparrals (ABA).

Rangers (AL) 1972—
Just as the name Senators seems to be a natural for a Washington, DC, team, Rangers seems to fit the bill for a Texas team. When the Washington Senators (the 1961-1971 version) moved to the Dallas-Fort Worth area, a new name was needed, and the results of a Name the Team contest produced Rangers.

Rangers, the legendary police force in Texas, is a popular team name in the state.

TOLEDO (OH)

Blue Stockings (AA) 1884
The team took its name from the color of its socks.

Crawfords (NAL) 1939
The Crawfords played the first half of the season only. *See* Pittsburgh Crawfords (NNL-2).

Crimson Coaches (NPBL) 1932/33
The team was sponsored by the Crimson Coaches Tobacco Company.

Jeeps (NBL) 1946/47-1947/48
The Jeeps were originally connected with the workers' recreation program at the Willys Jeep factory. They were then taken over and sponsored by the food service (Buddy's Box Lunch) that catered to workers in the Toledo area. Later, the Toledo Jeeps were sponsored by the more formal Toledo Sports Arena, Inc.

Jim White Chevrolets (NBL) 1941/42-1942/43
This team was sponsored by the Jim White Chevrolet dealership. The club disbanded on 12/14/42.

Maroons (NFL) 1922-1923
This team received its name from the color of its jerseys.

Maumees (AA) 1890
In 1888, the Toledo baseball team had a ballpark located at Presque Isle Park, near the mouth of the Maumee River and Bay. The team picked up the nickname Maumees, but it was also beginning to be called the Black Pirates of the Maumee Valley. The second nickname became the one in use in 1891 and 1892.

Red Man Tobaccos (ABL-1) 1930/31
Although often referred to as the Toledo Redmen (or Red Men), the following information, taken directly from one of the team's publicity posters, correctly explains the name:

Please, we appreciate being billed as the RED MAN TOBACCOS (not RED MEN). We realize that the word "Red Men" is the plural of Red Man and may without intent be substituted in error. Red Men, however, is the name of a National Fraternal Order and has no connection with Toledo's entry in the American Basketball League, the Red Man Tobaccos, sponsored by the Pinkerton Tobacco Company of Toledo, Ohio.

The Red Man Tobacco Basketball Club began as an industrial team in 1926/27, played as a semi-pro team in 1927/28 and 1928/29, and as a professional team beginning in 1929/30.

Tigers (NNL-1) 1923
The team disbanded on 7/15/23.

TONAWANDA (NY)

Kardex (APFA) 1921
At the turn of the century, business methods were being revolutionized in this country, and one of the pioneer companies in producing new items, such as the vertical file and the card-index system (Kar/dex), was the Rand Kardex Bureau, Inc. The company became part of Remington-Rand and then Sperry-Rand Corporation.

The Kardex team was sponsored by one of the company's plants in Tonawanda, just outside of Buffalo.

TORONTO (Ontario)

Arenas (NHL) 1917/18-1918/19
The Toronto NHL team played in the Mutual Street Arena and were thus called the Arenas.

Blizzard (NASL) 1979-1984
The Toronto club decided that it wanted a new name (it had been the Metros-Croatia) that was not ethnic but could be identified with Canada.

Club president Paul Morton explained, "We wanted a name which could meet the perception of Canada held by most North Americans and Europeans."

Blue Jays (AL) 1977—
When the Toronto club held its Name the Team contest in the summer of 1976, it was swamped with over 30,000 entries that produced in excess of 4,000 individual names.

The board of directors appointed a panel to narrow the list to ten names, and from that group the directors selected Blue Jays. When the list was narrowed, the most popular choice had been Blues. However, Blues had been the name of the University of Toronto sports teams since 1893, and the school was not happy with the possibility that the AL team would also be the Blues.

The winner of the contest was Dr. William Mills, of Etobicoke (Ontario), who was one of 154 who submitted Blue Jays. He received an all-expense-paid trip to the Blue Jays spring training camp, plus a pair of season tickets.

Falcons (NASL) 1968

Huskies (BAA) 1946/47
The Toronto entry in the BAA received its nickname on 8/20/46, but numerous references can be found to the team, both before and after, as the Toronto Maple Leafs basketball team.

Like most of the BAA teams, their owners also owned or controlled a hockey team and/or an arena. There are also references to the BAA itself as the Arena League. The Toronto Huskies were owned by the Maple Leaf Gardens.

Maple Leafs (NHL) 1926/27—
When Conn Smythe took over the Toronto St. Pats, one of his first acts was to change the name of the team.

Smythe was a very patriotic and spartan individual. He changed the team name to the name of the emblem of Canada, the maple leaf.

Metros (NASL) 1971-1974
Toronto is often referred to as Metro Toronto, after the metropolitan region of the city. The subway system is also called the Metro.

Metros-Croatia (NASL) 1975-1978
In 1975, the Croatian community saved the Metros from folding, and much to the objection of the NASL, added Croatia to the team name.

St. Patricks (NHL) 1919/20-1925/26
After several very bad seasons, the owners of the Arenas decided to rebuild the team, starting with the name. They gave it a new name, the St. Patricks, although it was frequently shortened to St. Pats.

It is uncertain as to why the name became St. Patricks. Some sources believe that it was in hopes of attracting more of Toronto's Irish population to the games.

Toros (WHA) 1973/74-1975/76
Toros is not the Spanish for "bull" in this instance; rather it is a shortened form of Toronto.

TRENTON (NJ)

Moose (EL) 1932/33
Moose (ABL-2) 1933/34
These teams were sponsored by a local lodge of the Loyal Order of Moose.

Moose (ABL-2) 1935/36
See Trenton Moose (EL).

Royal Bengals (ML-1) 1923/24-1924/25
See Passaic Bengal Tigers (ABL-2).

Royal Bengals (ABL-1) 1928/29
See Passaic Bengal Tigers (ABL-2).

Tigers (ABL-2) 1941/42-1945/46
See Passaic Bengal Tigers (ABL-2).

TRI-CITIES

Blackhawks (NBL) 1946/47-1948/49
Blackhawks (NBA) 1949/50-1950/51
The Tri-Cities Blackhawks began as the Buffalo Bisons at the beginning of the 1946/47 season. The reason for the move was a lack of attendance in Buffalo, where the Bisons had a 4-8 record.

The Tri-Cities consisted of Moline and Rock Island (IL) and Davenport (IA). The three towns are adjacent to one another on the Mississippi River. (Today, these three cities, along with Bettendorf [IA], form the Quad Cities and support a Class A baseball team.)

A group of civic leaders in the tri-city area established Tri-City Sports, Inc., to accept the franchise. Although a Name the Team contest was announced prior to the change, the author has not located any data concerning the contest. It is known that the name Blackhawks very quickly appeared, so the contest may not have been widely announced.

The name Blackhawks refers to the great Indian leader. *See* Chicago Black Hawks (NHL).

When the Tri-City Blackhawks moved to Milwaukee, the new owners decided to shorten the name to Hawks. *See* Buffalo Bisons (NBL).

TROY (NY)

Celtics (ABL-2) 1939/40-1940/41
The Celtics began the 1940/41 season in Troy but moved to Brooklyn. *See* New York Original Celtics (ABL-2).

Haymakers (ABL-2) 1938/39-1939/40
This team adopted the nickname of the famous baseball team that played in the National Association (NA).

The basketball team began the 1939/40 season as the Troy Haymakers but changed their name to Troy Celtics on 12/19/39.

See New York Original Celtics (ABL-2).

Haymakers (NA) 1871-1872
The Haymakers began as the Union Club of Rensselaer County (NY) and was formed in 1861 as a union of two clubs, one from Lansingburgh and the other from Troy. Today, Lansingburgh is part of Troy.

By 1866, the team was known as the Unions of Lansingburgh because most of the players were from Lansingburgh.

The nickname Haymakers is believed to have been coined in mid 1867, when they beat the Mutuals of New York. The New York team did not like the idea of being beaten by a bunch of country boys, a bunch of haymakers.

While the team was being referred to as Lansingburgh Unions or Lansingburgh Haymakers in upstate New York, fans and sports writers in other parts of the country found it was a lot easier to refer to the team as the Troy Haymakers.

A rivalry existed for many years over the name. Lansingburgh residents pointed out that most of the players were from their town and that the ballpark was also in their town. They complained that Troy claimed the team because it was successful.

Regardless of the debate, Haymakers is a unique nickname.

Trojans (NL) 1879-1882
This team adopted its city's name for a nickname. However, there were some references to the team as the New Haymakers.

Troy (ML-1) 1927/28
This was one of many of the early basketball teams that was known only by the name of its town or city.

TULSA (OK)

Roughnecks (NASL) 1978-1984

UNION CITY (NJ)

Reds (ML-2) 1931/32-1932/33
Reds (ABL-2) 1933/34
The Union City Reds were formed in the 1925/26 season and played most of their games in a ballroom known as *Palais de Danse*, in Union City. (Union City had just been formed by the merger of Union Hill and West Hoboken.)

Because the early references to the team are to the Redlegs, it may be assumed that it took its nickname from the color of its socks or leggings.

The Union City Reds became the Jersey Reds in 1934/35, giving them a broader fan base, because the team could play its home games in other communities.

UTAH

Jazz (NBA) 1979/80—
See New orleans Jazz (NBA).

Stars (ABA) 1970/71-1975/76
See Los Angeles Stars (ABA).

VANCOUVER (British Columbia)

Blazers (WHA) 1973/74-1974/75

Canucks (NHL) 1970/71—
The Vancouver NHL team adopted the name of the Vancouver Canucks of the Western Hockey League. The WHL team was disbanded when Vancouver got a NHL franchise. The term *Canuck* originally meant a French-Canadian but has become more generalized to mean a Canadian.

In its final year, the WHL team had set a new league attendance record, proving that Vancouver was ready for the NHL.

Royals (NASL) 1968

Whitecaps (NASL) 1974-1984
The nickname was selected for the white-capped mountains and the white-capped ocean waters that surround the city.

VIRGINIA

Squires (ABA) 1970/71-1975/76
A squire is a landowner, especially of a country estate, and goes back to colonial days.

The squires played home games in Richmond, Hampton Roads, and Norfolk.

WARREN (PA)

Oilers (MBC) 1936/37
This team was sponsored by the Hyvis Oil Company and thus was called Oilers. In 1937/38, it joined the NBL and some references are made to the team as the Warren Penn Oilers. However, Hyvis Oil had dropped its sponsorship, so the team was officially the Warren Penns for 1937/38 and 1938/39.

Warren Penns (a shortened form of Pennsylvania) avoids confusion with Warren (OH), which is a much larger city.

Penns (NBL) 1937/38-1938/39
The Penns moved to Cleveland on 2/10/38, with a 9-10 record, and became the Cleveland White Horses.
See Warren Oilers (MBC).

WASHINGTON (DC)

See also **Capital.**

Black Senators (NNL-2) 1938
This team adopted the name of the Washington Senators (AL). The club folded during the second half of the season.

Brewers (ABL-2) 1938/39-1941/42
The team was sponsored by the Christian Heurich Brewery of Washington, DC.

Bullets (NBA) 1974/75—
See Baltimore Bullets (NBA) 1973/74 and Baltimore Bullets (ABL-2).

Capitals (NHL) 1974/75—
When the NHL granted a franchise to Washington, Abe Pollin, owner of the new NHL club and of the Capital Bullets (NBA), decided to hold a Name the Team contest.

Over 12,000 entries were received. Among the final

names that Pollin considered were Domes, Cyclones, Streaks, and Comets. Comets had been the most popular choice, with 250 votes. Pollin ignored all of these and didn't even consider Pandas, which had been another fan favorite. Instead he chose Capitals.

More important, he chose Washington Capitals. A year earlier he had changed the name of his NBA Baltimore Bullets to the Capital Bullets (because they were going to play in the new Capital Centre in Landover, MD).

Pollin was criticized by some fans and sports writers because the most popular name submitted (Comets) had been overruled by the unanimous vote of Pollin and his wife. Also, they said, he had picked a nickname used by two now-defunct basketball teams.

On the second point, however, they were wrong. The two defunct teams (actually there were three) were named Capitol, not Capital. There is a difference, and Pollin knew that he was choosing Capital (which refers to the city) and not Capitol (which refers to the building).

Because eighty-eight people had sent in the name Capitals, a drawing was held, and Mrs. John Stolarick of Alexandria (VA) was declared winner of the first prize: two season tickets. Mrs. Stolarick, married to a civilian army engineer and the mother of four children, was raised in Regina, Saskatchewan, and was an avid hockey fan.

Three months after naming his hockey team, Pollin changed the name of the basketball team from Capital Bullets to Washington Bullets. Now the Washington Capitals (NHL) and the Washington Bullets (NBA) play their home games in the Capital Centre located in Landover (MD).

Capitols (BAA) 1946/47-1948/49
See Washington Capitols (ABA).

Capitols (ABL-3) 1961/62
See Washington Capitols (ABA).

Capitols (ABA) 1969/70
The ABA team was the third of three teams that took their nickname from the Capitol building in the nation's capital.

Capitol's (ABL-2) 1944/45
It is unknown as to why this team used the nickname in this way (with the 's). The team moved to Paterson (NJ) on 1/1/45 to become the Paterson Crescents.

Darts (NASL) 1970-1971

Diplomats (NASL) 1974-1980
The team's name was picked by Sandi Finci, wife of club president Mike Finci. "Just don't call us the Dips. That's all I ask," Mrs. Finci said when making the announcement.

The diplomatic corps is an integral part of the Washington scene.

Diplomats (NASL) 1981
This was a different franchise, but it adopted the nickname of the earlier team.

Elite Giants (NNL-2) 1936-1937
See Nashville Elite Giants (NNL-1).

Federals (USFL) 1983-1984
Washington is often called the Federal City. The team adopted this nickname.

Nationals (NA) 1873
Nationals (NA) 1875
See Washington Nationals (UA).

Nationals (UA) 1884
The first National Club started in Washington in 1860. National became associated with various Washington teams, and even in the later days of the Senators, Washington fans continued to refer to its major-league teams as the Nationals.

In 1905, when the name Senators was in use, a Name the Team contest was held. The winner, announced by Washington president Thomas C. Noyes, was F. L. McKenna, who wrote:

> My reasons for the name "Nationals" is that it has greater significance and will be more appreciated than "Senators" and incite the players to greater efforts. I believe the people of Washington will support a winning club. When Washington had a club called the "Nationals" it was a winner and the people were proud of it and supported it.

For the record, three names that were in the running were Climbers, Dixie, and Rough Riders.

Olympics (NA) 1871-1872

The Olympic club was formed in 1859, and its team took the name of the club.

Palace Five (ABL-1) 1925/26-1927/28

The Palace Five team was owned by George Preston Marshall, who would later own the Washington Redskins. Marshall owned the Palace Laundry in Washington. This team was sometimes referred to as the Palacians. On 6/14/28, Marshall sold his players and franchise to the Brooklyn Visitations, who had been playing in the Metropolitan League.

Potomacs (ECL) 1924

More than likely this team took its nickname from the river that flows past Washington (DC).

Redskins (NFL) 1937—

See Boston Braves (NFL) and Boston Redskins (NFL).

Senators (NL) 1888-1889

See Washington Senators (AL) 1961-1971.

Senators (AA) 1891

See Washington Senators (AL) 1961-1971.

Senators (NL) 1892-1899

See Washington Senators (AL) 1961-1971.

Senators (AL) 1901-1960

See Washington Senators (AL) 1961-1971.

Senators (AL) 1961-1971

In 1886, Washington got an NL franchise, after winning the Eastern League pennant in 1885. The team entered the NL as the Statesmen but changed their name to Senators in 1888. The Senators of 1888-1889 merged with the Cincinnati Reds to become the Cincinnati (NL) 1890-1943 team. Washington then had a Senators team in the AA (1891) and in the NL (1892-1899) before joining the AL in 1901.

In 1905, a contest was held that resulted in the "official" change of the Senators name to Nationals until 1944. However, the fans still referred to the team primarily as the Senators. *See* Washington Nationals (NA).

The Senators 1901-1960 moved to Minnesota and became the Twins. The Senators 1961-1971 moved to Texas and became the Rangers.

Senators (APFA) 1921

The football team adopted the name of the baseball teams.

Statesmen (NL) 1886-1887

See Washington Senators (NL).

Washington (AA) 1884

This was one of the early baseball teams that was known by its town or city name only.

Whips (NASL) 1968

This NASL team got its nickname as a result of a Name the Team contest.

WATERLOO (IA)

Hawks (NBL) 1948/49
Hawks (NBA) 1949/50

The Hawks were originally organized through the efforts of the local Rath meat-packing plant. While it would have been natural for Waterloo to use the nickname Blackhawks, they had to settle for the shortened form of Hawks, since the Tri-Cities team already had the nickname Blackhawks.

WESTCHESTER (NY)

See **New York Westchesters (ABL-2).**

WHITING (IN)

Ciesar All-Americans (MBC) 1936/37
Ciesar All-Americans (NBL) 1937/38

The owner was Eddie Ciesar, and his teams had numerous All-Americans, including John Wooden, later the coach of the great UCLA college basketball teams. In 1939/40, the team was briefly coached by baseball Hall of Famer Lou Boudreau, who also had played for the team in the previous season.

WICHITA (KS)

Wings (MISL) 1979/80—

WILKES-BARRE (PA)

Barons (ABL-2) 1938/39-1939/40

The Wilkes-Barre team takes its nickname from the

coal barons who lived in the area when "coal was king." The nickname has long been associated with teams in this area.

WILMINGTON (DE)

Cats (EL) 1931/32-1932/33
The team was sometimes known as the Hornets in 1931/32.

Blue Bombers (ABL-2) 1941/42
Blue Bombers (ABL-2) 1943/44
The Wilmington team was owned by the Carpenter family, which purchased the Philadelphia Phillies in 1944. The reason for the nickname is unknown. It may relate to the war industry of Wilmington, or it could have a relation to the basketball term *bomber*.

Bombers (ABL-2) 1944/45-1945/46
See Wilmington Blue Bombers (ABL-2).

Quicksteps (UA) 1884
The Quicksteps began the season in the Eastern League, moved up to the UA in August, but folded in September with a 2-16 record. The nickname Quicksteps was used by some of the early fire companies.

WINDSOR (Ontario)

Cooper Buses (MBC) 1935/36
The team was sponsored by the Cooper Bus Company.

WINNIPEG (Manitoba)

Jets (WHA) 1972/73-1978/79
Jets (NHL) 1979/80—
The Winnipeg team adopted the name that was used to identify the very popular recreational hockey leagues in Winnipeg—the Jets.

WORCESTER (MA)

Worcester (NL) 1880-1882
Although there are some references to Brown Stockings and Nationals, most sources agree on Worcester as the official name.

YONKERS (NY)

Chippewas (ML-1) 1922/23-1924/25
Although many sports teams, especially in basketball and football, have adopted nicknames that relate to the American Indian, this nickname seems a little out of place. The Chippewas are primarily in the Lake Superior region.

There is some doubt as to the team's name in 1923/24 and in 1924/25, but it is known that the name was Indians in the 1925/26 and 1926/27 seasons. Perhaps the team only spent the 1922/23 season as Chippewas.

Indians (ML-1) 1925/26-1926/27
See Yonkers Chippewas (ML-1).

Knights (ML-2) 1932/33
The team was sponsored by the Knights of Columbus. Some references were made to the team as Caseys (K.C.s).

YOUNGSTOWN (OH)

Bears (NBL) 1945/46-1946/47

Section 2

Professional Leagues

Baseball

National Association (NA) 1871-1875
National League (NL) 1876—
American Association (AA) 1882-1891
Union Association (UA) 1884
Players League (PL) 1890
American League (AL) 1901—
Federal League (FL) 1914-1915
National Negro League (NNL-1) 1920-1931
Eastern Colored League (ECL) 1923-1928
American Negro League (ANL) 1929
Negro Southern League (NSL) 1932
Negro National League (NNL-2) 1933-1948
Negro American League (NAL) 1937-1950

Basketball

Metropolitan Basketball League (ML-1) 1921/22-1927/28
American Basketball League (ABL-1) 1925/26-1930/31
Eastern Basketball League (EL) 1931/32-1932/33
Metropolitan Basketball League (ML-2) 1931/32-1932/33
National Professional Basketball League (NPBL) 1932/33
American Basketball League (ABL-2) 1933/34-1945/46
Midwest Basketball League (MBC) 1935/36-1936/37
National Basketball League (NBL) 1937/38-1948/49
Basketball Association of America (BAA) 1946/47-1948/49
National Basketball Association (NBA) 1949/50—
American Basketball League (ABL-3) 1961/62-1962/63
American Basketball Association (ABA) 1967/68-1975/76

Football

American Professional Football Association (APFA) 1920-1921
National Football League (NFL) 1922—
American Football League (AFL-1) 1926
American Football League (AFL-2) 1936-1937
American Football League (AFL-3) 1940-1941
All-American Football Conference (AAFC) 1946-1949
American Football League (AFL-4) 1960-1969
World Football League (WFL) 1974-1975
United States Football League (USFL) 1983-1985

Hockey

National Hockey League (NHL) 1917/18—
World Hockey Association (WHA) 1972/73-1978/79

Soccer

North American Soccer League (NASL) 1968-1984
Major Indoor Soccer League (MISL) 1978/79—

NATIONAL ASSOCIATION (NA) 1871-1875

Franchise Name	Were	Became
Brooklyn Atlantics 1872-1875		
Brooklyn Eckfords 1871-1872 (Replaced Ft. Wayne, which folded in late 1871. League struck 1871 record because of late entry.)		
Boston Red Stockings 1871-1875		
Chicago White Stockings 1871		Chicago White Stockings 1874-1875
Chicago White Stockings 1874-1875	Chicago White Stockings 1871	
Cleveland Forest Citys 1871-1872		
Elizabeth Resolutes 1873		
Fort Wayne Kekiongas 1871 (Team folded before the end of the season. Replaced by Brooklyn Eckfords.)		
Hartfords 1874-1875		
Keokuk Westerns 1875		
Lord Baltimores 1872-1874		
Middletown Mansfields 1872		

Franchise Name	**Were**	**Became**

New Havens
  1875

New York Mutuals
  1871-1875

Philadelphia Athletics
  1871-1875

Philadelphia Centennials
  1875

Philadelphias
  1873-1875

Rockford Forest Citys
  1871

St. Louis
  1875

St. Louis Reds
  1875

Troy Haymakers
  1871-1872

Washington Nationals
  1873

Washington Nationals
  1875

Washington Olympics
  1871-1872

NATIONAL LEAGUE (NL) 1876—

Franchise Name	Were	Became
Atlanta Braves 1966—	Milwaukee Braves 1953-1965 Boston Braves 1941-1952 Boston Bees 1936-1940 Boston Braves 1912-1935 Boston Pilgrims 1909-1911 Boston Doves 1907-1908 Boston Beaneaters 1883-1906 Boston Red Caps 1876-1882	
Baltimore Orioles 1892-1899	Baltimore Orioles (AA) 1890-1891 Brooklyn Gladiators (AA) 1890 (Brooklyn Gladiators disbanded on 8/3/90, and franchise moved to Baltimore.)	
Boston Beaneaters 1883-1906	Boston Red Caps 1876-1882	Boston Doves 1907-1908 Boston Pilgrims 1909-1911 Boston Braves 1912-1935 Boston Bees 1936-1940 Boston Braves 1941-1952 Milwaukee Braves 1953-1965 Atlanta Braves 1966—
Boston Bees 1936-1940	Boston Braves 1912-1935 Boston Pilgrims 1909-1911	Boston Braves 1941-1952 Milwaukee Braves 1953-1965

Franchise Name	Were	Became
	Boston Doves 1907-1908 Boston Beaneaters 1883-1906 Boston Red Caps 1876-1882	Atlanta Braves 1966—
Boston Braves 1912-1935	Boston Pilgrims 1909-1911 Boston Doves 1907-1908 Boston Beaneaters 1883-1906 Boston Red Caps 1876-1882	Boston Bees 1936-1940 Boston Braves 1941-1952 Milwaukee Braves 1953-1965 Atlanta Braves 1966—
Boston Braves 1941-1952	Boston Bees 1936-1940 Boston Braves 1912-1935 Boston Pilgrims 1909-1911 Boston Doves 1907-1908 Boston Beaneaters 1883-1906 Boston Red Caps 1876-1882	Milwaukee Braves 1953-1965 Atlanta Braves 1966—
Boston Doves 1907-1908	Boston Beaneaters 1883-1906 Boston Red Caps 1876-1882	Boston Pilgrims 1909-1911 Boston Braves 1912-1935 Boston Bees 1936-1940 Boston Braves 1941-1952 Milwaukee Braves 1953-1965 Atlanta Braves 1966—
Boston Pilgrims 1909-1911	Boston Doves 1907-1908 Boston Beaneaters 1883-1906 Boston Red Caps 1876-1882	Boston Braves 1912-1935 Boston Bees 1936-1940 Boston Braves 1941-1952

Franchise Name	Were	Became
		Milwaukee Braves 1953-1965 Atlanta Braves 1966—
Boston Red Caps 1876-1882		Boston Beaneaters 1883-1906 Boston Doves 1907-1908 Boston Pilgrims 1909-1911 Boston Braves 1912-1935 Boston Bees 1936-1940 Boston Braves 1941-1952 Milwaukee Braves 1953-1965 Atlanta Braves 1966—
Brooklyn Bridegrooms 1890-1898	Brooklyn Bridegrooms (AA) 1889 Brooklyns (AA) 1884-1888	Brooklyn Superbas 1899-1910 Brooklyn Infants 1911-1913 Brooklyn Robins 1914-1931 Brooklyn Dodgers 1932-1957 Los Angeles Dodgers 1958—
Brooklyn Dodgers 1932-1957	Brooklyn Robins 1914-1931 Brooklyn Infants 1911-1913 Brooklyn Superbas 1899-1910 Brooklyn Bridegrooms 1890-1898 Brooklyn Bridegrooms (AA) 1889 Brooklyns (AA) 1884-1888	Los Angeles Dodgers 1958—
Brooklyn Infants 1911-1913	Brooklyn Superbas 1899-1910	Brooklyn Robins 1914-1931

Franchise Name	Were	Became
	Brooklyn Bridegrooms 1890-1898 Brooklyn Bridegrooms (AA) 1889 Brooklyns (AA) 1884-1888	Brooklyn Dodgers 1932-1957 Los Angeles Dodgers 1958—
Brooklyn Robins 1914-1931	Brooklyn Infants 1911-1913 Brooklyn Superbas 1899-1910 Brooklyn Bridegrooms 1890-1898 Brooklyn Bridegrooms (AA) 1889 Brooklyns (AA) 1884-1888	Brooklyn Dodgers 1932-1957 Los Angeles Dodgers 1958—
Brooklyn Superbas 1899-1910	Brooklyn Bridegrooms 1890-1898 Brooklyn Bridegrooms (AA) 1889 Brooklyns (AA) 1884-1888	Brooklyn Infants 1911-1913 Brooklyn Robins 1914-1931 Brooklyn Dodgers 1932-1957 Los Angeles Dodgers 1958—
Buffalo Bisons 1879-1885		
Chicago Colts 1894-1897	Chicago White Stockings 1876-1893	Chicago Orphans 1898-1899 Chicago Cubs 1900—
Chicago Cubs 1900—	Chicago Orphans 1898-1899 Chicago Colts 1894-1897 Chicago White Stockings 1876-1893	
Chicago Orphans 1898-1899	Chicago Colts 1894-1897 Chicago White Stockings 1876-1893	Chicago Cubs 1900—
Chicago White Stockings 1876-1893		Chicago Colts 1894-1897

Franchise Name	Were	Became
		Chicago Orphans 1898-1899 Chicago Cubs 1900—
Cincinnati Redlegs 1944-1945	Cincinnati Reds 1890-1943 Cincinnati Reds (AA) 1882-1889 (Reds and Washington Senators of NL merged at end of 1889 season.)	Cincinnati Reds 1946—
Cincinnati Reds 1876-1880		
Cincinnati Reds 1890-1943	Cincinnati Reds (AA) 1882-1889 (Reds and Washington Senators of NL merged at end of 1889 season.)	Cincinnati Redlegs 1944-1945 Cincinnati Reds 1946—
Cincinati Reds 1946—	Cincinnati Redlegs 1944-1945 Cincinnati Reds 1890-1943 Cincinnati Reds (AA) 1882-1889 (Reds and Washington Senators of NL merged at end of 1889 season.)	
Cleveland Forest Cities 1879-1884		
Cleveland Spiders 1889-1899		
Detroit Wolverines 1881-1888		
Hartford Blues 1876-1877		
Houston Astros 1965—	Houston Colt .45s 1962-1964	
Houston Colt .45s 1962-1964		Houston Astros 1965—

Franchise Name	Were	Became
Indianapolis Hoosiers 1878		
Indianapolis Hoosiers 1887-1889	St. Louis Maroons 1885-1886 St. Louis Maroons (UA) 1884	
Kansas City Cowboys 1886		
Los Angeles Dodgers 1958—	Brooklyn Dodgers 1932-1957 Brooklyn Robins 1914-1931 Brooklyn Infants 1911-1913 Brooklyn Superbas 1899-1910 Brooklyn Bridegrooms 1890-1898 Brooklyn Bridegrooms (AA) 1889 Brooklyns (AA) 1884-1888	
Louisville Colonels 1876-1877		
Louisville Colonels 1892-1899	Louisville Colonels (AA) 1884-1891 Louisville Eclipse (AA) 1882-1883	
Milwaukee Braves 1953-1965	Boston Braves 1941-1952 Boston Bees 1936-1940 Boston Braves 1912-1935 Boston Pilgrims 1909-1911 Boston Doves 1907-1908 Boston Beaneaters 1883-1906 Boston Red Caps 1876-1882	Atlanta Braves 1966—

Franchise Name	Were	Became
Milwaukee Brewers 1878		
Montreal Expos 1969—		
New York Giants 1885-1957	New York Gothams 1883-1884 Troy Trojans 1879-1882	San Francisco Giants 1958—
New York Gothams 1883-1884	Troy Trojans 1879-1882	New York Giants 1885-1957 San Francisco Giants 1958—
New York Mets 1962—		
New York Mutuals 1876		
Philadelphia Athletics 1876		
Philadelphia Blue Jays 1944-1945	Philadelphia Phillies 1883-1943 Worcester 1880-1882	Philadelphia Phillies 1946—
Philadelphia Phillies 1883-1943	Worcester 1880-1882	Philadelphia Blue Jays 1944-1945 Philadelphia Phillies 1946—
Philadelphia Phillies 1946—	Philadelphia Blue Jays 1944-1945 Philadelphia Phillies 1883-1943 Worcester 1880-1882	
Pittsburgh Alleghenies 1887-1889	Pittsburgh Alleghenies (AA) 1882-1886	Pittsburgh Innocents 1890 Pittsburgh Pirates 1891—
Pittsburgh Innocents 1890	Pittsburgh Alleghenies 1887-1889	Pittsburgh Pirates 1891—

Franchise Name	Were	Became
	Pittsburgh Alleghenies (AA) 1882-1886	
Pittsburgh Pirates 1891—	Pittsburgh Innocents 1890 Pittsburgh Alleghenies 1887-1889 Pittsburgh Alleghenies (AA) 1882-1886	
Providence Grays 1878-1885		
St. Louis Browns 1876-1877		
St. Louis Browns 1892-1897	St. Louis Browns (AA) 1882-1891	St. Louis Perfectos 1898-1899 St. Louis Cardinals 1900—
St. Louis Cardinals 1900—	St. Louis Perfectos 1898-1899 St. Louis Browns 1892-1897 St. Louis Browns (AA) 1882-1891	
St. Louis Perfectos 1898-1899	St. Louis Browns 1892-1897 St. Louis Browns (AA) 1882-1891	St. Louis Cardinals 1900—
St. Louis Maroons 1885-1886	St. Louis Maroons (UA) 1884	Indianapolis Hoosiers 1887-1889
San Diego Padres 1969—		
San Francisco Giants 1958—	New York Giants 1885-1957 New York Gothams 1883-1884 Troy Trojans 1879-1882	
Syracuse Stars 1879		

Franchise Name	Were	Became
Troy Trojans 1879-1882		New York Gothams 1883-1884 New York Giants 1885-1957 San Francisco Giants 1958—
Washington Senators 1888-1889	Washington Statesmen 1886-1887	Cincinnati Reds 1890-1943 (Cincinnati Reds of AA and Senators merged at end of 1889 season.) Cincinnati Redlegs 1944-1945 Cincinnati Reds 1946—
Washington Senators 1892-1899	Washington Senators (AA) 1891	
Washington Statesmen 1886-1887		Washington Senators 1888-1889 Cincinnati Reds 1890-1943 (Cincinnati Reds of AA and Senators merged at end of 1889 season.) Cincinnati Redlegs 1944-1945 Cincinnati Reds 1946—
Worcester 1880-1882		Philadelphia Phillies 1883-1943 Philadelphia Blue Jays 1944-1945 Philadelphia Phillies 1946—

AMERICAN ASSOCIATION (AA) 1882-1891

Franchise Name	Were	Became
Baltimore Orioles 1882-1889 (Team folded in July 1889.)		
Baltimore Orioles 1890-1891	Brooklyn Gladiators 1890 (Moved to Baltimore on 8/3/90.)	Baltimore Orioles (NL) 1892-1899
Boston Reds 1891	Boston Reds (PL) 1890	
Brooklyns 1884-1888		Brooklyn Bridegrooms 1889 Brooklyn Bridegrooms (NL) 1890-1898 Brooklyn Superbas (NL) 1899-1910 Brooklyn Infants (NL) 1911-1913 Brooklyn Robins (NL) 1914-1931 Brooklyn Dodgers (NL) 1932-1957 Los Angeles Dodgers (NL) 1958—
Brooklyn Bridegrooms 1889	Brooklyns 1884-1888	Brooklyn Bridegrooms (NL) 1890-1898 Brooklyn Superbas (NL) 1899-1910 Brooklyn Infants (NL) 1911-1913 Brooklyn Robins (NL) 1914-1931 Brooklyn Dodgers (NL) 1932-1957 Los Angeles Dodgers (NL) 1958—
Brooklyn Gladiators 1890 (Team moved to Baltimore on 8/3/90.)		Baltimore Orioles 1890-1891 Baltimore Orioles (NL) 1892-1899

Franchise Name	Were	Became
Cincinnati Kelly's Killers 1891 (Team moved to Milwaukee in mid August of 1891.)		Milwaukee Brewers 1891
Cincinnati Reds 1882-1889		Cincinnati Reds (NL) 1890-1943 (Reds of AA merged with Washington Senators of NL at end of 1889 season.) Cincinnati Redlegs (NL) 1944-1945 Cincinnati Reds (NL) 1946—
Cleveland "Babies of the AA" 1887-1888		
Columbus Buckeyes 1883-1884		
Columbus Buckeyes 1889-1891		
Indianapolis Hoosiers 1884		
Kansas City Cowboys 1888-1889		
Louisville Colonels 1884-1891	Louisville Eclipse 1882-1883	Louisville Colonels (NL) 1892-1899
Louisville Eclipse 1882-1883		Louisville Colonels 1884-1891 Louisville Colonels (NL) 1892-1899
Milwaukee Brewers 1891	Cincinnati Kelly's Killers 1891 (Team moved to Milwaukee in mid August of 1891.)	

Franchise Name	Were	Became
New York Metropolitans 1883-1887		
Philadelphia Athletics 1882-1891		
Pittsburgh Alleghenies 1882-1886		Pittsburgh Alleghenies (NL) 1887-1889 Pittsburgh Innocents (NL) 1890 Pittsburgh Pirates (NL) 1891—
Richmond Virginias 1884 (Began season as Washington franchise and moved to Richmond with a 12-51 record.)	Washington 1884	
Rochester 1890		
St. Louis Browns 1882-1891		St. Louis Browns (NL) 1892-1897 St. Louis Perfectos (NL) 1898-1899 St. Louis Cardinals (NL) 1900—
Syracuse Stars 1890		
Toledo Blue Stockings 1884		
Toledo Maumees 1890		
Washington 1884 (Washington franchise moved to Richmond in midseason with a 12-51 record.)		Richmond Virginias 1884
Washington Senators 1891		Washington Senators (NL) 1892-1898

UNION ASSOCIATION (UA) 1884

Franchise Name	Were	Became
Altoona Pride 1884 (Altoona dropped out with a 6-19 record.)		
Baltimore Unions 1884		
Boston Unions 1884		
Chicago Unions 1884 (Chicago franchise moved to Pittsburgh in August 1884.)		Pittsburgh Unions 1884
Cincinnati Outlaw Reds 1884		
Kansas City Unions 1884		
Milwaukee Unions 1884 (Milwaukee dropped out with an 8-4 record.)		
Philadelphia Keystones 1884 (Philadelphia dropped out with a 21-46 record.)		
Pittsburgh Unions 1884	Chicago Unions 1884 (Chicago franchise moved to Pittsburgh in August 1884.)	

Franchise Name	Were	Became
St. Louis Maroons 1884		St. Louis Maroons (NL) 1885-1886 Indianapolis Hoosiers (NL) 1887-1889
St. Paul Saints 1884		
Washington Nationals 1884		
Wilmington Quicksteps 1884		

PLAYERS LEAGUE (PL) 1890

Franchise Name	Were	Became
Boston Reds 1890		Boston Reds (AA) 1891
Brooklyn Wonders 1890		
Buffalo Bisons 1890		
Chicago Pirates 1890		
Cleveland Infants 1890		
New York Giants 1890		
Philadelphia Quakers 1890		
Pittsburgh Burghers 1890		

AMERICAN LEAGUE (AL) 1901—

Franchise Name	Were	Became
Baltimore Orioles 1901-1902		New York Highlanders 1903-1912 New York Yankees 1913—
Baltimore Orioles 1954—	St. Louis Browns 1902-1953 Milwaukee Brewers 1901	
Boston Puritans 1905-1906	Boston Somersets 1901-1904	Boston Red Sox 1907—
Boston Red Sox 1907—	Boston Puritans 1905-1906 Boston Somersets 1901-1904	
Boston Somersets 1901-1904		Boston Puritans 1905-1906 Boston Red Sox 1907—
California Angels 1966—	Los Angeles Angels 1961-1965	
Chicago White Sox 1901—		
Cleveland Blues 1902-1904	Cleveland Bronchos 1901	Cleveland Naps 1905-1911 Cleveland Molly McGuires 1912-1914 Cleveland Indians 1915—
Cleveland Bronchos 1901		Cleveland Blues 1902-1904 Cleveland Naps 1905-1911 Cleveland Molly McGuires 1912-1914 Cleveland Indians 1915—

Franchise Name	Were	Became
Cleveland Indians 1915—	Cleveland Molly McGuires 1912-1914 Cleveland Naps 1905-1911 Cleveland Blues 1902-1904 Cleveland Bronchos 1901	
Cleveland Molly McGuires 1912-1914	Cleveland Naps 1905-1911 Cleveland Blues 1902-1904 Cleveland Bronchos 1901	Cleveland Indians 1915—
Cleveland Naps 1905-191	Cleveland Blues 1902-1904 Cleveland Bronchos 1901	Cleveland Molly McGuires 1912-1914 Cleveland Indians 1915—
Detroit Tigers 1901—		
Kansas City Athletics 1955-1967	Philadelphia Athletics 1901-1954	Oakland Athletics 1968—
Kansas City Royals 1969—		
Los Angeles Angels 1961-1965		California Angels 1966—
Milwaukee Brewers 1901		St. Louis Browns 1902-1953 Baltimore Orioles 1954—
Milwaukee Brewers 1970—	Seattle Pilots 1969	
Minnesota Twins 1961—	Washington Senators 1901-1960	
New York Highlanders 1903-1912	Baltimore Orioles 1901-1902	New York Yankees 1913—
New York Yankees 1913—	New York Highlanders 1903-1912	

Franchise Name	Were	Became
	Baltimore Orioles 1901-1902	
Oakland Athletics 1968—	Kansas City Athletics 1955-1967 Philadelphia Athletics 1901-1954	
Philadelphia Athletics 1901-1954		Kansas City Athletics 1955-1967 Oakland Athletics 1968—
St. Louis Browns 1902-1953	Milwaukee Brewers 1901	Baltimore Orioles 1954—
Seattle Pilots 1969		Milwaukee Brewers 1970—
Seattle Mariners 1977—		
Texas Rangers 1972—	Washington Senators 1961-1971	
Toronto Blue Jays 1977—		
Washington Senators 1901-1960		Minnesota Twins 1961—
Washington Senators 1961-1971		Texas Rangers 1972—

FEDERAL LEAGUE (FL) 1914-1915

Franchise Name	Were	Became
Baltimore Terrapins 1914-1915		
Brooklyn BrookFeds 1915	Brooklyn Tip Tops 1914	
Brooklyn Tip Tops 1914		Brooklyn BrookFeds 1915
Buffalo Blues 1915	Buffalo BufFeds 1914	
Buffalo BufFeds 1914		Buffalo Blues 1915
Chicago ChiFeds 1914		Chicago Whales 1915
Chicago Whales 1915	Chicago ChiFeds 1914	
Indianapolis Hoosiers 1914		Newark Peppers 1915
Kansas City Packers 1914-1915		
Newark Peppers 1915	Indianapolis Hoosiers 1914	
Pittsburgh Rebels 1914-1915		
St. Louis SlouFeds 1914		St. Louis Terriers 1915
St. Louis Terriers 1915	St. Louis SlouFeds 1914	

NEGRO NATIONAL LEAGUE-1 (NNL-1) 1920-1931

Franchise Name	Were	Became
Birmingham Black Barons 1924-1925		Birmingham Black Barons 1927-1930 Birmingham Black Barons (NAL) 1937-1938 Birmingham Black Barons (NAL) 1940-1950
Birmingham Black Barons 1927-1930	Birmingham Black Barons 1924-1925	Birmingham Black Barons 1937-1938 Birmingham Black Barons (NAL) 1940-1950
Chicago American Giants 1920-1931		(Chicago) Cole's American Giants (NSL) 1932 (Chicago) Cole's American Giants (NNL-2) 1933-1935 Chicago American Giants (NAL) 1937-1950
Chicago Giants 1920-1921		
(Cincinnati) Cuban Stars 1920-1922		Cuban Stars (West) (NNL-1) 1923-1930
Cleveland Browns 1924		
Cleveland Cubs 1931	Nashville Elite Giants (NNL-1) 1930	Nashville Elite Giants (NSL) 1932 Nashville Elite Giants (NNL-2) 1933-1934 Columbus Elite Giants (NNL-2) 1935

Franchise Name	Were	Became
		Washington Elite Giants (NNL-2) 1936-1937 Baltimore Elite Giants (NNL-2) 1938-1948 Baltimore Elite Giants (NAL) 1949-1950
Cleveland Elites 1926 (Played first half of season only.)		
Cleveland Hornets 1927		
Cleveland Tate Stars 1922		
Columbus Buckeyes 1921		
Cuban Stars (West) 1923-1930	(Cincinnati) Cuban Stars 1920-1922	
Dayton Marcos 1920		Dayton Marcos 1926 (Played first half of season only.)
Dayton Marcos 1926 (Played first half of season only.)	Dayton Marcos 1920	
Detroit Stars 1920-1931		
Indianapolis ABC's 1920-1926 (Did not play full season in 1924.)		Indianapolis ABC's 1931 Indianapolis ABC's (NSL) 1932 Indianapolis ABC's (NAL) 1938-1939 (Dropped out in early 1939 and replaced by

Franchise Name	Were	Became
		Toledo Crawfords for second half of season.)
Indianapolis ABC's 1931	Indianapolis ABC's 1920-1926 (Did not play full season in 1924.)	Indianapolis ABC's (NSL) 1932 Indianapolis ABC's (NAL) 1938-1939 (Dropped out in early 1939 and replaced by Toledo Crawfords for second half of season.)
Kansas City Monarchs 1920-1927		Kansas City Monarchs 1929-1930 Kansas City Monarchs (NAL) 1937-1950
Kansas City Monarchs 1929-1930	Kansas City Monarchs 1920-1927	Kansas City Monarchs (NAL) 1937-1950
Louisville White Sox 1931		
Memphis Red Sox 1924-1925 (Did not play full season in 1924.)		Memphis Red Sox 1927 Memphis Red Sox 1929-1930 Memphis Red Sox (NSL) 1932 Memphis Red Sox (NAL) 1937-1941 Memphis Red Sox (NAL) 1943-1950
Memphis Red Sox 1927	Memphis Red Sox 1924-1925 (Did not play full season in 1924.)	Memphis Red Sox 1929-1930 Memphis Red Sox (NSL) 1932 Memphis Red Sox (NAL) 1937-1941 Memphis Red Sox (NAL) 1943-1950
Memphis Red Sox 1929-1930	Memphis Red Sox 1927 Memphis Red Sox 1924-1925 (Did not play full season in 1924.)	Memphis Red Sox (NSL) 1932 Memphis Red Sox (NAL) 1937-1941 Memphis Red Sox (NAL) 1943-1950

Franchise Name	Were	Became
Milwaukee Bears 1923 (Did not play full season.)		
Nashville Elite Giants 1930		Cleveland Cubs 1931 Nashville Elite Giants (NSL) 1932 Nashville Elite Giants (NNL-2) 1933-1934 Columbus Elite Giants (NNL-2) 1935 Washington Elite Giants (NNL-2) 1936-1937 Baltimore Elite Giants (NNL-2) 1938-1948 Baltimore Elite Giants (NAL) 1949-1950
Pittsburgh Keystones 1922		
St. Louis Stars 1922-1931		St. Louis Stars (NAL) 1937 St. Louis Stars (NAL) 1939 New Orleans-St. Louis Stars (NAL) 1941 Harrisburg-St. Louis Stars (NNL-2) 1943 (Played first half of season only.)
St. Louis Giants 1920-1921		
Toledo Tigers 1923 (Disbanded 7/15/23.)		

EASTERN COLORED LEAGUE (ECL) 1923-1928

Franchise Name	Were	Became
Atlantic City Bacharach Giants 1923-1928		Atlantic City Bacharach Giants (ANL) 1929 Atlantic City Bacharach Giants (NNL-2) 1934 (Played second half of season only.)
Baltimore Black Sox 1923-1928		Baltimore Black Sox (ANL) 1929 Baltimore Black Sox (NNL-2) 1933-1934 (Did not play first half of 1934 season.)
Brooklyn Royal Giants 1923-1927		
Cuban Stars (East) 1923-1928		Cuban Stars (East) (ANL) 1929
Harrisburg Giants 1924-1927		
Hilldale 1923-1927		Hilldale (ANL) 1929
Newark Stars 1926 (Disbanded in mid-season with 1-10 record.)		
(New York) Lincoln Giants 1923-1926		(New York) Lincoln Giants 1928 (New York) Lincoln Giants (ANL) 1929
(New York) Lincoln Giants 1928	(New York) Lincoln Giants 1923-1926	(New York) Lincoln Giants (ANL) 1929
Philadelphia Tigers 1928		
Washington Potomacs 1924		

AMERICAN NEGRO LEAGUE (ANL) 1929

Franchise Name	Were	Became
Atlantic City Bacharach Giants 1929	Atlantic City Bacharach Giants (ECL) 1923-1928	Atlantic City Bacharach Giants (NNL-2) 1934
Baltimore Black Sox 1929	Baltimore Black Sox (ECL) 1923-1928	Baltimore Black Sox (NNL-2) 1933-1934 (Did not play first half of 1934 season.)
Cuban Stars (East) 1929	Cuban Stars (East) (ECL) 1923-1928	
Hilldale 1929	Hilldale (ECL) 1923-1927	
Homestead Grays 1929		Homestead Grays (NNL-2) 1935-1948
(New York) Lincoln Giants 1929	(New York) Lincoln Giants (ECL) 1928 (New York) Lincoln Giants (ECL) 1923-1926	

NEGRO SOUTHERN LEAGUE (NSL) 1932

Franchise Name	Were	Became
(Chicago) Cole's American Giants 1932	Chicago American Giants (NNL-1) 1920-1931	(Chicago) Cole's American Giants (NNL-2) 1933-1935 Chicago American Giants (NAL) 1937-1950
Columbus Turfs 1932 (Played second half of season only.)		
Indianapolis ABC's 1932	Indianapolis ABC's (NNL-1) 1931 Indianapolis ABC's (NNL-1) 1920-1926 (Did not play full season in 1924.)	Indianapolis ABC's (NAL) 1938-1939 (Dropped out in early 1939 and replaced by Toledo Crawford for second half of season.)
Louisville Black Caps 1932 (Played first half of season only.)		
Memphis Red Sox 1932	Memphis Red Sox (NNL-1) 1929-1930 Memphis Red Sox (NNL-1) 1927 Memphis Red Sox (NNL-1) 1924-1925 (Did not play full season in 1924.	Memphis Red Sox (NAL) 1937-1941 Memphis Red Sox (NAL) 1943-1950
Monroe Monarchs 1932		
Montgomery Grey Sox 1932		

Franchise Name	Were	Became
Nashville Elite Giants 1932	Cleveland Cubs (NNL-1) 1931 Nashville Elite Giants (NNL-1) 1930	Nashville Elite Giants (NNL-2) 1933-1934 Columbus Elite Giants (NNL-2) 1935 Washington Elite Giants (NNL-2) 1936-1937 Baltimore Elite Giants (NNL-2) 1938-1948 Baltimore Elite Giants (NAL) 1949-1950

NEGRO NATIONAL LEAGUE-2 (NNL-2) 1933-1948

Franchise Name	Were	Became
Atlantic City Bacharach Giants 1934 (Played second half of season only.)	Atlantic City Bacharach Giants (ANL) 1929 Atlantic City Bacharach Giants (ECL) 1923-1928	
Baltimore Black Sox 1933-1934 (Did not play first half of 1934 season.)	Baltimore Black Sox (ANL) 1929 Baltimore Black Sox (ECL) 1923-1928	
Baltimore Elite Giants 1938-1948	Washington Elite Giants 1936-1937 Columbus Elite Giants 1935 Nashville Elite Giants 1933-1934 Nashville Elite Giants (NSL) 1932 Cleveland Cubs (NNL-1) 1931 Nashville Elite Giants (NNL-1) 1930	Baltimore Elite Giants (NAL) 1949-1950
Brooklyn Eagles 1935		Newark Eagles 1936-1948 Houston Eagles (NAL) 1949-1950
(Chicago) Cole's American Giants 1933-1935	(Chicago) Cole's American Giants (NSL) 1932 Chicago American Giants (NNL-1) 1920-1931	Chicago American Giants (NAL) 1937-1950
Cleveland Giants 1933 (Joined league in Aug. 1933.)		

Franchise Name	Were	Became
Cleveland Red Sox 1934		
Columbus Blue Birds 1933 (Dropped out of league in midseason.)		
Columbus Elite Giants 1935	Nashville Elite Giants 1933-1934 Nashville Elite Giants (NSL) 1932 Cleveland Cubs (NNL-1) 1931 Nashville Elite Giants (NNL-1) 1930	Washington Elite Giants 1936-1937 Baltimore Elite Giants 1938-1948 Baltimore Elite Giants (NAL) 1949-1950
Detroit Stars 1933		
Harrisburg- St. Louis Stars 1943 (Played first half of season only.)	New Orleans- St. Louis Stars (NAL) 1941 St. Louis Stars (NAL) 1939 St. Louis Stars (NAL) 1937 St. Louis Stars (NNL-1) 1922-1931	
Homestead Grays 1935-1948	Homestead Grays (ANL) 1929	
Nashville Elite Giants 1933-1934	Nashville Elite Giants (NSL) 1932 Cleveland Cubs (NNL-1) 1931 Nashville Elite Giants (NNL-1) 1930	Columbus Elite Giants 1935 Washington Elite Giants 1936-1937 Baltimore Elite Giants 1938-1948 Baltimore Elite Giants (NAL) 1949/1950
Newark Dodgers 1934-1935		
Newark Eagles 1936-1948	Brooklyn Eagles 1935	Houston Eagles (NAL) 1949-1950

Franchise Name	**Were**	**Became**
New York Black Yankees 1936-1948 (Did not play first half of 1936 season.)		
New York Cubans 1935-1936		New York Cubans 1939-1948 New York Cubans (NAL) 1949-1950
New York Cubans 1939-1948	New York Cubans 1935-1936	New York Cubans (NAL) 1949-1950
Philadelphia Stars 1934-1948		Philadelphia Stars (NAL) 1949-1950
Pittsburgh Crawfords 1933-1938		Toledo Crawfords (NAL) 1939 (Played second half of season only.) Indianapolis Crawfords (NAL) 1940
Washington Black Senators 1938 (Team folded during second half of season.)		
Washington Homestead Grays (*See* Homestead Grays.)		
Washington Elite Giants 1936-1937	Columbus Elite Giants 1935 Nashville Elite Giants 1933-1934 Nashville Elite Giants (NSL) 1932 Cleveland Cubs (NNL-1) 1931 Nashville Elite Giants (NNL-1) 1930	Baltimore Elite Giants 1938-1948 Baltimore Elite Giants (NAL) 1949-1950

NEGRO AMERICAN LEAGUE (NAL) 1937-1950

Franchise Name	Were	Became
Atlanta Black Crackers 1938		
Baltimore Elite Giants 1949-1950	Baltimore Elite Giants (NNL-2) 1938-1948 Washington Elite Giants (NNL-2) 1936-1937 Columbus Elite Giants (NNL-2) 1935 Nashville Elite Giants (NNL-2) 1933-1934 Nashville Elite Giants (NSL) 1932 Cleveland Cubs (NNL-1) 1931 Nashville Elite Giants (NNL-1) 1930	
Birmingham Black Barons 1937-1938	Birmingham Black Barons (NNL-1) 1927-1930 Birmingham Black Barons (NNL-1) 1924-1925	Birmingham Black Barons 1940-1950
Birmingham Black Barons 1940-1950	Birmingham Black Barons 1937-1938 Birmingham Black Barons (NNL-1) 1927-1930 Birmingham Black Barons (NNL-1) 1924-1925	
Chicago American Giants 1937-1950	(Chicago) Cole's American Giants (NNL-2) 1933-1935	

Franchise Name	Were	Became
	(Chicago) Cole's American Giants (NSL) 1932 Chicago American Giants (NNL-1) 1920-1931	
Cincinnati Buckeyes 1942		Cleveland Buckeyes 1943-1948 Louisville Buckeyes 1949 Cleveland Buckeyes 1950 (Disbanded at end of first half of season.)
Cincinnati Clowns 1943		Indianapolis-Cincinnati Clowns 1944 Cincinnati Clowns 1945 Indianapolis Clowns 1946-1950
Cincinnati Clowns 1945	Indianapolis-Cincinnati Clowns 1944 Cincinnati Clowns 1943	Indianapolis Clowns 1946-1950
Cincinnati Tigers 1937		
Cleveland Bears 1930-1940		
Cleveland Buckeyes 1943-1948	Cincinnati Buckeyes 1942	Louisville Buckeyes 1949 Cleveland Buckeyes 1950 (Disbanded at end of first half of season.)
Cleveland Buckeyes 1950 (Disbanded at end of first half of season.)	Louisville Buckeyes 1949 Cleveland Buckeyes 1943-1948 Cincinnati Buckeyes 1942	

Franchise Name	Were	Became
Detroit Stars 1937		
Houston Eagles 1949-1950	Newark Eagles (NNL-2) 1936-1948 Brooklyn Eagles (NNL-2) 1935	
Indianapolis ABC's 1938-1939 (Dropped out in early 1939 and replaced by Toledo Crawfords for second half of season.)	Indianapolis ABC's (NSL) 1932 Indianapolis ABC's (NNL-1) 1931 Indianapolis ABC's (NNL-1) 1920-1926 (Did not play full season in 1924.)	
Indianapolis Athletics 1937		
Indianapolis- Cincinnati Clowns 1944	Cincinnati Clowns 1943	Cincinnati Clowns 1945 Indianapolis Clowns 1946-1950
Indianapolis Clowns 1946-1950	Cincinnati Clowns 1945 Indianapolis- Cincinnati Clowns 1944 Cincinnati Clowns 1943	
Indianapolis Crawfords 1940	Toledo Crawfords 1939 (Played second half of season only.) Pittsburgh Crawfords (NNL-2) 1933-1938	
Jacksonville Red Caps 1938 (Played first half of season only.)		Jacksonville Red Caps 1941-1942 (Dropped out of league in early 1942 season.)
Jacksonville Red Caps 1941-1942 (Dropped out of league in early 1942 season.)	Jacksonville Red Caps 1938 (Played first half of season only.)	

Franchise Name	Were	Became
Kansas City Monarchs 1937-1950	Kansas City Monarchs (NNL-2) 1929-1930 Kansas City Monarchs (NNL-2) 1920-1927	
Louisville Buckeyes 1949	Cleveland Buckeyes 1943-1948 Cincinnati Buckeyes 1942	Cleveland Buckeyes 1950 (Disbanded at end of first half of season.)
Memphis Red Sox 1937-1941	Memphis Red Sox (NSL) 1932 Memphis Red Sox (NNL-1) 1929-1930 Memphis Red Sox (NNL-1) 1927 Memphis Red Sox (NNL-1) 1924-1925 (Did not play full season in 1924.)	Memphis Red Sox 1943-1950
Memphis Red Sox 1943-1950	Memphis Red Sox 1937-1941 Memphis Red Sox (NSL) 1932 Memphis Red Sox (NNL-1) 1929-1930 Memphis Red Sox (NNL-1) 1927 Memphis Red Sox (NNL-1) 1924-1925 (Did not play full season in 1924.)	
New Orleans- St. Louis Stars 1941	St. Louis Stars 1939 St. Louis Stars 1937 St. Louis Stars (NNL-1) 1922-1931	Harrisburg- St. Louis Stars (NNL-2) 1943 (Played first half of season only.)
New York Cubans 1949-1950	New York Cubans (NNL-2) 1939-1948 New York Cubans (NNL-2) 1935-1936	
Philadelphia Stars 1949-1950	Philadelphia Stars (NNL-2) 1934-1948	

Franchise Name	Were	Became
St. Louis Stars 1937	St. Louis Stars (NNL-1) 1922-1931	St. Louis Stars 1939 New Orleans- St. Louis Stars 1941 Harrisburg- St. Louis Stars (NNL-2) 1943 (Played first half of season only.)
St. Louis Stars 1939	St. Louis Stars 1937 St. Louis Stars (NNL-1) 1922-1931	New Orleans- St. Louis Stars 1941 Harrisburg- St. Louis Stars (NNL-2) 1943 (Played first half of season only.)
Toledo Crawfords 1939 (Played second half of season only.)	Pittsburgh Crawfords (NNL-2) 1933-1938	Indianapolis Crawfords 1940

METROPOLITAN BASKETBALL LEAGUE (ML-1) 1921/22-1927/28

Franchise Name	Were	Became
Albany 1927/28		
Brooklyn Dodgers 1921/22-1922/23		
Brooklyn Pros 1921/22-1922/23		
Brooklyn Visitations 1921/22-1927/28		Brooklyn Visitations (ABL-1) 1927/28-1930/31 (Visitations played in two leagues from 1/3/28 until end of 1927/28 season.) Brooklyn Visitations (ML-2) 1931/32-1932/33 Brooklyn Visitations (ABL-2) 1933/34-1938/39 (Brooklyn played as the Paterson Visitations for 1 game in 1936/37.) Baltimore Clippers (ABL-2) 1939/40-1940/41
(Brooklyn) Greenpoint Knights 1921/22-1926/27 (Dropped out before end of first half of 1926/27 season.)		
(Brooklyn) West Brooklyn Assumption Triangles 1926/27 (Dropped out early in second half of 1926/27 season.)		
Catskill 1927/28		

Franchise Name	Were	Became
Elizabeth 1922/23		
Hudson 1927/28		
Kingston Colonials 1924/25	Passaic 1923/24-1924/25 (Moved to Kingston on 11/23/24.)	
Kingston Colonials 1926/27-1927/28		
New York Celtics 1922/23 (Dropped out on 11/17/22 to join the original Eastern League, which folded in second half of season.)		
New York McDowell Lyceum 1921/22-1922/23		
New York Pros 1925/26 (Dropped out before end of first half of season.)		
Newark Bears 1925/26		
Passaic 1923/24-1924/25 (Moved to Kingston on 11/23/24.)		Kingston Colonials 1924/25
Passaic Mets 1925/26	Perth Amboy Mets 1925/26 (Moved to Passaic in late January 1926.)	
Paterson Crescents 1926/27		
Paterson Legionnaires 1922/23-1925/26		

Franchise Name	Were	Became
Paterson Pats 1927/28 (Played 2 games and dropped out of league.)		
Paterson Powers Five Brothers 1921/22		
Perth Amboy Mets 1925/26 (Moved to Passaic in late January 1926.)		Passaic Mets 1925/26
Trenton Royal Bengals 1923/24-1924/25		
Troy 1927/28		
Yonkers Chippewas 1922/23-1924/25 (Did not play first half of 1922/23 season.)		Yonkers Indians 1925/26-1926/27
Yonkers Indians 1925/26-1926/27	Yonkers Chippewas 1922/23-1924/25 (Did not play first half of 1922/23 season.)	

AMERICAN BASKETBALL LEAGUE-1 (ABL-1) 1925/26-1930/31

Franchise Name	Were	Became
Baltimore Orioles 1926/27		
Boston Whirlwinds 1925/26 (Played first half of season only.)		
Brooklyn Arcadians 1925/26-1926/27 (Dropped out in 1926 with 0-5 record. Replaced by Brooklyn Celtics.)		
Brooklyn Celtics 1926/27 (Celtics replace Arcadians. Assume their 0-5 record and finish with 13-8 for first half and 19-2 for the second half.)		New York Celtics 1927/28 New York Celtics 1929/30 (Celtics dropped out 12/10/29 with a 5-5 record.)
Brooklyn Visitations 1927/28-1930/31	Washington Palace Five 1925/26-1927/28 (Washington team sold to Brooklyn Visitations 1/3/28. Washington record was 6-14.)	
Buffalo Germans 1925/26		
Chicago Bruins 1925/26-1930/31		
Cleveland Rosenblums 1925/26-1930/31 (Dropped out on 12/8/30 with 6-6 record.)		

Franchise Name	Were	Became
Detroit Cardinals 1927/28 (Dropped out on 1/3/28 with 5-13 record.)		
Detroit Pulaski Post Five 1925/26-1926/27 (Dropped out in mid-December 1926 with 0-6 record.)		
Fort Wayne Caseys 1925/26		Fort Wayne Hoosiers 1926/27-1930/31
Fort Wayne Hoosiers 1926/27-1930/31	Fort Wayne Caseys 1925/26	
New York Celtics 1927/28	Brooklyn Celtics 1926/27 (Celtics replaced Arcadians. Assumed their 0-5 record and finished 13-8 for first half and 19-2 for second half.)	New York Celtics 1929/30 (Celtics dropped out 12/10/29 with a 5-5 record.)
New York Celtics 1929/30 (Celtics dropped out 12/10/29 with a 5-5 record.)	New York Celtics 1927/28 Brooklyn Celtics 1926/27 (Celtics replaced Arcadians. Assumed their 0-5 record and finished 13-8 for first half and 19-2 for second half.)	
New York Hakoahs 1928/29		
Paterson Crescents 1929/30-1930/31 (Dropped out on 12/30/30 with a 9-9 record.)		
Paterson Whirlwinds 1928/29		

Franchise Name	Were	Became
Philadelphia Phillies 1926/27 (Renamed Warriors on 1/20/27.)		Philadelphia Warriors 1926/27-1927/28
Philadelphia Warriors 1926/27-1927/28	Philadelphia Phillies 1926/27 (Renamed Warriors on 1/20/27.)	
Rochester Centrals 1925/26-1930/31		
Syracuse All-Americans 1929/30 (Dropped out on 1/6/30 with 4-16 record. Forfeited last 4 games for 4-20 record.)		
Toledo Red Man Tobaccos 1930/31		
Trenton Royal Bengals 1928/29		
Washington Palace Five 1925/26-1927/28 (Sold to Brooklyn Visitations on 1/3/28. Record was 6-14.)		

EASTERN BASKETBALL LEAGUE (EL) 1931/32-1932/33

Franchise Name	Were	Became
Bridgeton (NJ) 1931/32-1932/33		
Camden 1931/32		
Philadelphia Jasper Jewels 1931/32-1932/33		
Philadelphia Moose 1931/32-1932/33		
Philadelphia Sphas 1931/32-1932/33		Philadelphia Hebrews (ABL-2) 1933/34-1936/37 Philadelphia Sphas (ABL-2) 1937/38-1945/46
Philadelphia WPEN A.C. 1932/33		
Trenton Moose 1932/33		Trenton Moose (ABL-2) 1933/34
Wilmington Cats 1931/32-1932/33 (Dropped out 11/20/33 with 2-4 record.)		

METROPOLITAN BASKETBALL LEAGUE-2 (ML-2) 1931/32-1932/33

Franchise Name	Were	Became
Bronx Braves 1932/33 (second half). (Played 11 games with a 5-6 record in the second half of season.)	Brooklyn Americans 1932/33 (second half). (Began second half of season and posted 2-7 record. Became Bronx Braves before end of second half.) Brooklyn Hill House 1932/33 (first half). (Played 4 games and posted 2-2 record.) Brooklyn Americans 1932/33 (first half). (Began first half of season and posted 1-10 record. Became Brooklyn Hill House before end of first half.)	Bronx Americans (ABL-2) 1933/34
Brooklyn Americans 1932/33 (first half). (Began first half of season and posted 1-10 record. Became Brooklyn Hill House before end of first half.)		Brooklyn Hill House 1932/33 (first half). (Played 4 games and posted 2-2 record.) Brooklyn Americans 1932/33 (second half). (Began second half of season and posted 2-7 record. Became Bronx Braves before end of second half.) Bronx Braves 1932/33 (second half). (Played 11 games with 5-6 record in the second half of season.) Bronx Americans (ABL-2) 1933/34
Brooklyn Americans 1932/33 (second half). (Began second half of season and posted 2-7 record. Became Bronx Braves before end of second half.)	Brooklyn Hill House 1932/33 (first half). (Played 4 games and posted 2-2 record.) Brooklyn Americans 1932/33(first half). (Began first half of	Bronx Braves 1932/33 (second half). (Played 11 games with a 5-6 record in the second half of season.) Bronx Americans (ABL-2) 1933/34

Franchise Name	Were	Became
	season and posted 1-10 record. Became Brooklyn Hill House before end of first half.)	
Brooklyn Hill House 1932/33 (first half). (Played 4 games and posted 2-2 record.)	Brooklyn Americans 1932/33 (first half). (Began first half of season and posted 1-10 record. Became Brooklyn Hill House before end of first half.)	Brooklyn Americans 1932/33 (second half). (Began second half of season and posted 2-7 record. Became Bronx Braves before end of second half.)
		Bronx Braves 1932/33 (second half). (Played 11 games with 5-6 record in the second half of season.)
		Bronx Americans (ABL-2) 1933/34
Brooklyn Jewels 1931/32-1932/33		Brooklyn Jewels (ABL-2) 1933/34
		New York Jewels (ABL-2) 1934/35-1935/36
		Brooklyn Jewels (ABL-2) 1936/37
		New Haven Jewels (ABL-2) 1937/38 (Moved to New York City on 11/30/37 with a 4-2 record.)
		New York Jewels (ABL-2) 1937/38-1941/42 (Disbanded in early 1941/42 season with 1-6 record.)
		New York Jewels (ABL-2) 1942/43
		New York Americans (ABL-2) 1943/44
		New York Westchesters (ABL-2) 1944/45 (Moved to Brooklyn as the New York Gothams on 1/20/45.)
		New York Gothams 1944/45-1945/46

Franchise Name	Were	Became
Brooklyn Jewish Center 1931/32		
Brooklyn Visitations 1931/32-1932/33	Brooklyn Visitations (ABL-1) 1927/28-1930/31 (Visitations played in two leagues from 1/3/28 until end of 1927/28 season.) Brooklyn Visitations (ML-1) 1921/22-1927/28	Brooklyn Visitations (ABL-2) 1933/34-1938/39 (Brooklyn played as the Paterson Visitations for 1 game in 1936/37.) Baltimore Clippers (ABL-2) 1939/40-1940/41
Hoboken Lisas 1931/32-1932/33		North Hudson Thourots (ABL-2) 1933/34 (Moved to Camden on 11/23/33 with a 0-2 record.) Camden Brewers (ABL-2) 1933/34 (Moved to New Britain on 1/8/34 with a 2-10 overall record.) New Britain Palace (ABL-2) 1933/34 New Britain Jackaways (ABL-2) 1934/35 (Disbanded on 1/18/35.)
Jamaica St. Monicas 1931/32-1932/33 (Dropped out at end of first half of 1932/33 season.)		
Jersey City Diamonds 1932/33 (Played second half of season only.)		
Long Island Pros 1931/32-1932/33 (Dropped out at end of first half of 1932/33 season.)		

Franchise Name	Were	Became
Paterson Continentals 1932/33 (Played first half of season only.)		
Union City Reds 1931/32-1932/33		Union City Reds (ABL-2) 1933/34 Jersey Reds (ABL-2) 1934/35-1939/40 (Disbanded on 1/24/40.)
Yonkers Knights 1932/33		

NATIONAL PROFESSIONAL BASKETBALL LEAGUE (NPBL) 1932/33

Franchise Name	Were	Became
Akron Firestones 1932/33		Akron Firestones (MBC) 1935/36 Akron Firestone Non-Skids (MBC) 1936/37 Akron Firestone Non-Skids (NBL) 1937/38-1940/41
Akron Goodyears 1932/33		Akron Goodyear Regulars (MBC) 1936/37 Akron Goodyear Wingfoots (NBL) 1937/38-1941/42
Fort Wayne Firemen 1932/33		
Indianapolis Kautskys 1932/33		Indianapolis Kautskys (MBC) 1935/36-1936/37 Indianapolis Kautskys (NBL) 1937/38-1939/40 Indianapolis Kautskys (NBL) 1941/42 (Suspended operations for World War II: 1942/43-1944/45.) Indianapolis Kautskys (NBL) 1945/46-1947/48 Indianapolis Jets (BAA) 1948/49
Kokomo Kelts 1932/33 (Dropped out 1/16/33 with 2-3 record.)		
Lorain Fisher Foods 1932/33 (Dropped out 12/15/32 with 0-1 record.)		

Franchise Name	**Were**	**Became**

Muncie Whys
  1932/33
  (Joined league in
  midseason.)

South Bend Guardsmen
  1932/33

Toledo Crimson
  Coaches
  1932/33

AMERICAN BASKETBALL LEAGUE-2 (ABL-2)
1933/34-1945/46

Franchise Name	Were	Became
Atlantic City Sand Snipers 1936/37 (Dropped out 12/21/36 with 0-10 record.)		
Baltimore Bullets 1944/45-1946/47		Baltimore Bullets (BAA) 1947/48-1948/49 Baltimore Bullets (NBA) 1949/50-1954/55 (Disbanded on 11/27/54 with 3-11 record.)
Baltimore Clippers 1939/40-1940/41	Brooklyn Visitations (ABL-2) 1933/34-1938/39 (Brooklyn played as the Paterson Visitations for 1 game in 1936/37.) Brooklyn Visitations (ML-2) 1931/32-1932/33 Brooklyn Visitations (ABL-1) 1927/28-1930/31 (Visitations played in two leagues from 1/3/28 until end of season.) Brooklyn Visitations (ML-1) 1921/22-1927/28	
Boston Trojans 1934/35		
Bronx Americans 1933/34	Bronx Braves (ML-2) 1932/33 (second half). (Played 11 games with 5-6 record in the second half of season.) Brooklyn Americans (ML-2) 1932/33 (second half). (Began second half of season and posted 2-7 record. Became Bronx Braves before end of second half.)	

Franchise Name	Were	Became
	Brooklyn Hill House (ML-2) 1932/33 (first half). (Played 4 games and posted 2-2 record.) Brooklyn Americans (ML-2) 1932/33 (first half). (Began first half of season and posted 1-10 record. Became Brooklyn Hill House before end of first half.)	
Bronx Yankees 1937/38 (Changed name early in season.)		New York Yankees 1937/38 (Played first half of season only. Disbanded on 1/11/38.)
Brooklyn Celtics 1940/41	Troy Celtics 1939/40-1940/41 (Began 1940/41 season as Troy Celtics. Moved to Brooklyn.) Troy Haymakers 1938/39-1939/40 (Began 1939/40 season as Troy Haymakers. Changed name to Celtics on 12/19/39.) New York Original Celtics 1936/37-1937/38 (Did not play first half of 1936/37 season.)	
Brooklyn Indians 1942/43	Camden Indians 1942/43 (Moved to Brooklyn on 1/18/43.) Washington Blue Bombers 1941/42	Wilmington Blue Bombers 1943/44 Wilmington Bombers 1944/45-1945/46
Brooklyn Indians 1943/44 (Played first half of 1943/44 season only.)		

Franchise Name	Were	Became
Brooklyn Jewels 1933/34	Brooklyn Jewels (ML-2) 1931/32-1932/33	New York Jewels 1934/35-1935/36 Brooklyn Jewels 1936/37 New Haven Jewels 1937/38 (Moved to New York City on 11/30/37 with 4-2 record.) New York Jewels 1937/38-1941/42 (Disbanded in early 1941/42 season with 1-6 record.) New York Jewels 1942/43 New York Americans 1943/44 New York Westchesters 1944/45 (Moved to Brooklyn as New York Gothams on 1/20/45.) New York Gothams 1944/45-1945/46
Brooklyn Jewels 1936/37	New York Jewels 1934/35-1935/36 Brooklyn Jewels 1933/34 Brooklyn Jewels (ML-2) 1931/32-1932/33	New Haven Jewels 1937/38 (Moved to New York City on 11/30/37 with 4-2 record.) New York Jewels 1937/38-1941/42 (Disbanded in early 1941/42 season with 1-6 record.) New York Jewels 1942/43 New York Americans 1943/44 New York Westchesters 1944/45 (Moved to Brooklyn as New York Gothams on 1/20/45.) New York Gothams 1944/45-1945/46

Franchise Name	Were	Became
Brooklyn Visitations 1933/34-1938/39 (Brooklyn played as the Paterson Visitations for 1 game in the the 1936/37 season.)	Brooklyn Visitations (ML-2) 1931/32-1932/33 Brooklyn Visitations (ABL-1) 1927/28-1930/31 (Visitations played in two leagues from 1/3/28 until end of season.) Brooklyn Visitations (ML-1) 1921/22-1927/28	Baltimore Clippers 1939/40-1940/41
Camden Brewers 1933/34 (Moved to New Britain on 1/8/34 with a 2-10 record.)	North Hudson Thourots 1933/34 (Moved to Camden on 11/23/33 with a 0-2 record.) Hoboken Lisas (ML-2) 1931/32-1932/33	New Britain Palace 1933/34 New Britain Jackaways 1934/35 (Disbanded on 1/18/75.)
Camden Indians 1942/43 (Moved to Brooklyn on 1/18/43.)	Willington Blue Bombers 1941/42	Brooklyn Indians 1942/43 Wilmington Blue Bombers 1943/44 Wilmington Bombers 1944/45-1945/46
Harrisburg Senators 1942/43		
Jersey Reds 1934/35-1939/40 (Disbanded on 1/24/40.)	Union City Reds 1933/34 Union City Reds (ML-2) 1931/32-1932/33	
Kingston Colonials 1935/36-1939/40 (Disbanded on 12/19/39.)		
Newark Joe Fays 1933/34		Newark Mules 1934/35 (Moved to New Britain on 1/18/35 when the New Britain Jackaways disbanded.)

Franchise Name	Were	Became
		New Britain Mules 1934/35
Newark Mules 1934/35 (Newark moved to New Britain on 1/18/35 when the New Britain Jackaways disbanded.)	Newark Joe Fays 1933/34	New Britain Mules 1934/35
New Britain Jackaways 1934/35 (Disbanded on 1/18/35.)	New Britain Palace 1933/34 Camden Brewers 1933/34 (Moved to New Britain on 1/8/34 with a 2-10 overall record.) North Hudson Thourots 1933/34 (Moved to Camden on 11/23/33 with a 0-2 record.) Hoboken Lisas (ML-2) 1931/32-1932/33	
New Britain Mules 1934/35	Newark Mules 1934/35 (Newark moved to New Britain on 1/18/35 when New Britain Jackaways disbanded.) Newark Joe Fays 1933/34	
New Britain Palace 1933/34	Camden Brewers 1933/34 (Moved to New Britain on 1/8/34 with a 2-10 overall record.) North Hudson Thourots 1933/34 (Moved to Camden on 11/23/34 with a 0-2 record.) Hoboken Lisas (ML-2) 1931/32-1932/33	New Britain Jackaways 1934/35 (Disbanded on 1/18/35.)

Franchise Name	Were	Became
New Haven Jewels 1937/38 (Moved to New York City on 11/30/37 with 4-2 record.)	Brooklyn Jewels 1936/37 New York Jewels 1934/35-1935/36 Brooklyn Jewels 1933/34 Brooklyn Jewels (ML-2) 1931/32-1932/33	New York Jewels 1937/38-1941/42 (Disbanded early in 1941/42 season with a 1-6 record.) New York Jewels 1942/43 New York Americans 1943/44 New York Westchesters 1944/45 (Moved to Brooklyn as the New York Gothams on 1/20/45.)
New York Americans 1943/44	New York Jewels 1942/43 New York Jewels 1937/38-1941/42 (Disbanded early in 1941/42 season with a 1-6 record.) New Haven Jewels 1937/38 (Moved to New York City on 11/30/37 with a 4-2 record.) Brooklyn Jewels 1936/37 New York Jewels 1934/35-1935/36 Brooklyn Jewels 1933/34 Brooklyn Jewels (ML-2) 1931/32-1932/33	New York Westchesters 1944/45 (Moved to Brooklyn as the New York Gothams on 1/20/45.) New York Gothams 1944/45-1945/46
New York Gothams 1944/45-1945/46	New York Westchesters 1944/45 (Moved to Brooklyn as the New York Gothams on 1/20/45.) New York Americans 1943/44 New York Jewels 1942/43	

Franchise Name	Were	Became
	New York Jewels 1937/38-1941/42 (Disbanded early in 1941/42 season with a 1-6 record.) New Haven Jewels 1937/38 (Moved to New York City on 11/30/37 with a 4-2 record.) Brooklyn Jewels 1936/37 New York Jewels 1934/35-1935/36 Brooklyn Jewels 1933/34 Brooklyn Jewels (ML-2) 1931/32-1932/33	
New York Jewels 1934/35-1935/36	Brooklyn Jewels 1933/34 Brooklyn Jewels (ML-2) 1931/32-1932/33	Brooklyn Jewels 1936/37 New Haven Jewels 1937/38 (Moved to New York City on 11/30/37 with a 4-2 record.) New York Jewels 1937/38-1941/42 (Disbanded early in 1941/42 season with a 1-6 record.) New York Jewels 1942/43 New York Americans 1943/44 New York Westchesters 1944/45 (Moved to Brooklyn as the New York Gothams on 1/20/45.) New York Gothams 1944/45-1945/46
New York Jewels 1937/38-1941/42 (Disbanded early in 1941/42 season with a 1-6 record.)	New Haven Jewels 1937/38 (Moved to New York City on 11/30/37 with a 4-2 record.) Brooklyn Jewels 1936/37	New York Jewels 1942/43 New York Americans 1943/44 New York Westchesters 1944/45

Franchise Name	Were	Became
	New York Jewels 1934/35-1935/36 Brooklyn Jewels 1933/34 Brooklyn Jewels (ML-2) 1931/32-1932/33	(Moved to Brooklyn as the New York Gothams on 1/20/45.) New York Gothams 1944/45-1945/46
New York Jewels 1942/43	New York Jewels 1937/38-1941/42 (Disbanded early in 1941/42 season with a 1-6 record.) New Haven Jewels 1937/38 (Moved to New York City on 11/30/37 with a 4-2 record.) Brooklyn Jewels 1936/37 New York Jewels 1934/35-1935/36 Brooklyn Jewels 1933/34 Brooklyn Jewels (ML-2) 1931/32-1932/33	New York Americans 1943/44 New York Westchesters 1944/45 (Moved to Brooklyn as the New York Gothams on 1/20/45.) New York Gothams 1944/45-1945/46
New York Original Celtics 1936/37-1937/38 (Did not play first half of 1936/37 season.)		Troy Haymakers 1938/39-1939/40 (Began 1939/40 season as Troy Haymakers. Changed name to Troy Celtics on 12/19/39.) Troy Celtics 1939/40-1940/41 (Began 1940/41 season as Troy Celtics. Moved to Brooklyn.) Brooklyn Celtics 1940/41
New York Westchesters 1944/45 (Moved to Brooklyn as the New York Gothams on 1/20/45.)	New York Americans 1943/44 New York Jewels 1942/43 New York Jewels 1937/38-1941/42 (Disbanded early in	New York Gothams 1944/45-1945/46

Franchise Name	Were	Became
	1941/42 season with a 1-6 record.) New Haven Jewels 1937/38 (Moved to New York City on 11/30/37 with a 4-2 record.) Brooklyn Jewels 1936/37 New York Jewels 1934/35-1935/36 Brooklyn Jewels 1933/34 Brooklyn Jewels (ML-2) 1931/32-1932/33	
New York Yankees 1937/38 (Played first half of season only. Disbanded 1/11/38.)	Bronx Yankees 1937/38 (Changed name early in season.)	
North Hudson Thourots 1933/34 (Moved to Camden on 11/23/33 with a 0-2 record.)	Hoboken Lisas (ML-2) 1931/32-1932/33	Camden Brewers 1933/34 (Moved to New Britain on 1/8/34 with a 2-10 overall record.) New Britain Palace 1933/34 New Britain Jackaways 1934/35 (Disbanded 1/18/35.)
Passaic Bengal Tigers 1941/42 (Moved to Trenton in early part of season.)		Trenton Tigers 1941/42-1945/46
Passaic Reds 1935/36	Trenton Moose 1935/36 (Moved to Passaic on 1/2/36.) Paterson Panthers 1935/36 (Moved to Trenton on 12/13/35.)	

Franchise Name	Were	Became
Paterson Crescents 1944/45-1945/46	Washington Capitol's 1944/45 (Moved to Paterson on 1/1/45.)	
Paterson Panthers 1935/36 (Moved to Trenton) on 12/13/35.)		Trenton Moose 1935/36 (Moved to Passaic on 1/2/36.) Passaic Reds 1935/36.
Paterson Visitations 1936/37 (Brooklyn Visitations played 1 game as Paterson, lost it, and returned to Brooklyn on 11/23/36.)	(*See* Brooklyn Visitations.)	(*See* Brooklyn Visitations.)
Philadelphia Hebrews 1933/34-1936/37	Philadelphia Sphas (EL) 1931/32-1932/33	Philadelphia Sphas 1937/38-1945/46
Philadelphia Sphas 1937/38-1945/46	Philadelphia Hebrews 1933/34-1936/37 Philadelphia Sphas (EL) 1931/32-1932/33	
Trenton Moose 1935/36 (Moved to Passaic on 1/2/36.)	Paterson Panthers 1935/36 (Moved to Trenton on 12/13/35.)	Passaic Reds 1935/36
Trenton Moose 1933/34	Trenton Moose (EL) 1932/33	
Trenton Tigers 1941/42-1945/46	Passaic Bengal Tigers 1941/42 (Moved to Trenton early in 1941/42 season.)	
Troy Celtics 1939/40-1940/41	Troy Haymakers 1938/39-1939/40	Brooklyn Celtics 1940/41

Franchise Name	Were	Became
(Began 1940/41 season as Troy Celtics. Moved to Brooklyn.)	(Began 1939/40 season as Troy Haymakers. Changed name to Troy Celtics on 12/19/39.) New York Original Celtics 1936/37-1937/38 (Did not play first half of 1936/37 season.)	
Troy Haymakers 1938/39-1939/40 (Began 1939/40 season as Troy Haymakers. Changed name to Troy Celtics on 12/19/39.)	New York Original Celtics 1936/37-1937/38 (Did not play first half of 1936/37 season.)	Troy Celtics 1939/40-1940/41 (Began 1940/41 season as Troy Celtics. Moved to Brooklyn.) Brooklyn Celtics 1940/41
Union City Reds 1933/34	Union City Reds (ML-2) 1931/32-1932/33	Jersey Reds 1934/35-1939/40 (Disbanded on 1/24/40.)
Washington Brewers 1938/39-1941/42		
Washington Capitol's 1944/45 (Moved to Paterson on 1/1/45.)		Paterson Crescents 1944/45
Wilkes-Barre Barons 1938/39-1939/40 (Disbanded on 2/2/40.)		
Wilmington Blue Bombers 1941/42		Camden Indians 1942/43 (Moved to Brooklyn 1/18/43.) Brooklyn Indians 1942/43 Wilmington Blue Bombers 1943/44 Wilmington Bombers 1944/45-1945/46

Franchise Name	Were	Became
Wilmington Blue Bombers 1943/44	Brooklyn Indians 1942/43 Camden Indians 1942/43 (Moved to Brooklyn 1/18/43.) Wilmington Blue Bombers 1941/42	Wilmington Bombers 1944/45-1945/46
Wilmington Bombers 1944/45-1945/46	Wilmington Blue Bombers 1943/44 Brooklyn Indians 1942/43 Camden Indians 1942/43 (Moved to Brooklyn on 1/18/43.) Wilmington Blue Bombers 1941/42	

MIDWEST BASKETBALL CONFERENCE (MBC)
1935/36-1936/37

Franchise Name	Were	Became
Akron Firestones 1935/36	Akron Firestones (NPBL) 1932/33	Akron Firestone Non-Skids (NBL) 1936/37 Akron Firestone Non-Skids (NBL) 1937/38-1940/41
Akron Firestone Non-Skids 1936/37	Akron Firestones (MBC) 1935/36 Akron Firestones (NPBL) 1932/33	Akron Firestone Non-Skids (NBL) 1937/38-1940/41
Akron Goodyear Regulars 1936/37	Akron Goodyears (NPBL) 1932/33	Akron Goodyear Wingfoots (NBL) 1937/38-1941/42
Buffalo Bisons 1935/36		
Chicago Duffy Florals 1935/36-1936/37		
Columbus Athletic Supplys 1936/37		Columbus Athletic Supplys (NBL) 1937/38
Dayton London Bobbys 1936/37		
Dayton Metros 1935/36		
Detroit Altes Lagers 1936/37	Detroit Hed-Aids 1935/36	
Detroit Hed-Aids 1935/36		Detroit Altes Lagers 1936/37
Fort Wayne General Electrics 1936/37		Fort Wayne General Electrics (NBL) 1937/38

Franchise Name	Were	Became
Indianapolis Kautskys 1935/36-1936/37	Indianapolis Kautskys (NPBL) 1932/33	Indianapolis Kautskys (NBL) 1937/38-1939/40 Indianapolis Kautskys (NBL) 1941/42 (Suspended operations for World War II: 1942/43-1944/45.) Indianapolis Kautskys (NBL) 1945/46-1947/48 Indianapolis Jets (BAA) 1948/49
Indianapolis U. S. Tires 1935/36-1936/37		
Pittsburgh YMHA 1935/36-1936/37		
Warren Oilers 1936/37		Warren Penns (NBL) 1937/38-1938/39 (Moved to Cleveland on 2/10/38 with a 9-10 record.) Cleveland White Horses (NBL) 1938/39 Detroit Eagles (NBL) 1939/40-1940/41
Whiting Ciesar All-Americans 1936/37		Whiting Ciesar All-Americans (NBL) 1937/38 Hammond Ciesar All-Americans (NBL) 1938/39-1940/41
Windsor Cooper Buses 1935/36		

NATIONAL BASKETBALL LEAGUE (NBL) 1937/38-1948/49

Franchise Name	Were	Became
Akron Firestone Non-Skids 1937/38-1940/41	Akron Firestone Non-Skids (MBC) 1936/37 Akron Firestones (MBC) 1935/36 Akron Firestones (NPBL) 1932/33	
Akron Goodyear Wingfoots 1937/38-1941/42	Akron Goodyear Regulars (MBC) 1936/37 Akron Goodyears (NPBL) 1932/33	
Anderson Duffey Packers 1946/47-1948/49		Anderson Packers (NBA) 1949/50
Buffalo Bisons 1937/38		
Buffalo Bisons 1946/47 (Franchise moved 12/27/46 with a 4-8 record.)		Tri-Cities Blackhawks (NBL) 1946/47-1948/49 Tri-Cities Blackhawks (NBA) 1949/50-1950/51 Milwaukee Hawks (NBA) 1951/52-1954/55 St. Louis Hawks (NBA) 1955/56-1967/68 Atlanta Hawks (NBA) 1968/69—
Chicago American Gears 1944/45-1946/47		Chicago American Gears 1947/48 (Began 1947/48 season as part of 16-team Professional Basketball League of America. League folded on 11/13/47 after 3 weeks.)
Chicago Bruins 1939/40-1941/42		
Chicago Studebakers 1942/43		

Franchise Name	Were	Became
Cincinnati Comellos 1937/38	Richmond King Clothiers 1937/38 (Moved to Cincinnati before end of season.)	
Cleveland Allmen Transfers 1944/45-1945/46		
Cleveland Chase Brass 1943/44		
Cleveland White Horses 1938/39	Warren Penns 1937/38-1938/39 (Moved to Cleveland 2/10/38 with a 9-10 record.) Warren Oilers (MBC) 1936/37	Detroit Eagles 1939/40-1940/41
Columbus Athletic Supplys 1937/38	Columbus Athletic Supplys (MBC) 1936/37	
Dayton Metros 1937/38		
Dayton Rens 1948/49 (Replaced Detroit Vagabond Kings, who disbanded on 12/17/48.)		
Denver Nuggets 1948/49		Denver Nuggets (NBA) 1949/50
Detroit Eagles 1939/40-1940/41	Cleveland White Horses 1938/39 Warren Penns 1937/38-1938/39 (Moved to Cleveland 2/10/38 with a 9-10 record.) Warren Oilers (MBC) 1936/37	

Franchise Name	Were	Became
Detroit Gems 1946/47		
Detroit Vagabond Kings 1948/49 (Disbanded 12/17/48 with 2-17 record. Replaced by Dayton Rens.)		
Flint Dow A. C. 1947/48	Midland Dow A. C. 1947/48 (Moved to Flint in early part of season.) Youngstown Bears 1945/46-1946/47 Pittsburgh Raiders 1944/45	
Fort Wayne General Electrics 1937/38	Fort Wayne General Electrics (MBC) 1936/37	
Fort Wayne Zollner Pistons 1941/42-1947/48		Fort Wayne Pistons (BAA) 1948/49 Fort Wayne Pistons (NBA) 1949/50-1956/57 Detroit Pistons (NBA) 1957/58—
Hammond Calumet Buccaneers 1948/49		
Hammond Ciesar All-Americans 1938/39-1940/41	Whiting Ciesar All-Americans 1937/38 Whiting Ciesar All-Americans (MBC) 1936/37	
Indianapolis Kautskys 1937/38-1939/40	Indianapolis Kautskys (MBC) 1935/36-1936/37 Indianapolis Kautskys (NPBL) 1932/33	Indianapolis Kautskys 1941/42 (Suspended operations for World War II: 1942/43- 1944/45.)

Franchise Name	Were	Became
		Indianapolis Kautskys 1945/46-1947/48 Indianapolis Jets (BAA) 1948/49
Indianapolis Kautskys 1941/42 (Suspended operations for World War II: 1942/43-1944/45.)	Indianapolis Kautskys 1937/38-1939/40 Indianapolis Kautskys (MBC) 1935/36-1936/37 Indianapolis Kautskys (NPBL) 1932/33	Indianapolis Kautskys 1945/46-1947/48 Indianapolis Jets (BAA) 1948/49
Indianapolis Kautskys 1945/46-1947/48	Indianapolis Kautskys 1941/42 (Suspended operations for World War II: 1942/43-1944/45.) Indianapolis Kautskys 1937/38-1939/40 Indianapolis Kautskys (MBC) 1935/36-1936/37 Indianapolis Kautskys (NPBL) 1932/33	Indianapolis Jets (BAA) 1948/49
Kankakee Gallagher Trojans 1937/38		
Midland Dow A. C. 1947/48 (Moved to Flint in early part of season.)	Youngstown Bears 1945/46-1946/47 Pittsburgh Raiders 1944/45	Flint Dow A. C. 1947/48
Minneapolis Lakers 1947/48		Minneapolis Lakers (BAA) 1948/49 Minneapolis Lakers (NBA) 1949/50-1959/60 Los Angeles Lakers (NBA) 1960/61—

Franchise Name	Were	Became
Oshkosh All-Stars 1937/38-1948/49		
Pittsburgh Raiders 1944/45		Youngstown Bears 1945/46-1946/47 Midland Dow A. C. 1947/48 (Moved to Flint in early part of season.) Flint Dow A. C. 1947/48
Pittsburgh Pirates 1937/38-1938/39		
Richmond King Clothiers 1937/38 (Moved to Cincinnati before end of season.)		Cincinnati Comellos 1937/38
Rochester Royals 1945/46-1947/48		Rochester Royals (BAA) 1948/49 Rochester Royals (NBA) 1949/50-1956/57 Cincinnati Royals (NBA) 1957/58-1971/72 Kansas City- Omaha Kings (NBA) 1972/73-1974/75 Kansas City Kings (NBA) 1975/76-1984/85 Sacramento Kings (NBA) 1985/86—
Sheboygan Red Skins 1938/39-1948/49		Sheboygan Red Skins (NBA) 1949/50
Syracuse Nationals 1946/47-1948/49		Syracuse Nationals (NBA) 1949/50-1962/63 Philadelphia 76ers (NBA) 1963/64—

Franchise Name	Were	Became
Toledo Jeeps 1946/47-1948/49		Waterloo Hawks 1948/49 Waterloo Hawks (NBA) 1949/50
Toledo Jim White Chevrolets 1941/42-1942/43 (Disbanded on 12/14/42 with 0-4 record.)		
Tri-Cities Blackhawks 1946/47	Buffalo Bisons 1946/47 (Moved to Tri-Cities 12/27/46 with 4-8 record.)	Tri-Cities Blackhawks (NBA) 1949/50-1950/51 Milwaukee Hawks (NBA) 1951/52-1954/55 St. Louis Hawks (NBA) 1955/56-1967/68 Atlanta Hawks (NBA) 1968/69—
Warren Penns 1937/38-1938/39 (Moved to Cleveland 2/10/38 with a 9-10 record.)	Warren Oilers (MBC) 1936/37	Cleveland White Horses 1938/39 Detroit Eagles 1939/40-1940/41
Waterloo Hawks 1948/49	Toledo Jeeps 1946/47-1947/48	Waterloo Hawks (NBA) 1949/50
Whiting Ciesar All-Americans 1937/38	Whiting Ciesar All-Americans (MBC) 1936/37	Hammond Ciesar All-Americans 1938/39-1940/41
Youngstown Bears 1945/46-1946/47	Pittsburgh Raiders 1944/45	Midland Dow A. C. 1947/48 (Moved to Flint in early part of season.) Flint Dow A. C. 1947/48

BASKETBALL ASSOCIATION OF AMERICA (BAA) 1946/47-1948/49

Franchise Name	Were	Became
Baltimore Bullets 1947/48-1948/49	Baltimore Bullets (ABL-2) 1944/45-1946/47	Baltimore Bullets (NBA) 1949/50-1954/55 (Disbanded on 11/27/54 with a 3-11 record.)
Boston Celtics 1946/47-1948/49		Boston Celtics (NBA) 1949/50—
Chicago Stags 1946/47-1948/49		Chicago Stags (NBA) 1949/50
Cleveland Rebels 1946/47		
Detroit Falcons 1946/47		
Fort Wayne Pistons 1948/49	FortWayne Zollner Pistons (NBL) 1941/42-1947/48	Fort Wayne Pistons (NBA) 1949/50-1956/57 Detroit Pistons (NBA) 1957/58—
Indianapolis Jets 1948/49	Indianapolis Kautskys (NBL) 1945/46-1947/48 (Suspended operations for World War II: 1942/43-1944/45.) Indianapolis Kautskys (NBL) 1941/42 Indianapolis Kautskys (NBL) 1937/38-1939/40 Indianapolis Kautskys (MBC) 1935/36-1936/37 Indianapolis Kautskys (NPBL) 1932/33	
Minneapolis Lakers 1948/49	Minneapolis Lakers (NBL) 1947/48	Minneapolis Lakers (NBA) 1949/50-1959/60 Los Angeles Lakers (NBA) 1960/61—

Franchise Name	Were	Became
New York Knickerbockers 1946/47-1948/49		New York Knickerbockers (NBA) 1949/50—
Philadelphia Warriors 1946/47-1948/49		Philadelphia Warriors (NBA) 1949/50-1961/62 San Francisco Warriors (NBA) 1962/63-1970/71 Golden State Warriors (NBA) 1971/72—
Pittsburgh Ironmen 1946/47		
Providence Steamrollers 1946/47-1948/49		
Rochester Royals 1948/49	Rochester Royals (NBL) 1945/46-1947/48	Rochester Royals (NBA) 1949/50-1956/57 Cincinnati Royals (NBA) 1957/58-1971/72 Kansas City- Omaha Kings (NBA) 1972/73-1974/75 Kansas City Kings (NBA) 1975/76-1984/85 Sacramento Kings (NBA) 1985/86—
St. Louis Bombers 1946/47-1948/49		St. Louis Bombers (NBA) 1949/50
Toronto Huskies 1946/47		
Washington Capitols 1946/47-1948/49		Washington Capitols (NBA) 1949/50-1950/51 (Disbanded on 1/9/51 with a 10-25 record.)

NATIONAL BASKETBALL ASSOCIATION (NBA) 1949/50—

Franchise Name	Were	Became
Anderson Packers 1949/50	Anderson Duffey Packers (NBL) 1946/47-1948/49	
Atlanta Hawks 1968/69—	St. Louis Hawks 1955/56-1967/68 Milwaukee Hawks 1951/52-1954/55 Tri-Cities Blackhawks 1949/50-1950/51 Tri-Cities Blackhawks (NBL) 1946/47-1948/49 Buffalo Bisons (NBL) 1946/47 (Moved to Tri-Cities on 12/27/46 with a 4-8 record.)	
Baltimore Bullets 1940/50-1954/55 (Disbanded on 11/27/54 with 3-11 record.)	Baltimore Bullets (BAA) 1947/48-1948/49 Baltimore Bullets (ABL-2) 1944/45-1946/47	
Baltimore Bullets 1963/64-1972/73	Chicago Zephyrs 1962/63 Chicago Packers 1961/62	Capital Bullets 1973/74 Washington Bullets 1974/75—
Boston Celtics 1949/50—	Boston Celtics (BAA) 1946/47-1948/49	
Buffalo Braves 1970/71-1977/78		San Diego Clippers 1978/79-1983/84 Los Angeles Clippers 1984/85—
Capital Bullets 1973/74	Baltimore Bullets 1963/64-1972/73 Chicago Zephyrs 1962/63 Chicago Packers 1961/62	Washington Bullets 1974/75—

Franchise Name	Were	Became
Charlotte Hornets 1988/89—		
Chicago Bulls 1966/67—		
Chicago Packers 1961/62		Chicago Zephyrs 1962/63 Baltimore Bullets 1963/64-1972/73 Capital Bullets 1973/74 Washington Bullets 1974/75—
Chicago Stags 1949/50	Chicago Stags (BAA) 1946/47-1948/49	
Chicago Zephyrs 1962/63	Chicago Packers 1961/62	Baltimore Bullets 1963/64-1972/73 Capital Bullets 1973/74 Washington Bullets 1974/75—
Cincinnati Royals 1957/58-1971/72	Rochester Royals 1949/50-1956/57 Rochester Royals (BAA) 1948/49 Rochester Royals (NBL) 1945/46-1947/48	Kansas City- Omaha Kings 1972/73-1974/75 Kansas City Kings 1975/76-1984/85 Sacramento Kings 1985/86—
Cleveland Cavaliers 1970/71—		
Dallas Mavericks 1980/81—		
Denver Nuggets 1949/40	Denver Nuggets (NBL) 1948/49	
Denver Nuggets 1976/77—	Denver Nuggets (ABA) 1967/68-1975/76	
Detroit Pistons 1957/58—	Fort Wayne Pistons 1949/50-1956/57 Fort Wayne Pistons (BAA) 1948/49	

Franchise Name	Were	Became
	Fort Wayne Zollner Pistons (NBL) 1941/42-1947/48	
Fort Wayne Pistons 1949/50-1956/57	Fort Wayne Pistons (BAA) 1948/49 Fort Wayne Zollner Pistons (NBL) 1941/42-1947/48	Detroit Pistons 1957/58—
Golden State Warriors 1971/72—	San Francisco Warriors 1962/63-1970/71 Philadelphia Warriors 1949/50-1961/62 Philadelphia Warriors (BAA) 1946/47-1948/49	
Houston Rockets 1971/72—	San Diego Rockets 1967/68-1970/71	
Indiana Pacers 1976/77—	Indiana Pacers (ABA) 1967/68-1975/76	
Indianapolis Olympians 1949/50-1952/53	(*See* main entry. Team was actually an NBL franchise that replaced the Indianapolis Jets BAA franchise when the BAA and NBL merged.)	
Kansas City Kings 1975/76-1984/85	Kansas City- Omaha Kings 1972/73-1974/75 Cincinnati Royals 1957/58-1971/72 Rochester Royals 1949/50-1956/57 Rochester Royals (BAA) 1948/49 Rochester Royals (NBL) 1945/46-1947/48	Sacramento Kings 1985/86—
Kansas City- Omaha Kings 1972/73-1974/75	Cincinnati Royals 1957/58-1971/72	Kansas City Kings 1975/76-1984/85

Franchise Name	Were	Became
	Rochester Royals 1949/50-1956/57 Rochester Royals (BAA) 1948/49 Rochester Royals (NBL) 1945/46-1947/48	Sacramento Kings 1985/86—
Los Angeles Clippers 1984/85—	San Diego Clippers 1978/79-1983/84 Buffalo Braves 1970/71-1977/78	
Los Angeles Lakers 1960/61—	Minneapolis Lakers 1949/50-1959/60 Minneapolis Lakers (BAA) 1948/49 Minneapolis Lakers (NBL) 1947/48	
Miami Heat 1988/89—		
Milwaukee Bucks 1968/69—		
Milwaukee Hawks 1951/52-1954/55	Tri-Cities Blackhawks 1949/50-1950/51 Tri-Cities Blackhawks (NBL) 1946/47-1948/49 Buffalo Bisons (NBL) 1946/47 (Moved to Tri-Cities on 12/27/46 with a 4-8 record.)	St. Louis Hawks 1955/56-1967/68 Atlanta Hawks 1968/69—
Minneapolis Lakers 1949/50-1959/60	Minneapolis Lakers (BAA) 1948/49 Minneapolis Lakers (NBL) 1947/48	Los Angeles Lakers 1960/61—
Minnesota Timberwolves 1989/90—		
New Jersey Nets 1977/78—	New York Nets 1976/77	

Franchise Name	Were	Became
	New York Nets (ABA) 1968/69-1975/76 New Jersey Americans (ABA) 1967/68	
New Orleans Jazz 1974/75-1978/79		Utah Jazz 1979/80—
New York Knickerbockers 1949/50—	New York Knickerbockers (BAA) 1946/47-1948/49	
New York Nets 1976/77	New York Nets (ABA) 1968/69-1975/76 New Jersey Americans (ABA) 1967/68	New Jersey Nets 1977/78—
Orlando Magic 1989/90—		
Philadelphia Warriors 1949/50-1961/62	Philadelphia Warriors (BAA) 1946/47-1948/49	San Francisco Warriors 1962/63-1970/71 Golden State Warriors 1971/72
Philadelphia 76ers 1963/64—	Syracuse Nationals 1949/50-1962/63 Syracuse Nationals (NBL) 1946/47-1948/49	
Phoenix Suns 1968/69—		
Portland Trail Blazers 1970/71—		
Rochester Royals 1949/50-1956/57	Rochester Royals (BAA) 1948/49 Rochester Royals (NBL) 1945/46-1947/48	Cincinnati Royals 1957/58-1971/72 Kansas City-Omaha Kings 1972/73-1974/75 Kansas City Kings 1975/76-1984/85 Sacramento Kings 1985/86—
Sacramento Kings 1985/86—	Kansas City Kings 1975/76-1984/85	

Franchise Name	Were	Became
	Kansas City-Omaha Kings 1972/73-1974/75 Cincinnati Royals 1957/58-1971/72 Rochester Royals 1949/50-1956/57 Rochester Royals (BAA) 1948/49 Rochester Royals (NBL) 1945/46-1947/48	
St. Louis Bombers 1949/50	St. Louis Bombers (BAA) 1946/47-1948/49	
St. Louis Hawks 1955/56-1967/68	Milwaukee Hawks 1951/52-1954/55 Tri-Cities Blackhawks 1949/50-1950/51 Tri-Cities Blackhawks (NBL) 1946/47-1948/49 Buffalo Bisons (NBL) 1946/47 (Moved to Tri-Cities on 12/27/46 with a 4-8 record.)	Atlanta Hawks 1968/69—
San Antonio Spurs 1976/77—	San Antonio Spurs (ABA) 1973/74-1975/76 Dallas Chapparrals (ABA) 1971/72-1972/73 Texas Chaparrals (ABA) 1970/71 Dallas Chaparrals (ABA) 1967/68-1969/70	
San Diego Clippers 1978/79-1983/84	Buffalo Braves 1970/71-1977/78	Los Angeles Clippers 1984/85—
San Diego Rockets 1967/68-1970/71		Houston Rockets 1971/72—
San Francisco Warriors 1962/63-1970/71	Philadelphia Warriors 1949/50-1961/62 Philadelphia Warriors (BAA) 1946/47-1948/49	Golden State Warriors 1971/72—

Franchise Name	Were	Became
Seattle Supersonics 1967/68—		
Sheboygan Red Skins 1949/50	Sheboygan Red Skins (NBL) 1938/39-1948/49	
Syracuse Nationals 1949/50-1962/63	Syracuse Nationals (NBL) 1946/47-1948/49	Philadelphia 76ers 1963/64—
Tri-Cities Blackhawks 1949/50-1950/51	Tri-Cities Blackhawks (NBL) 1946/47-1948/49 Buffalo Bisons (NBL) 1946/47 (Moved to Tri-Cities on 12/27/46 with a 4-8 record.)	Milwaukee Hawks 1951/52-1954/55 St. Louis Hawks 1955/56-1967/68 Atlanta Hawks 1968/69—
Utah Jazz 1979/80—	New Orleans Jazz 1974/75-1978/79	
Washington Bullets 1974/75—	Capital Bullets 1973/74 Baltimore Bullets 1963/64-1972/73 Chicago Zephyrs 1962/63 Chicago Packers 1961/62	
Washington Capitols 1949/50-1950/51 (Disbanded on 1/9/51 with a 10-25 record.)	Washington Capitols (BAA) 1946/47-1948/49	
Waterloo Hawks 1949/50	Waterloo Hawks (NBL) 1948/49 Toledo Jeeps (NBL) 1946/47-1947/48	

AMERICAN BASKETBALL LEAGUE-3 (ABL-3)
1961/62-1962/63

Franchise Name	Were	Became
Chicago Majors 1961/62-1962/63		
Cleveland Pipers 1961/62		
Hawaii Chiefs 1961/62		Long Beach Chiefs 1962/63
Kansas City Steers 1961/62-1962/63		
Long Beach Chiefs 1962/63	Hawaii Chiefs 1961/62	
Los Angeles Jets 1961/62 (Folded in second half of 1961/62 season.)		
New York Tapers 1961/62	Washington Capitols 1961/62 (Moved to New York in midseason.)	Philadelphia Tapers 1962/63
Oakland Oaks 1962/63	San Francisco Saints 1961/62	
Philadelphia Tapers 1962/63	New York Tapers 1961/62 Washington Capitols 1961/62 (Moved to New York in midseason.)	
Pittsburgh Rens 1961/62-1962/63		
San Francisco Saints 1961/62		Oakland Oaks 1962/63
Washington Capitols 1961/62 (Moved to New York in midseason.)		New York Tapers 1961/62 Philadelphia Tapers 1962/63

AMERICAN BASKETBALL ASSOCIATION (ABA) 1967/68-1975/76

Franchise Name	Were	Became
Anaheim Amigos 1967/68		Los Angeles Stars 1968/69-1969/70 Utah Stars 1970/71-1975/76 (Folded after 16 games of 1975/76 season.)
Carolina Cougars 1969/70-1973/74	Houston Mavericks 1967/68-1968/69	Spirits of St. Louis 1974/75-1975/76
Dallas Chaparrals 1967/68-1969/70		Texas Chaparrals 1970/71 Dallas Chaparrals 1971/72-1972/73 San Antonio Spurs 1973/74-1975/76 San Antonio Spurs (NBA) 1976/77—
Dallas Chaparrals 1971/72-1972/73	Texas Chaparrals 1970/71 Dallas Chaparrals 1967/68-1969/70	San Antonio Spurs 1973/74-1975/76 San Antonio Spurs (NBA) 1976/77—
Denver Nuggets 1974/75-1975/76	Denver Rockets 1967/68-1973/74	Denver Nuggets (NBA) 1976/77—
Denver Rockets 1967/68-1973/74		Denver Nuggets 1974/75-1975/76 Denver Nuggets (NBA) 1976/77—
Floridians 1970/71-1971/72	Miami Floridians 1968/69-1969/70 Minnesota Muskies 1967/68	
Houston Mavericks 1967/68-1968/69		Carolina Cougars 1969/70-1973/74 Spirits of St. Louis 1974/75-1975/76
Indiana Pacers 1967/68-1975/76		Indiana Pacers (NBA) 1976/77—

Franchise Name	Were	Became
Kentucky Colonels 1967/68-1975/76		
Los Angeles Stars 1968/69-1969/70	Anaheim Amigos 1967/68	Utah Stars 1970/71-1975/76 (Team folded after 16 games of 1975/76 season.)
Memphis Pros 1970/71-1971/72	New Orleans Buccaneers 1967/68-1969/70	Memphis Tams 1972/73-1973/74 Memphis Sounds 1974/75
Memphis Sounds 1974/75	Memphis Tams 1972/73-1973/74 Memphis Pros 1970/71-1971/72 New Orleans Buccaneers 1967/68-1969/70	
Memphis Tams 1972/73-1973/74	Memphis Pros 1970/71-1971/72 New Orleans Buccaneers 1967/68-1969/70	Memphis Sounds 1974/75
Miami Floridians 1968/69-1969/70	Minnesota Muskies 1967/68	Floridians 1970/71-1971/72
Minnesota Muskies 1967/68		Miami Floridians 1968/69-1969/70 Floridians 1970/71-1971/72
Minnesota Pipers 1968/69	Pittsburgh Pipers 1967/68	Pitttsburgh Pipers 1969/70 Pittsburgh Condors 1970/71-1971/72
New Jersey Americans 1967/68		New York Nets 1968/69-1975/76 New York Nets (NBA) 1976/77 New Jersey Nets (NBA) 1977/78—
New Orleans Buccaneers 1967/68-1969/70		Memphis Pros 1970/71-1971/72 Memphis Tams 1972/73-1973/74

Franchise Name	Were	Became
		Memphis Sounds 1974/75
New York Nets 1968/69-1975/76	New Jersey Americans 1967/68	New York Nets (NBA) 1976/77 New Jersey Nets (NBA) 1977/78—
Oakland Oaks 1967/68-1968/69		Washington Capitols 1969/70 Virginia Squires 1970/71-1975/76
Pittsburgh Condors 1970/71-1971/72	Pittsburgh Pipers 1969/70 Minnesota Pipers 1968/69 Pittsburgh Pipers 1967/68	
Pittsburgh Pipers 1967/68		Minnesota Pipers 1968/69 Pittsburgh Pipers 1969/70 Pittsburgh Condors 1970/71-1971/72
Pittsburgh Pipers 1969/70	Minnesota Pipers 1968/69 Pittsburgh Pipers 1967/68	Pittsburgh Condors 1970/71-1971/72
(St. Louis) Spirits of St. Louis 1974/75	Carolina Cougars 1969/70-1973/74 Houston Mavericks 1967/68-1968/69	
San Antonio Spurs 1973/74-1975/76	Dallas Chaparrals 1971/72-1972/73 Texas Chaparrals 1970/71 Dallas Chaparrals 1967/68-1969/70	San Antonio Spurs (NBA) 1976/77—
San Diego Conquistadors 1972/73-1974/75		San Diego Sails 1975/76 (Folded early in season with a 3-8 record.)

Franchise Name	Were	Became
San Diego Sails 1975/76 (Folded early in season with 3-8 record.)		San Diego Conquistadors 1972/73-1974/75
Texas Chaparrals 1970/71	Dallas Chaparrals 1967/68-1969/70	Dallas Chaparrals 1971/72-1972/73 San Antonio Spurs 1973/74-1975/76 San Antonio Spurs (NBA) 1976/77—
Utah Stars 1970/71-1975/76 (Folded after 16 games of 1975/76 season.)	Los Angeles Stars 1968/69-1969/70 Anaheim Amigos 1967/68	
Virginia Squires 1970/71-1975/76	Washington Capitols 1969/70 Oakland Oaks 1967/68-1968/69	
Washington Capitols 1969/70	Oakland Oaks 1967/68-1968/69	Virginia Squires 1970/71-1975/76

AMERICAN PROFESSIONAL FOOTBALL ASSOCIATION (APFA) 1920-1921

Franchise Name	Were	Became
Akron Pros 1920-1921		Akron Pros (NFL) 1922-1925 Akron Indians (NFL) 1926
Buffalo All-Americans 1920-1921		Buffalo All-Americans (NFL) 1922-1923 Buffalo Bisons (NFL) 1924-1925 Buffalo Rangers (NFL) 1926 Buffalo Bisons (NFL) 1927 (Suspended operations for 1928.) Buffalo Bisons (NFL) 1929
Canton Bulldogs 1920-1921		Canton Bulldogs (NFL) 1922-1923 Cleveland Bulldogs (NFL) 1924/1925 (Suspended operations for 1926.) Cleveland Bulldogs (NFL) 1927
Chicago Cardinals 1921	(Chicago) Racine Cardinals 1920	Chicago Cardinals (NFL) 1922-1943 Chicago-Pittsburgh Card-Pitt (NFL) 1944 Chicago Cardinals (NFL) 1945-1959 St. Louis Cardinals (NFL) 1960-1987 Phoenix Cardinals (NFL) 1988—
Chicago Staleys 1921	Decatur Staleys 1920	Chicago Bears (NFL) 1922—
Chicago Tigers 1920		

Franchise Name	Were	Became
(Chicago) Racine Cardinals 1920		Chicago Cardinals 1921
		Chicago Cardinals (NFL) 1922-1943
		Chicago-Pittsburgh Card-Pitt (NFL) 1944
		Chicago Cardinals (NFL) 1945-1959
		St. Louis Cardinals (NFL) 1960-1987
		Phoenix Cardinals (NFL) 1988—
Cincinnati Celts 1921		
Cleveland Indians 1920-1921		
Columbus Panhandles 1920-1921		Columbus Panhandles (NFL) 1922-1924
		Columbus Tigers (NFL) 1925-1926
Dayton Triangles 1920-1921		Dayton Triangles (NFL) 1922-1929
		Brooklyn Dodgers (NFL) 1930-1943
		Brooklyn Tigers (NFL) 1944 (Merged with Boston Yanks on 4/10/45.)
		Boston Yanks (NFL) (1944)-1945
		New York Bulldogs (NFL) 1949
		New York Yanks (NFL) 1950-1951
Decatur Staleys 1920		Chicago Staleys 1921
		Chicago Bears 1922—
Detroit Heralds 1920		

Franchise Name	Were	Became
Detroit Tigers 1921		
Evansville Crimson Giants 1921		Evansville Crimson Giants (NFL) 1922
Green Bay Packers 1921		Green Bay Packers (NFL) 1922—
Hammond Pros 1920-1921		Hammond Pros (NFL) 1922-1926
Louisville Brecks 1921		Louisville Brecks (NFL) 1922-1923
Minneapolis Marines 1921		Minneapolis Marines (NFL) 1922-1924
Muncie Flyers 1920-1921		
New York Giants 1921		
Rochester Jeffersons 1920-1921		Rochester Jeffersons (NFL) 1922-1925
Rock Island Independents 1920-1921		Rock Island Independents (NFL) 1922-1925 Rock Island Independents (AFL-1) 1926
Tonawanda Kardex 1921		
Washington Senators 1921		

NATIONAL FOOTBALL LEAGUE (NFL) 1922—

Franchise Name	Were	Became
Akron Indians 1926	Akron Pros 1922-1925 Akron Pros (APFA) 1920-1921	
Akron Pros 1922-1925	Akron Pros (APFA) 1920-1921	Akron Indians 1926
Atlanta Falcons 1966—		
Baltimore Colts 1950	Baltimore Colts (AAFC) 1947-1949 Miami Seahawks (AAFC) 1946	
Baltimore Colts 1953-1983		Indianapolis Colts 1984—
Boston Braves 1932		Boston Redskins 1933-1936 Washington Redskins 1937—
Boston Bulldogs 1929	Pottsville Maroons 1925-1928	
Boston Patriots 1970	Boston Patriots (AFL-4) 1960-1969	New England Patriots 1971—
Boston Redskins 1933-1936	Boston Braves 1932	Washington Redskins 1937—
Boston Yanks 1944-1948	(Brooklyn Tigers merged with Yanks on 4/10/45. Refer to Tiger entry for additional data.)	New York Bulldogs 1949 New York Yanks 1950-1951
Brooklyn Dodgers 1930-1943	Dayton Triangles 1922-1929 Dayton Triangles (APFA) 1920-1921	Brooklyn Tigers 1944 (Tigers merged with Boston Yanks on 4/10/45. Refer to Tiger entry for additional data.)

Franchise Name	Were	Became
Brooklyn Lions 1926		
Brooklyn Tigers 1944	Brooklyn Dodgers 1930-1943 Dayton Triangles 1922-1929 Dayton Triangles (APFA) 1920-1921	(Merged with the Boston Yanks on 4/10/45.) Boston Yanks (1944)-1948 New York Bulldogs 1949 New York Yanks 1950-1951
Buffalo All-Americans 1922-1923	Buffalo All-Americans (APFA) 1920-1921	Buffalo Bisons 1924-1925 Buffalo Rangers 1926 Buffalo Bisons 1927 (Suspended operations for 1928.) Buffalo Bisons 1929
Buffalo Bills 1970—	Buffalo Bills (AFL-4) 1960-1969	
Buffalo Bisons 1924-1925	Buffalo All-Americans 1922-1923 Buffalo All-Americans 1920-1921	Buffalo Rangers 1926 Buffalo Bisons 1927 (Suspended operations for 1928.) Buffalo Bisons 1929
Buffalo Bisons 1927 (Suspended operations for 1928.)	Buffalo Rangers 1926 Buffalo Bisons 1924-1925 Buffalo All-Americans 1922-1923 Buffalo All-Americans (APFA) 1920-1921	Buffalo Bisons 1929
Buffalo Bisons 1929	Buffalo Bisons 1927 (Suspended operations for 1928.)	

Franchise Name	Were	Became
	Buffalo Rangers 1926 Buffalo Bisons 1924-1925 Buffalo All-Americans 1922-1923 Buffalo All-Americans (APFA) 1920-1921	
Buffalo Rangers 1926	Buffalo Bisons 1924-1925 Buffalo All-Americans 1922-1923 Buffalo All-Americans (APFA) 1920-1921	Buffalo Bisons 1927 (Suspended operations for 1928.) Buffalo Bisons 1929
Canton Bulldogs 1922-1923	Canton Bulldogs (APFA) 1920-1921	Cleveland Bulldogs 1924-1925 (Suspended operations for 1926.) Cleveland Bulldogs 1927
Canton Bulldogs 1925-1926		
Chicago Bears 1922—	Chicago Staleys (APFA) 1921 Decatur Staleys (APFA) 1920	
Chicago Cardinals 1922-1943	Chicago Cardinals (APFA) 1921 (Chicago) Racine Cardinals (APFA) 1920	Chicago-Pittsburgh Card-Pitt 1944 Chicago Cardinals 1945-1959 St. Louis Cardinals 1960-1987 Phoenix Cardinals 1988—
Chicago Cardinals 1945-1959	Chicago-Pittsburgh Card-Pitt 1944 Chicago Cardinals 1922-1943 Chicago Cardinals (APFA) 1921 (Chicago) Racine Cardinals (APFA) 1920	St. Louis Cardinals 1960-1987 Phoenix Cardinals 1988—

Franchise Name	Were	Became
Chicago-Pittsburgh Card-Pitt 1944	Chicago Cardinals 1922-1943 Chicago Cardinals (APFA) 1921 (Chicago) Racine Cardinals (APFA) 1920	Chicago Cardinals 1945-1959 St. Louis Cardinals 1960-1987 Phoenix Cardinals 1988—
Cincinnati Bengals 1970—	Cincinnati Bengals (AFL-4) 1968-1969	
Cincinnati Reds 1933-1934		St. Louis Gunners 1934 (Reds folded and were replaced by the Gunners on 11/5/34.)
Cleveland Browns 1950—	Cleveland Browns (AAFC) 1946-1949	
Cleveland Bulldogs 1924-1925 (Suspended operations for 1926.)	Canton Bulldogs 1922-1923 Canton Bulldogs (APFA) 1920-1921	Cleveland Bulldogs 1927
Cleveland Bulldogs 1927	Cleveland Bulldogs 1924-1925 (Suspended operations for 1926.) Canton Bulldogs 1922-1923 Canton Bulldogs (APFA) 1920-1921	
Cleveland Indians 1923		
Cleveland Indians 1931		
Cleveland Rams 1937-1942 (Suspended operations for 1943.)	Cleveland Rams (AFL-2) 1936	Cleveland Rams 1944-1945 Los Angeles Rams 1946—
Cleveland Rams 1944-1945	Cleveland Rams 1937-1942 (Suspended operations for 1943.)	Los Angeles Rams 1946—

Franchise Name	Were	Became
	Cleveland Rams (AFL-2) 1936	
Columbus Panhandles 1922-1924	Columbus Panhandles (APFA) 1920-1921	Columbus Tigers 1925-1926
Columbus Tigers 1925-1926	Columbus Panhandles 1922-1924 Columbus Panhandles (APFA) 1920-1921	
Dallas Cowboys 1960—		
Dallas Texans 1952		
Dayton Triangles 1922-1929	Dayton Triangles (APFA) 1920-1921	Brooklyn Dodgers 1930-1943 Brooklyn Tigers 1944 (Merged with Boston Yanks on 4/10/45. Refer to Tiger entry for additional data.)
Denver Broncos 1970—	Denver Broncos (AFL-4) 1960-1969	
Detroit Lions 1934—	Portsmouth Spartans 1930-1933	
Detroit Panthers 1925-1926		
Detroit Wolverines 1928		
Duluth Eskimos 1926-1927	Duluth Kelleys 1923-1925	
Duluth Kelleys 1923-1925		Duluth Eskimos 1926-1927
Evansville Crimson Giants 1922	Evansville Crimson Giants (APFA) 1921	

Franchise Name	Were	Became
Frankford Yellow Jackets 1924-1931 (Team did not play in 1932.)		Philadelphia Eagles 1933-1942 Philadelphia-Pittsburgh Steagles 1943 Philadelphia Eagles 1944—
Green Bay Packers 1922—	Green Bay Packers (APFA) 1921	
Hammond Pros 1922-1926	Hammond Pros (APFA) 1920-1921	
Hartford Blues 1926		
Houston Oilers 1970—	Houston Oilers (AFL-4) 1960-1969	
Indianapolis Colts 1984—	Baltimore Colts 1953-1983	
Kansas City Blues 1924		Kansas City Cowboys 1925-1926
Kansas City Chiefs 1970—	Kansas City Chiefs (AFL-4) 1963-1969 Dallas Texans (AFL-4) 1960-1962	
Kansas City Cowboys 1925-1926	Kansas City Blues 1924	
Kenosha Maroons 1924	Toledo Maroons 1922-1923	
Los Angeles Buccaneers 1926		
Los Angeles Raiders 1982—	Oakland Raiders 1970-1981 Oakland Raiders (AFL-4) 1960-1969	
Los Angeles Rams 1946—	Cleveland Rams 1944-1945 (Suspended operations for 1943.)	

Franchise Name	Were	Became
	Cleveland Rams 1937-1942 Cleveland Rams (AFL-2) 1936	
Louisville Brecks 1922-1923	Louisville Brecks (APFA) 1921	
Louisville Colonels 1926		
Miami Dolphins 1970—	Miami Dolphins (AFL-4) 1960-1969	
Milwaukee Badgers 1922-1926		
Minneapolis Marines 1922-1924	Minneapolis Marines (APFA) 1921	
Minneapolis Red Jackets 1929-1930		
Minnesota Vikings 1961—		
New England Patriots 1971—	Boston Patriots 1970 Boston Patriots (AFL-4) 1960-1969	
New Orleans Saints 1967—		
New York Bulldogs 1949	Boston Yanks 1944-1948 (Brooklyn Tigers merged with Yanks on 4/10/45. Refer to Tiger entry for additional data.)	New York Yanks 1950-1951
New York Giants 1925—		
New York Jets 1970—	New York Jets (AFL-4) 1963-1969 New York Titans (AFL-4) 1960-1962	

Franchise Name	Were	Became
New York Yankees 1927-1928	New York Yankees (AFL-1) 1926	
New York Yanks 1950-1951	New York Bulldogs 1949 Boston Yanks 1944-1948 (Merged with Brooklyn Tigers on 4/10/.45. Refer to Tiger entry for additional data.)	
Newark Tornadoes 1930	Orange Tornadoes 1929	
Oakland Raiders 1970-1981	Oakland Raiders (AFL-4) 1960-1969	Los Angeles Raiders 1982—
Oorang Indians 1922-1923		
Orange Tornadoes 1929		Newark Tornadoes 1930
Philadelphia Eagles 1933-1942	Frankford Yellow Jackets 1924-1931 (Did not play in 1932.)	Philadelphia-Pittsburgh Steagles 1943 Philadelphia Eagles 1944—
Philadelphia Eagles 1944—	Philadelphia-Pittsburgh Steagles 1943 Philadelphia Eagles 1933-1942 Frankford Yellow Jackets 1924-1931 (Did not play in 1932.)	
Philadelphia-Pittsburgh Steagles 1943	Philadelphia Eagles 1933-1942 Frankford Yellow Jackets 1924-1931 (Did not play in 1932.)	Philadelphia Eagles 1944—
Phoenix Cardinals 1988—	St. Louis Cardinals 1960-1987	

Franchise Name	Were	Became
	Chicago Cardinals 1945-1959 Chicago-Pittsburgh Card-Pitt 1944 Chicago Cardinals 1922-1943 Chicago Cardinals (APFA) 1921 (Chicago) Racine Cardinals (APFA) 1920	
Pittsburgh Pirates 1933-1938		Pittsburgh Steelers 1939-1942 Philadelphia-Pittsburgh Steagles 1943 Chicago-Pittsburgh Card-Pitt 1944 Pittsburgh Steelers 1945—
Pittsburgh Steelers 1939-1942	Pittsburgh Pirates 1933-1938	Philadelphia-Pittsburgh Steagles 1943 Chicago-Pittsburgh Card-Pitt 1944 Pittsburgh Steelers 1945—
Pittsburgh Steelers 1945—	Chicago-Pittsburgh Card-Pitt 1944 Philadelphia-Pittsburgh Steagles 1943 Pittsburgh Steelers 1939-1942 Pittsburgh Pirates 1933-1938	
Portsmouth Spartans 1930-1933		Detroit Lions 1934—
Pottsville Maroons 1925-1928		Boston Bulldogs 1929

Franchise Name	Were	Became
Providence Steam Roller 1925-1931		
Racine Legion 1922-1924		
Racine Tornadoes 1926		
Rochester Jeffersons 1922-1925	Rochester Jeffersons (APFA) 1920-1921	
Rock Island Independents 1922-1925	Rock Island Independents (APFA) 1920-1921	Rock Island Independents (AFL-1) 1926
St. Louis All-Stars 1923		
St. Louis Cardinals 1960-1987	Chicago Cardinals 1945-1959 Chicago-Pittsburgh Card-Pitt 1944 Chicago Cardinals 1922-1943 Chicago Cardinals (APFA) 1921 (Chicago) Racine Cardinals (APFA) 1920	Phoenix Cardinals 1988—
St. Louis Gunners 1934	Cincinnati Reds 1933-1934 (Cincinnati moved to St. Louis on 11/5/34 and played 3 games.)	
San Diego Chargers 1970—	San Diego Chargers (AFL-4) 1961-1969 Los Angeles Chargers (AFL-4) 1960	
San Francisco 49ers 1950—	San Francisco 49ers (AAFC) 1946-1949	
Seattle Seahawks 1976—		

Franchise Name	Were	Became
Staten Island Stapes 1931-1932	Staten Island Stapletons 1929-1930	
Staten Island Stapletons 1929-1930		Staten Island Stapes 1931-1932
Tampa Bay Buccaneers 1976—		
Toledo Maroons 1922-1923		Kenosha Maroons 1924
Washington Redskins 1937—	Boston Redskins 1933-1936 Boston Braves 1932	

AMERICAN FOOTBALL LEAGUE-1 (AFL-1) 1926

Franchise Name	Were	Became
Boston Bulldogs 1926		
Brooklyn Horsemen 1926		
Chicago Bulls 1926		
Cleveland Panthers 1926		
Los Angeles Wildcats 1926		
New York Yankees 1926		New York Yankees (NFL) 1927-1928
Newark Bears 1926		
Philadelphia Quakers 1926		
Rock Island Independents 1926	Rock Island Independents (NFL) 1922-1925 Rock Island Independents (APFA) 1920-1921	

AMERICAN FOOTBALL LEAGUE-2 (AFL-2) 1936-1937

Franchise Name	Were	Became
Boston Shamrocks 1936-1937		
Brooklyn Tigers 1936		Rochester Tigers 1936-1937 (Brooklyn moved to Rochester on 11/13/36 after Rochester Braves folded.)
Cincinnati Bengals 1937		
Cleveland Rams 1936		Cleveland Rams (NFL) 1937-1942 (Suspended operations for 1943.) Cleveland Rams (NFL) 1944-1945 Los Angeles Rams (NFL) 1946—
Los Angeles Bulldogs 1937		
New York Yanks 1936-1937		
Pittsburgh Americans 1936-1937		
Rochester Braves 1936 (Syracuse Braves moved to Rochester with 1-5 record, lost one game as Rochester Braves, and folded on 11/5/36.)	Syracuse Braves 1936 (Syracuse had a 1-5 record and moved to Rochester.)	

Franchise Name	Were	Became
Rochester Tigers 1936-1937	Brooklyn Tigers 1936 (Brooklyn moved to Rochester on 11/13/36 after Rochester Braves folded.)	
Syracuse Braves 1936 (Syracuse had a 1-5 record and moved to Rochester.)		Rochester Braves 1936 (Syracuse Braves moved to Rochester with a 1-5 record, lost 1 game as Rochester Braves, and folded on 11/5/36.)

AMERICAN FOOTBALL LEAGUE-3 (AFL-3) 1940-1941

Franchise Name	Were	Became
Boston Bears 1940		
Buffalo Indians 1940		Buffalo Tigers 1941
Buffalo Tigers 1941	Buffalo Indians 1940	
Cincinnati Bengals 1940-1941		
Columbus Bullies 1940-1941		
Milwaukee Chiefs 1940-1941		
New York Americans 1941	New York Yanks 1940	
New York Yanks 1940		New York Americans 1941

ALL-AMERICAN FOOTBALL CONFERENCE (AAFC) 1946-1949

Franchise Name	Were	Became
Baltimore Colts 1947-1949	Miami Seahawks 1946	Baltimore Colts (NFL) 1950
Brooklyn Dodgers 1946-1948 (Merged with New York Yankees for 1949.)		
Buffalo Bills 1947-1949	Buffalo Bisons 1946	
Buffalo Bisons 1946		Buffalo Bills 1947-1949
Chicago Hornets 1949	Chicago Rockets 1946-1948	
Chicago Rockets 1946-1948		Chicago Hornets 1949
Cleveland Browns 1946-1949		Cleveland Browns (NFL) 1950—
Los Angeles Dons 1946-1949		
Miami Seahawks 1946		Baltimore Colts 1947-1949 Baltimore Colts (NFL) 1950
New York Yankees 1946-1949		
San Francisco 49ers 1946-1949		San Francisco 49ers (NFL) 1950—

AMERICAN FOOTBALL LEAGUE-4 (AFL-4) 1960-1969

Franchise Name	Were	Became
Boston Patriots 1960-1969		Boston Patriots (NFL) 1970 New England Patriots (NFL) 1971—
Buffalo Bills 1960-1969		Buffalo Bills (NFL) 1970—
Cincinnati Bengals 1968-1969		Cincinnati Bengals (NFL) 1970—
Dallas Texans 1960-1962		Kansas City Chiefs 1963-1969 Kansas City Chiefs (NFL) 1970—
Denver Broncos 1960-1969		Denver Broncos (NFL) 1970—
Houston Oilers 1960-1969		Houston Oilers (NFL) 1970—
Kansas City Chiefs 1963-1969	Dallas Texans 1960-1962	Kansas City Chiefs (NFL) 1970—
Los Angeles Chargers 1960		San Diego Chargers 1961-1969 San Diego Chargers (NFL) 1970—
Miami Dolphins 1966-1969		Miami Dolphins (NFL) 1970—
New York Jets 1963-1969	New York Titans 1960-1962	New York Jets (NFL) 1970—
New York Titans 1960-1962		New York Jets 1963-1969 New York Jets (NFL) 1970—
Oakland Raiders 1960-1969		Oakland Raiders (NFL) 1970-1988 Los Angeles Raiders (NFL) 1982—
San Diego Chargers 1961-1969	Los Angeles Chargers 1960	San Diego Chargers (NFL) 1970—

WORLD FOOTBALL LEAGUE (WFL) 1974-1975

Franchise Name	Were	Became
Birmingham Americans 1974		
Birmingham Vulcans 1975		
Charlotte Hornets 1974-1975	New York Stars 1974	
Chicago Fire 1974 (Disbanded with 7-12 record. One game unplayed.)		
Chicago Wind 1975 (Folded with a 1-4 record.)		
Detroit Wheels 1974 (Folded with a 1-13 record.)		
Florida Blazers 1974		
Hawaiians 1974-1975		
Houston Texans 1974		Shreveport Steamer 1974-1975
Jacksonville Sharks 1974 (Folded with a 4-10 record.)		
Jacksonville Express 1975		
Memphis Southmen 1974-1975		

Franchise Name	Were	Became
New York Stars 1974		Charlotte Hornets 1974-1975
Philadelphia Bell 1974-1975		
Portland Storm 1974		
Portland Thunder 1975		
San Antonio Wings 1975		
Shreveport Steamer 1974-1975	Houston Texans 1974	
Southern California Sun 1974-1975		

UNITED STATES FOOTBALL LEAGUE (USFL) 1983-1985

Franchise Name	Were	Became
Arizona Outlaws 1985 (Wranglers and Oklahoma Outlaws merged 1984 teams!)	Arizona Wranglers 1984 Chicago Blitz 1983 (Blitz and Wranglers exchanged franchises for 1984 season.)	
Arizona Wranglers 1983 (Blitz and Wranglers exchanged franchises for 1984 season.)		Chicago Blitz 1984
Arizona Wranglers 1984	Chicago Blitz 1983 (Blitz and Wranglers exchanged franchises for 1984 season.)	Arizona Outlaws 1985 (Arizona Wranglers and Oklahoma Outlaws merged 1984 teams.)
Baltimore Stars 1985	Philadelphia Stars 1983-1984 (Stars and Pittsburgh Maulers merged at end of 1984 season.)	
Birmingham Stallions 1983-1984		
Boston Breakers 1983		New Orlean Breakers 1984 Portland Breakers 1985
Chicago Blitz 1983 (Blitz and Wranglers exchanged franchises for 1984 season.)		Arizona Wranglers 1984 Arizona Outlaws 1985 (Arizona Wranglers and Oklahoma Outlaws merged 1984 teams.)
Chicago Blitz 1984	Arizona Wranglers 1983 (Blitz and Wranglers exchanged franchises for 1984 season.)	

Franchise Name	Were	Became
Denver Gold 1983-1985		
Houston Gamblers 1984-1985		
Jacksonville Bulls 1984-1985		
Los Angeles Express 1983-1985		
Memphis Showboats 1984-1985		
Michigan Panthers 1983-1984		Oakland Invaders 1985 (Panthers merged with Invaders.)
New Orleans Breakers 1984	Boston Breakers 1983	Portland Breakers 1985
New Jersey Generals 1983-1985		
Oakland Invaders 1983-1985 (Michigan Panthers merged with Invaders for 1985 season.)		
Oklahoma Outlaws 1984		Arizona Outlaws 1985 (Arizona Wranglers and Oklahoma Outlaws merged 1984 teams.)
Orlando Renegades 1985	Washington Federals 1983-1984	
Philadelphia Stars 1983-1984 (Stars and Pittsburgh Maulers merged at end of 1984 season.)		Baltimore Stars 1985

Franchise Name	Were	Became
Pittsburgh Maulers 1984 (Philadelphia Stars and Pittsburgh merged at end of 1984 season.)		Baltimore Stars 1985
Portland Breakers 1985	New Orleans Breakers 1984 Boston Breakers 1983	
San Antonio Gunslingers 1984-1985		
Tampa Bay Bandits 1983-1985		
Washington Federals 1983-1984		Orlando Renegades 1985

NATIONAL HOCKEY LEAGUE (NHL) 1917/18—

Franchise Name	Were	Became
Atlanta Flames 1972/73-1979/80		Calgary Flames 1980/81—
Boston Bruins 1924/25—		
Brooklyn Americans 1941/42	New York Americans 1925/26-1940/41 Hamilton Tigers 1920/21-1924/25 Quebec Bulldogs 1919/20	
Buffalo Sabres 1970/71—		
California Golden Seals 1970/71-1975/76	Oakland Seals 1967/68-1969/70 California Seals 1967/68 (Team changed name to Oakland Seals in midseason.)	Cleveland Barons 1976/77-1977/78 (Team merged with Minnesota North Stars for 1978/79.)
California Seals 1967/68		Oakland Seals 1967/68-1969/70 (Team changed name to Oakland Seals in midseason.) California Golden Seals 1970/71-1975/76 Cleveland Barons 1976/77-1977/78 (Team merged with Minnesota North Stars for 1978/79.)
Calgary Flames 1980/81—	Atlanta Flames 1972/73-1979/80	
Chicago Black Hawks 1926/27—		
Cleveland Barons 1976/77-1977/78	California Golden Seals 1970/71-1975/76	

Franchise Name	Were	Became
(Team merged with the Minnesota North Stars for 1978/79.)	Oakland Seals 1967/68-1969/70 California Seals 1967/68 (Team changed name to Oakland Seals in midseason.)	
Colorado Rockies 1976/77-1981/82	Kansas City Scouts 1974/75-1975/76	New Jersey Devils 1982/83—
Detroit Cougars 1926/27-1929/30		Detroit Falcons 1930/31-1932/33 Detroit Red Wings 1933/34—
Detroit Falcons 1930/31-1932/33	Detroit Cougars 1926/27-1929/30	Detroit Red Wings 1933/34—
Detroit Red Wings 1933/34—	Detroit Falcons 1930/31-1932/33 Detroit Cougars 1926/27-1929/30	
Edmonton Oilers 1979/80—	Edmonton Oilers (WHA) 1972/73-1978/79 Alberta Oilers (WHA) 1972/73 (Team changed name to Edmonton during the season.)	
Hamilton Tigers 1920/21-1924/25	Quebec Bulldogs 1919/20	New York Americans 1925/26-1940/41 Brooklyn Americans 1941/42
Hartford Whalers 1979/80—	New England Whalers (WHA) 1972/73-1978/79	
Kansas City Scouts 1974/75-1975/76		Colorado Rockies 1976/77-1981/82 New Jersey Devils 1982/83—
Los Angeles Kings 1967/68—		

Franchise Name	Were	Became
Minnesota North Stars 1967/68—	(Cleveland Barons were merged with Minnesota for the 1978/79 season.)	
Montreal Canadiens 1917/18—		
Montreal Maroons 1924/25-1937/38		
Montreal Wanderers 1917/18		
New Jersey Devils 1982/83—	Colorado Rockies 1976/77-1981/82 Kansas City Scouts 1974/75-1975/76	
New York Americans 1925/26-1940/41	Hamilton Tigers 1920/21-1924/25 Quebec Bulldogs 1919/20	Brooklyn Americans 1941/42
New York Islanders 1972/73—		
New York Rangers 1926/27—		
Oakland Seals 1967/68-1969/70	California Seals 1967/68 (Team changed name to Oakland Seals in midseason.)	California Golden Seals 1970/71-1975/76 Cleveland Barons 1976/77-1977/78 (Team merged with Minnesota North Stars for 1978/79 season.)
Ottawa Senators 1917/18-1930/31 (Team dropped out for 1931/32 season.)		Ottawa Senators 1932/33-1933/34 St. Louis Eagles 1934/35
Ottawa Senators 1932/33-1933/34	Ottawa Senators 1917/18-1930/31 (Team dropped out for 1931/32 season.)	St. Louis Eagles 1934/35

Franchise Name	**Were**	**Became**
Philadelphia Flyers 1967/68—		
Philadelphia Quakers 1930/31	Pittsburgh Pirates 1925/26-1929/30	
Pittsburgh Penguins 1967/68—		
Pittsburgh Pirates 1925/26-1929/30		Philadelphia Quakers 1930/31
Quebec Bulldogs 1919/20		Hamilton Tigers 1920/21-1924/25 New York Americans 1925/26-1940/41 Brooklyn Americans 1941/42
Quebec Nordiques 1979/80—	Quebec Nordiques (WHA) 1972/73-1978/79	
St. Louis Blues 1967/68—		
St. Louis Eagles 1934/35	Ottawa Senators 1932/33-1933/34 (Team dropped out for 1931/32 season.) Ottawa Senators 1917/18-1930/31	
San Jose Sharks 1991/92—		
Toronto Arenas 1917/18-1918/19		Toronto St. Patricks 1919/20-1925/26 Toronto Maple Leafs 1926/27—
Toronto Maple Leafs 1926/27—	Toronto St. Patricks 1919/20-1925/26 Toronto Arenas 1917/18-1918/19	
Toronto St. Patricks 1919/20-1925/26	Toronto Arenas 1917/18-1918/19	Toronto Maple Leafs 1926/27—

Franchise Name	Were	Became
Vancouver Canucks 1970/71—		
Washington Capitals 1974/75—		
Winnipeg Jets 1979/80—	Winnipeg Jets (WHA) 1972/73-1978/79	

WORLD HOCKEY ASSOCIATION (WHA) 1972/73-1978/79

Franchise Name	Were	Became
Alberta Oilers 1972/73		Edmonton Oilers 1972/73-1978/79 Edmonton Oilers (NHL) 1979/80—
Baltimore Blades 1974/75	Michigan Stags 1974/75 (Moved to Baltimore on 1/23/75.)	
Birmingham Bulls 1976/77-1978/79	Toronto Toros 1973/74-1975/76 Ottawa Nationals 1972/73	
Calgary Stampeders 1975/76-1976/77		
Chicago Cougars 1972/73-1974/75		
Cincinnati Stingers 1975/76-1978/79		
Cleveland Crusaders 1972/73-1975/76		
Denver Spurs 1975/76		Ottawa Civics 1975/76 (Denver moved to Ottawa on 1/2/76 but later disbanded with a 14-26-1 record.)
Edmonton Oilers 1972/73-1978/79	Alberta Oilers 1972/73	Edmonton Oilers (NHL) 1979/80—
Houston Aeros 1972/73-1977/78		
Indianapolis Racers 1974/75-1978/79 (Disbanded on 12/15/78 with a 5-18-2 record.)		

Franchise Name	Were	Became
Jersey Knights 1973/74	New York Golden Blades 1973/74 New York Raiders 1972/73	San Diego Mariners 1974/75-1976/77
Los Angeles Sharks 1972/73-1973/74		
Michigan Stags 1974/75 (Moved to Baltimore on 1/23/75.)		Baltimore Blades 1974/75
Minnesota Fighting Saints 1972/73-1975/76 (Disbanded on 2/28/76 with a 30-25-4 record.)		
New England Whalers 1972/73-1978/79		Hartford Whalers (NHL) 1979/80—
New York Golden Blades 1973/74	New York Raiders 1972/73	Jersey Knights 1973/74 San Diego Mariners 1974/75-1976/77
New York Raiders 1972/73		New York Golden Blades 1973/74 Jersey Knights 1973/74 San Diego Mariners 1974/75-1976/77
Ottawa Civics 1975/76 (Denver moved to Ottawa on 1/2/76 but later disbanded with a 14-26-1 record.)	Denver Spurs 1975/76	
Ottawa Nationals 1972/73		Toronto Toros 1973/74-1975/76 Birmingham Bulls 1976/77-1978/79

Franchise Name	Were	Became
Philadelphia Blazers 1972/73		Vancouver Blazers 1973/74-1974/75
Phoenix Roadrunners 1974/75-1976/77		
Quebec Nordiques 1972/73-1978/79		Quebec Nordiques (NHL) 1979/80—
San Diego Mariners 1974/75-1976/77	Jersey Knights 1973/74 New York Golden Blades 1973/74 New York Raiders 1972/73	
Toronto Toros 1973/74-1975/76	Ottawa Nationals 1972/73	Birmingham Bulls 1976/77-1978/79
Vancouver Blazers 1973/74-1974/75	Philadelphia Blazers 1972/73	
Winnipeg Jets 1972/73-1978/79		Winnipeg Jets (NHL) 1979/80—

NORTH AMERICAN SOCCER LEAGUE (NASL) 1968-1984

Franchise Name	Were	Became
(Team) America 1983		
Atlanta Apollos 1973		
Atlanta Chiefs 1968-1972		
Atlanta Chiefs 1979-1980	Colorado Caribous 1978	
Baltimore Bays 1968-1969		
Baltimore Comets 1974-1975		San Diego Jaws 1976 Las Vegas Quicksilver 1977 San Diego Sockers 1978-1984 San Diego Sockers (MISL) 1984/85—
Boston Beacons 1968		
Boston Minutemen 1974-1976		
Calgary Boomers 1981	Memphis Rouges 1978-1980	
California Surf 1978-1981	St. Louis Stars 1968-1977	
Chicago Mustangs 1968		
Chicago Sting 1975-1984		Chicago Sting (MISL) 1982/83 (Played summer season with NASL and winter season with MISL.) Chicago Sting (MISL) 1984/85-1987/88

Franchise Name	Were	Became
Cleveland Stokers 1968		
Colorado Caribous 1978		Atlanta Chiefs 1979-1980
Connecticut Bicentennials 1977	Hartford Bicentennials 1975-1976	Oakland Stompers 1978 Edmonton Drillers 1979-1982
Dallas Tornado 1968-1981		
Denver Dynamo 1974-1975		Minnesota Kicks 1976-1981
Detroit Cougars 1968		
Detroit Express 1978-1980		Washington Diplomats 1981
Edmonton Drillers 1979-1982	Oakland Stompers 1978 Connecticut Bicentennials 1977 Hartford Bicentennials 1975-1976	
Fort Lauderdale Strikers 1977-1983	Miami Toros 1973-1976 Miami Gatos 1972 Washington Darts 1970-1971	Minnesota Strikers 1984 Minnesota Strikers (MISL) 1984/85-1987/88
Golden Bay Earthquakes 1983-1984	Golden Bay Earthquakes (MISL) 1982/83 (Played summer season with NASL and winter season with MISL.) San Jose Earthquakes 1974-1982	

Franchise Name	Were	Became
Hartford Bicentennials 1975-1976		Connecticut Bicentennials 1977 Oakland Stompers 1978 Edmonton Drillers 1979-1982
(Team) Hawaii 1977	San Antonio Thunder 1975-1976	Tulsa Roughnecks 1978-1984
Houston Hurricane 1978-1980		
Houston Stars 1968		
Jacksonville Tea Men 1981-1982	New England Tea Men 1978-1980	
Kansas City Spurs 1968-1970		
Las Vegas Quicksilver 1977	San Diego Jaws 1976 Baltimore Comets 1974-1975	San Diego Sockers 1978-1984 San Diego Sockers (MISL) 1984/85—
Los Angeles Aztecs 1974-1981		
Los Angeles Wolves 1968		
Memphis Rouges 1978-1980		Calgary Boomers 1981
Miami Gatos 1972	Washington Darts 1970-1971	Miami Toros 1973-1976 Fort Lauderdale Strikers 1977-1983 Minnesota Strikers 1984 Minnesota Strikers (MISL) 1984/85-1987/88

Franchise Name	Were	Became
Miami Toros 1973-1976	Miami Gatos 1972 Washington Darts 1970-1971	Fort Lauderdale Strikers 1977-1983 Minnesota Strikers 1984 Minnesota Strikers (MISL) 1984/85-1987/88
Minnesota Kicks 1976-1981	Denver Dynamos 1974-1975	
Minnesota Strikers 1984	Fort Lauderdale Strikers 1977-1983 Miami Toros 1973-1976 Miami Gatos 1972 Washington Darts 1970-1971	Minnesota Strikers (MISL) 1984/85-1987/88
Montreal Manic 1981-1983	Philadelphia Fury 1978-1980	
Montreal Olympique 1971-1973		
New England Tea Men 1978-1980		Jacksonville Tea Men 1981-1982
New York Cosmos 1971-1984		New York Cosmos (MISL) 1984/85 (Folded on 2/22/85 with an 11-22 record.)
New York Generals 1968		
Oakland Clippers 1968		
Oakland Stompers 1978	Connecticut Bicentennials 1977 Hartford Bicentennials 1975-1976	Edmonton Drillers 1979-1982
Philadelphia Atoms 1973-1976		

Franchise Name	Were	Became
Philadelphia Fury 1978-1980	Montreal Manic 1981-1983	
Portland Timbers 1975-1982		
Rochester Lancers 1970-1980		
St. Louis Stars 1968-1977		California Surf 1978-1981
San Antonio Thunder 1975-1976		(Team) Hawaii 1977 Tulsa Roughnecks 1978-1984
San Diego Jaws 1976	Baltimore Comets 1974-1975	Las Vegas Quicksilver 1977 San Diego Sockers 1978-1984 San Diego Sockers (MISL) 1984/85—
San Diego Sockers 1978-1984	Las Vegas Quicksilver 1977 San Diego Jaws 1976 Baltimore Comets 1974-1975	San Diego Sockers (MISL) 1984/85—
San Diego Toros 1968		
San Jose Earthquakes 1974-1982		Golden Bay Earthquakes (MISL) 1982/83 (Played summer season in NASL and winter season in MISL.) Golden Bay Earthquakes 1983-1984
Seattle Sounders 1974-1983		

Franchise Name	Were	Became
Tampa Bay Rowdies 1975-1984		
Toronto Blizzard 1979-1984		
Toronto Falcons 1968		
Toronto Metros 1971-1974		Toronto Metros-Croatia 1975-1978
Toronto Metros-Croatia 1975-1978	Toronto Metros 1971-1974	
Tulsa Roughnecks 1978-1984	(Team) Hawaii 1977 San Antonio Thunder 1975-1976	
Vancouver Royals 1968		
Vancouver Whitecaps 1974-1984		
Washington Darts 1970-1971		Miami Gatos 1972 Miami Toros 1973-1976 Fort Lauderdale Strikers 1977-1983 Minnesota Strikers 1984 Minnesota Strikers (MISL) 1984/85-1987/88
Washington Diplomats 1974-1980		
Washington Diplomats 1981	Detroit Express 1978-1980	
Washington Whips 1968		

MAJOR INDOOR SOCCER LEAGUE (MISL) 1978/79—

Franchise Name	Were	Became
Baltimore Blast 1980/81—	Houston Summit 1978/79-1979/80	
Buffalo Stallions 1979/80-1983/84		
Chicago Horizon 1980/81		
Chicago Sting 1982/83	Chicago Sting (NASL) 1975-1984 (Played summer season with NASL and winter season with MISL.)	
Chicago Sting 1984/85-1987/88	Chicago Sting (NASL) 1975-1984 (Played summer season with NASL and winter season with MISL.)	
Cincinnati Kids 1978/79		
Cleveland Crunch 1989/90—		
Cleveland Force 1978/79-1987/88		
Dallas Sidekicks 1984/85—		
Denver Avalanche 1980/81-1981/82		Tacoma Stars 1983/84—
Detroit Lightning 1979/80		San Francisco Fog 1980/81 Kansas City Comets 1981/82—
Golden Bay Earthquakes 1982/83	San Jose Earthquakes (NASL) 1974-1982	Golden Bay Earthquakes (NASL) 1983-1984

Franchise Name	Were	Became
	(Played summer season with NASL and winter season with MISL.)	
Hartford Hellions 1979/80-1980/81		Memphis Americans 1981/82-1983/84 Las Vegas Americans 1984/85
Houston Summit 1978/79-1979/80		Baltimore Blast 1980/81—
Kansas City Comets 1981/82—	San Francisco Fog 1980/81 Detroit Lightning 1979/80	
Las Vegas Americans 1984/85	Memphis Americans 1981/82-1983/84 Hartford Hellions 1979/80-1980/81	
Los Angeles Lazers 1984/85		
Memphis Americans 1981/82-1983/84	Hartford Hellions 1979/80-1980/81	Las Vegas Americans 1984/85
Minnesota Strikers 1984/85-1987/88	Minnesota Strikers (NASL) 1984 Fort Lauderdale Strikers (NASL) 1977-1983 Miami Toros (NASL) 1973-1976 Miami Gatos (NASL) 1972 Washington Darts (NASL) 1970-1971	
New Jersey Rockets 1981/82		
New York Arrows 1978/79-1983/84		

Franchise Name	Were	Became
New York Cosmos 1984/85 (Folded on 2/22/85 with an 11-22 record.)	New York Cosmos (NASL) 1971-1984	
New York Express 1986/87 (Folded on 2/17/87 with a 3-23 record.)		
Philadelphia Fever 1978/79-1981/82		
Phoenix Inferno 1980/81-1982/83		Phoenix Pride 1983/84
Phoenix Pride 1983/84	Phoenix Inferno 1980/81-1982/83	
Pittsburgh Spirit 1978/79-1979/80 (Team was granted a leave of absence for 1980/81 season.)		Pittsburgh Spirit 1981/82-1985/86
Pittsburgh Spirit 1981/82-1985/86	Pittsburgh Spirit 1978/79-1979/80 (Team was granted a leave of absence for 1980/81 season.)	
St. Louis Steamers 1979/80-1987/88		
St. Louis Storm 1989/90—		
San Diego Sockers 1982/83	San Diego Sockers (NASL) 1978-1984 (Team played summer season with NASL and winter season with MISL.) Las Vegas Quicksilver (NASL) 1977 San Diego Jaws (NASL) 1976 Baltimore Comets (NASL) 1974-1975	

Franchise Name	Were	Became
San Diego Sockers 1984/85—	San Diego Sockers (NASL) 1978-1984 Las Vegas Quicksilver (NASL) 1977 San Diego Jaws (NASL) 1976 Baltimore Comets (NASL) 1974-1975	
San Francisco Fog 1980/81	Detroit Lightning 1979/80	Kansas City Comets 1981/82—
Tacoma Stars 1983/84—	Denver Avalanche 1980/81-1981/82	
Wichita Wings 1979/80—		

Section 3

Index of Nicknames

ABC's
Indianapolis (NAL)
Indianapolis (NNL-1) 1920-1926
Indianapolis (NNL-1) 1931
Indianapolis (NSL)

Aeros
Houston (WHA)

Albany
Albany (ML-1)

All-Americans (*See also* **Ciesar
All-Americans**)
Buffalo (APFA)
Buffalo (NFL)
Syracuse (ABL-1)

All-Stars (*See also* **Cuban Stars,
North Stars, Stars, Tate Stars**)
Oshkosh (NBL)
St. Louis (NFL)

Allegheny(s)
Pittsburgh (AA)
Pittsburgh (NL)

Allmen Transfers
Cleveland (NBL)

Altes Lagers
Detroit (MBC)

America (*See* **Team America**)

American Gears
Chicago (NBL)

American Giants (*See also* **Cole's
American Giants**)
Chicago (NAL)
Chicago (NNL-1)

Americans
Birmingham (WFL)
Bronx (ABL-2)
Brooklyn (ML-2)
Brooklyn (NHL)
Las Vegas (MISL)
Memphis (MISL)
New Jersey (ABA)
New York (ABL-2)
New York (AFL-3)
New York (NHL)
Pittsburgh (AFL-2)

Amigos
Anaheim (ABA)

Angels
California (AL)
Los Angeles (AL)

Apollos
Atlanta (NASL)

Arcadians
Brooklyn (ABL-1)

Arenas
Toronto (NHL)

Arrows
New York (MISL)

Assumption Triangles
(Brooklyn) West Brooklyn (ML-1)

Athletic Supplys
Columbus (MBC)
Columbus (NBL)

Athletics
Indianapolis (NAL)
Kansas City (AL)
Oakland (AL)
Philadelphia (AA)
Philadelphia (AL)
Philadelphia (NA)
Philadelphia (NL)

Atlantics
Brooklyn (NA)

Atoms
Philadelphia (NASL)

Avalanche
Denver (MISL)

Aztecs
Los Angeles (NASL)

"Babies of the AA"
Cleveland (AA)

Bacharach Giants
Atlantic City (ANL)
Atlantic City (ECL)
Atlantic City (NNL-2)

Badgers
Milwaukee (NFL)

Barons (*See also* **Black Barons**)
Cleveland (NHL)
Wilkes-Barre (ABL-2)

Bandits
Tampa Bay (USFL)

Bays
Baltimore (NASL)

Beacons
Boston (NASL)

Beaneaters
Boston (NL)

Bears
Boston (AFL-3)
Chicago (NFL)
Cleveland (NAL)
Milwaukee (NNL-1)
Newark (AFL-1)
Newark (ML-1)
Youngstown (NBL)

Bees
Boston (NL)

Bell
Philadelphia (WFL)

Bengals (*See also* **Bengal Tigers,
Tigers**)
Cincinnati (AFL-2)
Cincinnati (AFL-3)
Cincinnati (AFL-4)
Cincinnati (NFL)

Bengal Tigers (*See also* **Bengals,
Tigers**)
Passaic (ABL-2)

Bicentennials (*See also*
Centennials)
Connecticut (NASL)
Hartford (NASL)

Bills
Buffalo (AAFC)
Buffalo (AFL-4)
Buffalo (NFL)

Bisons
Buffalo (AAFC)
Buffalo (MBC)
Buffalo (NBL) 1937/38
Buffalo (NBL) 1946/47
Buffalo (NFL) 1924/25
Buffalo (NFL) 1927
Buffalo (NFL) 1929

Buffalo (NL)

Buffalo (PL)

Black Barons (*See also* Barons)
Birmingham (NAL) 1937-1938
Birmingham (NAL) 1940-1950
Birmingham (NNL-1) 1924-1925
Birmingham (NNL-1) 1927-1930

Black Caps
Louisville (NSL)

Black Crackers
Atlanta (NAL)

Black Senators (*See also* Senators)
Washington (NNL-2)

Black Sox
Baltimore (ANL)
Baltimore (ECL)
Baltimore (NNL-2)

Blackhawks/Black Hawks
Chicago (NHL)
Tri-Cities (NBA)
Tri-Cities (NBL)

Blades
Baltimore (WHA)

Blast
Baltimore (MISL)

Blazers (*See also* Trail Blazers)
Florida (WFL)
Philadelphia (WHA)
Vancouver (WHA)

Blitz
Chicago (USFL) 1983
Chicago (USFL) 1984

Blizzard
Toronto (NASL)

Blue Birds
Columbus (NNL-2)

Blue Bombers (*See also* Bombers)
Wilmington (ABL-2) 1941/42
Wilmington (ABL-2) 1943/44

Blue Jays
Philadelphia (NL)
Toronto (AL)

Blue Stockings
Toledo (AA)

Blues
Buffalo (FL)

Cleveland (AL)
Hartford (NFL)
Hartford (NL)
Kansas City (NFL)
St. Louis (NHL)

Bombers (*See also* Blue Bombers)
St. Louis (BAA)
St. Louis (NBA)
Wilmington (ABL-2)

Boomers
Calgary (NASL)

Braves
Atlanta (NL)
Boston (NL) 1912-1935
Boston (NL) 1941-1952
Bronx (ML-2)
Buffalo (NBA)
Milwaukee (NL)
Rochester (AFL-2)
Syracuse (AFL-2)

Breakers
Boston (USFL)
New Orleans (USFL)
Portland (USFL)

Brecks
Louisville (APFA)
Louisville (NFL)

Brewers
Camden (ABL-2)
Milwaukee (AA)
Milwaukee (AL) 1901
Milwaukee (AL) 1970—
Milwaukee (NL)
Washington (ABL-2)

Bridegrooms
Brooklyn (AA)
Brooklyn (NL)

Bridgeton
Bridgeton (EL)

Bronchos
Cleveland (AL)
Denver (AFL-4)
Denver (NFL)

Brooklyns
Brooklyn (AA)

Browns
Cleveland (AAFC)

Cleveland (NFL)
Cleveland (NNL-1)
St. Louis (AA)
St. Louis (AL)
St. Louis (NL) 1876-1877
St. Louis (NL) 1892-1897

Bruins
Boston (NHL)
Chicago (ABL-1)
Chicago (NBL)

Buccaneers (*See also* Calumet Buccaneers)
Los Angeles (NFL)
New Orleans (ABA)
Tampa Bay (NFL)

Buckeyes
Cincinnati (NAL)
Cleveland (NAL) 1943-1948
Cleveland (NAL) 1950
Columbus (AA) 1883-1884
Columbus (AA) 1889-1891
Columbus (NNL-1)
Louisville (NAL)

Bucks
Milwaukee (NBA)

Bulldogs
Boston (AFL-1)
Boston (NFL)
Canton (APFA)
Canton (NFL) 1922-1923
Canton (NFL) 1925-1926
Cleveland (NFL) 1924-1925
Cleveland (NFL) 1927
Los Angeles (AFL-2)
New York (NFL)
Quebec (NHL)

Bullets
Baltimore (ABL-2)
Baltimore (BAA)
Baltimore (NBA) 1949/50-1954/55
Baltimore (NBL) 1963/64-1972/73
Capital (NBA)
Washington (NBA)

Bullies
Columbus (AFL-3)

Bulls
Birmingham (WHA)
Chicago (AFL-1)

Chicago (NBA)
Jacksonville (USFL)

Burghers
Pittsburgh (PL)

Calumet Buccaneers (*See also* Buccaneers)
Hammond (NBL)

Camden
Camden (EL)

Canadiens
Montreal (NHL)

Canucks
Vancouver (NHL)

Capitals
Washington (NHL)

Capitols/Capitol's
Washington (ABA)
Washington (ABL-2)
Washington (ABL-3)
Washington (BAA)
Washington (NBA)

Cardinals
Chicago (APFA)
Chicago (NFL) 1922-1943
Chicago (NFL) 1945-1959
(Chicago) Racine (APFA)
Detroit (ABL-1)
Phoenix (NFL)
St. Louis (NFL)
St. Louis (NL)

Card-Pitt
Chicago-Pittsburgh (NFL)

Caribous
Colorado (NASL)

Caseys
Fort Wayne (ABL-1)

Catskill
Catskill (ML-1)

Cats
Wilmington (EL)

Cavaliers
Cleveland (NBA)

Celtics (*See also* Original Celtics)
Boston (BAA)
Boston (NBA)

Brooklyn (ABL-1)
Brooklyn (ABL-2)
New York (ABL-1) 1927/28
New York (ABL-1) 1929/30
New York (ML-1)
Troy (ABL-2)

Celts (*See also* Kelts)
Cincinnati (APFA)
Cincinnati (NFL)

Centennials (*See also* Bicentennials)
Philadelphia (NA)

Centrals
Rochester (ABL-1)

Chaparrals (*See also* Roadrunners)
Dallas (ABA) 1967/68-1969/70
Dallas (ABA) 1971/72-1972/73
Texas (ABA)

Chargers
Los Angeles (AFL-4)
San Diego (AFL-4)
San Diego (NFL)

Chase Brass
Cleveland (NBL)

Chevrolets (Jim White)
Toledo (NBL)

Chiefs
Atlanta (NASL) 1968-1972
Atlanta (NASL) 1979-1980
Hawaii (ABL-3)
Kansas City (AFL-4)
Kansas City (NFL)
Long Beach (ABL-3)
Milwaukee (AFL-3)

Chippewas
Yonkers (ML-1)

Ciesar All-Americans (*See also* All-Americans)
Hammond (NBL)
Whiting (MBC)
Whiting (NBL)

Civics
Ottawa (WHA)

Clippers
Baltimore (ABL-1)

Los Angeles (NBA)
Oakland (NASL)
San Diego (NBA)

Clowns
Cincinnati (NAL) 1943
Cincinnati (NAL) 1945
Indianapolis (NAL)
Indianapolis-Cincinnati (NAL)

Cole's American Giants (*See also* American Giants)
Chicago (NNL-2)
Chicago (NSL)

Colonels
Kentucky (ABA)
Louisville (AA)
Louisville (NFL)
Louisville (NL) 1876-1877
Louisville (NL) 1892-1899

Colonials
Kingston (ABL-2)
Kingston (ML-1) 1924/25
Kingston (ML-1) 1926/27-1927/28

Colt .45s
Houston (NL)

Colts
Baltimore (AAFC)
Baltimore (NFL) 1950
Baltimore (NFL) 1953-1983
Chicago (NL)
Indianapolis (NFL)

Comellos
Cincinnati (NBL)

Comets
Baltimore (NASL)
Kansas City (MISL)

Condors
Pittsburgh (ABA)

Conquistadors
San Diego (ABA)

Continentals
Paterson (ML-2)

Cooper Buses
Windsor (MBC)

Cosmos
New York (MISL)
New York (NASL)

Cougars
Carolina (ABA)
Chicago (WHA)
Detroit (NASL)
Detroit (NHL)

Cowboys
Dallas (NFL)
Kansas City (AA)
Kansas City (NFL)
Kansas City (NL)

Crawfords
Indianapolis (NAL)
Pittsburgh (NNL-2)
Toledo (NAL)

Crescents
Paterson (ABL-1)
Paterson (ABL-2)
Paterson (ML-1)

Crimson Coaches
Toledo (NPBL)

Crimson Giants
Evansville (APFA)
Evansville (NFL)

Crunch
Cleveland (MISL)

Crusaders
Cleveland (WHA)

Cubans
New York (NAL)
New York (NNL-2) 1935-1936
New York (NNL-2) 1939-1948

Cuban Stars (*See also* All-Stars, North Stars, Stars, Tate Stars)
Cincinnati (NNL-1)
Cuban Stars (East)
Cuban Stars (ANL)
Cuban Stars (ECL)
Cuban Stars (West)
Cuban Stars (NNL-1)

Cubs
Chicago (NL)
Cleveland (NNL-1)

Darts
Washington (NASL)

Devils
New Jersey (NHL)

Diamonds
Jersey City (ML-2)

Diplomats
Washington (NASL) 1974-1980
Washington (NASL) 1980

Dodgers
Brooklyn (AAFC)
Brooklyn (ML-1)
Brooklyn (NFL)
Brooklyn (NL)
Los Angeles (NL)
Newark (NNL-2)

Dolphins
Miami (AFL-4)
Miami (NFL)

Dons
Los Angeles (AAFC)

Doves
Boston (NL)

Dow Athletic Club (A. C.)
Flint (NBL)
Midland (NBL)

Drillers
Edmonton (NASL)

Duffey Packers (*See also* Packers)
Anderson (NBL)

Duffy Florals
Chicago (MBC)

Dynamo
Denver (NASL)

Eagles
Brooklyn (NNL-2)
Detroit (NBL)
Houston (NAL)
Newark (NNL-2)
Philadelphia (NFL) 1933-1942
Philadelphia (NFL) 1944—
St. Louis (NHL)

Earthquakes
Golden Bay (MISL)
Golden Bay (NASL)
San Jose (NASL)

Eckfords
Brooklyn (NA)

Eclipse
Louisville (AA)

Elite Giants
Baltimore (NAL)
Baltimore (NNL-2)
Columbus (NNL-2)
Nashville (NNL-1)
Nashville (NSL)
Washington (NNL-2)

Elites
Cleveland (NNL-1)

Elizabeth
Elizabeth (ML-1)

Eskimos
Duluth (NFL)

Expos
Montreal (NL)

Express
Detroit
Jacksonville (WFL)
Los Angeles (USFL)
New York (MISL)

Falcons
Atlanta (NFL)
Detroit (BAA)
Detroit (NHL)
Toronto (NASL)

Federals
Washington (USFL)

Federals (Feds in combination)
Brooklyn: BrookFeds (FL)
Buffalo: BufFeds (FL)
Chicago: ChiFeds (FL)
St. Louis: SlouFeds (FL)

Fever
Philadelphia (MISL)

Fighting Saints
Minnesota (WHA)

Fire
Chicago (WFL)

Firemen
Fort Wayne (NPBL)

Firestone Non-Skids
Akron (MBC)
Akron (NBL)

Firestones
Akron (MBC)
Akron (NPBL)

Fisher Foods
Lorain (NPBL)

Flames
Atlanta (NHL)
Calgary (NHL)

Florals (*See* **Duffy Florals**)

Floridians
Floridians (ABA)
Miami (ABA)

Flyers
Muncie (APFA)
Philadelphia (NHL)

Fog
San Francisco (MISL)

Force
Cleveland (MISL)

Forest City/Forest Citys
Cleveland (NA)
Cleveland (NL)
Rockford (NA)

Forty-niners (49ers)
San Francisco (AAFC)
San Francisco (NFL)

Fury
Philadelphia (NASL)

Gallagher Trojans
Kankakee (NBL)

Gamblers
Houston (USFL)

Gatos
Miami (NASL)

Gears (*See* **American Gears**)

Gems
Detroit (NBL)

General Electrics
Fort Wayne (MBC)
Fort Wayne (NBL)

Generals
New Jersey (USFL)
New York (NASL)

Germans
Buffalo (ABL-1)

Giants (*See also* **American
Giants, Bacharach Giants, Cole's**

**American Giants, Crimson
Giants, Elite Giants, Lincoln
Giants, Royal Giants)**
Chicago (NNL-1)
Cleveland (NNL-2)
Harrisburg (ECL)
New York (APFA)
New York (NFL)
New York (NL)
New York (PL)
St. Louis (NNL-1)
San Francisco (NL)

Gladiators
Brooklyn (AA)

Gold
Denver (USFL)

Golden Blades
New York (WHA)

Golden Seals
California (NHL)

Goodyear Regulars
Akron (MBC)

Goodyear Wingfoots
Akron (NBL)

Goodyears
Akron (NPBL)

Gothams
New York (ABL-2)
New York (NL)

Grays
Homestead (ANL)

Homestead (NNL-2)
Providence (NL)

Grey Sox
Montgomery (NSL)

Guardsmen
South Bend (NPBL)

Gunners
St. Louis (NFL)

Gunslingers
San Antonio (USFL)

Hakoahs
New York (ABL-1)

Hartfords
Hartford (NA)

Hawaii (*See* **Team Hawaii**)

Hawaiians
Hawaiians (WFL)

Hawks
Atlanta (NBA)
Milwaukee (NBA)
St. Louis (NBA)
Waterloo (NBA)
Waterloo (NBL)

Haymakers
Troy (ABL-2)
Troy (NA)

Heat
Miami (NBA)

Hebrews
Philadelphia (ABL-2)

Hed-Aids
Detroit (MBC)

Hellions
Hartford (MISL)

Heralds
Detroit (APFA)

Highlanders
New York (AL)

Hilldale
Hilldale (ANL)
Hilldale (ECL)

Hill House
Brooklyn (ML-2)

Hoosiers
Fort Wayne (ABL-1)
Indianapolis (AA)
Indianapolis (FL)
Indianapolis (NL) 1878
Indianapolis (NL) 1887-1889

Horizon
Chicago (MISL)

Hornets
Charlotte (NBA)
Charlotte (WFL)
Chicago (AAFC)
Cleveland (NNL-1)

Horsemen
Brooklyn (AFL-1)

Hudson
Hudson (ML-1)

Hurricane
Houston (NASL)

Huskies
Toronto (BAA)

Independents
Rock Island (APFA)
Rock Island (AFL-1)
Rock Island (NFL)

Indians
Akron (NFL)
Brooklyn (ABL-2) 1942/43
Brooklyn (ABL-2) 1943/44
Buffalo (AFL-3)
Camden (ABL-2)
Cleveland (AL)
Cleveland (APFA)
Cleveland (NFL) 1923
Cleveland (NFL) 1931
Oorang (NFL)
Yonkers (ML-1)

Infants
Brooklyn (NL)
Cleveland (PL)

Inferno
Phoenix (MISL)

Innocents
Pittsburgh (NL)

Invaders
Oakland (USFL)

Ironmen
Pittsburgh (BAA)

Islanders
New York (NHL)

Jackaways
New Britain (ABL-2)

Jasper Jewels
Philadelphia (ML-2)

Jaws
San Diego (NASL)

Jazz
New Orleans (NBA)

Utah (NBA)

Jeeps
Toledo (NBL)

Jeffersons
Rochester (APFA)
Rochester (NFL)

Jets
Indianapolis (BAA)
Los Angeles (ABL-3)
New York (AFL-4)
New York (NFL)
Winnipeg (WHA)
Winnipeg (NHL)

Jewels
Brooklyn (ABL-2) 1933/34
Brooklyn (ABL-2) 1936/37
Brooklyn (ML-2)
New Haven (ABL-2)
New York (ABL-2) 1934/35-1935/36
New York (ABL-2) 1937/38-1941/42
New York (ABL-2) 1942/43

Jewish Center
Brooklyn (ML-2)

Jim White Chevrolets
Toledo (NBL)

Joe Fays
Newark (ABL-2)

Kardex
Tonawanda (APFA)

Kautskys
Indianapolis (MBC)
Indianapolis (NBL) 1937/38-1939/40
Indianapolis (NBL) 1941/42
Indianapolis (NBL) 1945/46-1947/48
Indianapolis (NPBL)

Kekiongas
Fort Wayne (NA)

Kelleys
Duluth (NFL)

Kelly's Killers
Cincinnati (AA)

Kelts (*See also* **Celts**)
Kokomo (NPBL)

Keystones
Philadelphia (UA)
Pittsburgh (NNL-1)

Kicks
Minnesota (NASL)

Kids
Cincinnati (MISL)

King Clothiers
Richmond (NBL)

Kings (*See also* **Vagabond Kings**)
Kansas City (NBA)
Kansas City-Omaha (NBA)
Los Angeles (NHL)
Sacramento (NBA)

Knickerbockers
New York (BAA)
New York (NBA)

Knights
(Brooklyn) Greenpoint (ML-1)
Jersey (WHA)
Yonkers (ML-2)

Lancers
Rochester (NASL)

Lakers
Los Angeles (NBA)
Minneapolis (BAA)
Minneapolis (NBA)
Minneapolis (NBL)

Lazers
Los Angeles (MISL)

Legion
Racine (NFL)

Legionnaires
Paterson (ML-1)

Lightning
Detroit (MISL)

Lincoln Giants
(New York) Lincoln Giants (ANL)
(New York) Lincoln Giants
 (ECL) 1923-1926
(New York) Lincoln Giants (ECL) 1928

Lions
Brooklyn (NFL)
Detroit (NFL)

Lisas
Hoboken (ML-2)

London Bobbys
Dayton (MBC)

Lord Baltimores
(Baltimore) Lord Baltimores (NA)

Magic
Orlando (NBA)

Majors
Chicago (ABL-3)

Mansfields
Middletown (NA)

Manic
Montreal (NASL)

Maple Leafs
Toronto (NHL)

Marcos
Dayton (NNL-1) 1920
Dayton (NNL-1) 1926

Marines
Minneapolis (APFA)
Minneapolis (NFL)

Mariners
San Diego (WHA)
Seattle (AL)

Maroons
Kenosha (NFL)
Montreal (NHL)
Pottsville (NFL)
St. Louis (NL)
St. Louis (UA)
Toledo (NFL)

Maulers
Pittsburgh (USFL)

Maumees
Toledo (AA)

Mavericks
Dallas (NBA)
Houston (ABA)

McDowell Lyceum
New York (ML-1)

Mets (*See also* Metropolitans)
New York (NL)
Passaic (ML-1)
Perth Amboy (ML-1)

Metropolitans (*See also* Mets)
New York (AA)

Metros
Dayton (MBC)

Dayton (NBL)
Toronto (NASL)

Metros-Croatia
Toronto (NASL)

Minutemen
Boston (NASL)

Molly Maguires
Cleveland (AL)

Monarchs
Kansas City (NAL)
Kansas City (NNL-1) 1920-1927
Kansas City (NNL-1) 1929-1930
Monroe (NSL)

Moose
Philadelphia (EL)
Trenton (ABL-2) 1933/34
Trenton (ABL-2) 1935/36
Trenton (EL)

Mules
Newark (ABL-2)
New Britain (ABL-2)

Muskies
Minnesota (ABA)

Mustangs
Chicago (NASL)

Mutuals
New York (NA)
New York (NL)

Naps
Cleveland (AL)

Nationals
Ottawa (WHA)
Syracuse (NBA)
Syracuse (NBL)
Washington (NA) 1873
Washington (NA) 1875
Washington (UA)

"No Nicknames" (or teams with city or regional names only. All teams are listed elsewhere in alphabetical sequence.)
Albany (ML-1)
Bridgeton (EL)
Brooklyns (AA)
Camden (EL)
Elizabeth (ML-1)

Floridians (ABA)
Hartford (NA)
Hawaiians (WFL)
Hilldale (ANL)
Hilldale (ECL)
Hudson (ML-1)
Lord Baltimore (NA)
New Havens (NA)
Passaic (ML-1)
Philadelphias (NA)
Rochester (AA)
St. Louis (NA)
Team America (NASL)
Team Hawaii (NASL)
Troy (ML-1)
Washington (AA)
Worcester (NA)

Non-Skids (*See* Firestone Non-Skids)

Nordiques
Quebec (NHL)
Quebec (WHA)

North Stars (*See also* All-Stars, Cuban Stars, Stars, Tate Stars)
Minnesota (NHL)

Nuggets
Denver (ABA)
Denver (NBA) 1949/50
Denver (NBA) 1976/77—
Denver (NBL)

Oaks
Oakland (ABA)
Oakland (ABL-3)

Oilers
Alberta (WHA)
Edmonton (NHL)
Edmonton (WHA)
Houston (AFL-4)
Houston (NFL)
Warren (MBC)

Olympians
Indianapolis (NBA)

Olympics
Washington (NA)

Olympique
Montreal (NASL)

Red Man Tobacco
Toledo (ABL-1)

Red Sox
Boston (AL)
Cleveland (NNL-2)
Memphis (NAL) 1937-1941
Memphis (NAL) 1943-1950
Memphis (NNL-1) 1924-1925
Memphis (NNL-1) 1927
Memphis (NNL-1) 1929-1930
Memphis (NSL)

Red Stockings
Boston (NA)

Red Wings
Detroit (NHL)

Redlegs
Cincinnati (NL)

Reds (*See also* Outlaw Reds)
Boston (AA)
Boston (PL)
Cincinnati (AA)
Cincinnati (NFL)
Cincinnati (NL) 1876-1880
Cincinnati (NL) 1890-1943
Cincinnati (NL) 1946—
Jersey (ABL-2)
Passaic (ABL-2)
St. Louis (NA)
Union City (ABL-2)
Union City (ML-2)

Redskins/Red Skins
Boston (NFL)
Sheboygan (NBA)
Sheboygan (NBL)
Washington (NFL)

Renegades
Orlando (USFL)

Rens
Dayton (NBL)
Pittsburgh (ABL-3)

Resolutes
Elizabeth (NA)

Roadrunners (See also Chaparrals)
Phoenix (WHA)

Robins
Brooklyn (NL)

Rockets
Chicago (AAFC)
Denver (ABA)
Houston (NBA)
New Jersey (MISL))
San Diego (NBA)

Rockies
Colorado (NHL)

Rosenblums
Cleveland (ABL-1)

Rouges
Memphis (NASL)

Roughnecks
Tulsa (NASL)

Rowdies
Tampa Bay (NASL)

Royal Bengals (*See also* Bengals, Tigers)
Trenton (ML-1)

Royal Giants (*See also* Giants)
Brooklyn (ECL)

Royals
Cincinnati (NBA)
Kansas City (AL)
Rochester (BAA)
Rochester (NBA)
Rochester (NBL)
Vancouver (NASL)

Sabres
Buffalo (NHL)

Sails
San Diego (ABA)

St. Louis
St. Louis (NA)

St. Monicas
(New York) Jamaica (ML-2)

St. Patricks
Toronto (NHL)

Saints (*See also* Fighting Saints)
New Orleans (NFL)
St. Paul (UA)
San Francisco (ABL-3)

Sand Snipers
Atlantic City (ABL-2)

Scouts
Kansas City (NHL)

Seahawks
Miami (AAFC)
Seattle (NFL)

Seals (*See also* Golden Seals)
California (NHL)
Oakland (NHL)

Senators (*See also* Black Senators)
Harrisburg (ABL-2)
Ottawa (NHL) 1917/18-1930/31
Ottawa (NHL) 1932/33-1933/34
Washington (AA)
Washington (AL) 1901-1960
Washington (AL) 1961-1971
Washington (APFA)
Washington (NL) 1888-1889
Washington (NL) 1892-1899

Seventy-sixers (76ers)
Philadelphia (NBA)

Shamrocks
Boston (AFL-2)

Sharks
Jacksonville (WFL)
Los Angeles (WHA)
San Jose (NHL)

Sidekicks
Dallas (MISL)

Showboats
Memphis (USFL)

Sockers
San Diego (MISL) 1982-83
San Diego (MISL) 1984/85—
San Diego (NASL)

Somersets
Boston (AL)

Sounders
Seattle (NASL)

Sounds
Memphis (ABA)

Southmen
Memphis (WFL)

Spartans
Portsmouth (NFL)

Sphas
Philadelphia (ABL-2)
Philadelphia (EL)

Spiders
Cleveland (NL)

Spirit
Pittsburgh (MISL) 1978/79-1979/80
Pittsburgh (MISL) 1981/82-1985/86

Spirits of St. Louis
St. Louis (ABA)

Spurs
Denver (WHA)
Kansas City (NASL)
San Antonio (ABA)
San Antonio (NBA)

Squires
Virginia (ABA)

Stags
Chicago (BAA)
Chicago (NBA)
Michigan (WHA)

Staleys
Chicago (APFA)
Decatur (APFA)

Stallions
Birmingham (USFL)
Buffalo (MISL)

Stampeders
Calgary (WHA)

Stapes
Staten Island (NFL)

Stapletons
Staten Island (NFL)

**Stars (*See also* All-Stars, Cuban
Stars, North Stars, Tate Stars)**
Baltimore (USFL)
Detroit (NAL)
Detroit (NNL-1)
Detroit (NNL-2)
Harrisburg-St. Louis (NNL-2)
Houston (NASL)
Los Angeles (ABA)
New Orleans-St. Louis (NAL)
New York (WFL)
Newark (ECL)
Philadelphia (NAL)

Philadelphia (NNL-2)
Philadelphia (USFL)
St. Louis (NAL) 1937
St. Louis (NAL) 1939
St. Louis (NASL)
St. Louis (NNL-1)
Syracuse (AA)
Syracuse (NL)
Tacoma (MISL)
Utah (ABA)

Statesmen
Washington (NL)

Steagles
Philadelphia-Pittsburgh (NFL)

Steamer/Steamers
St. Louis (MISL)
Shreveport (WFL)

Steam Roller/Steamrollers
Providence (BAA)
Providence (NFL)

Steelers
Pittsburgh (NFL) 1939-1942
Pittsburgh (NFL) 1945—

Steers
Kansas City (ABL-3)

Sting
Chicago (MISL) 1982/83
Chicago (MISL) 1984/85-1987/88
Chicago (NASL)

Stingers
Cincinnati (WHA)

Stokers
Cleveland (NASL)

Stompers
Oakland (NASL)

Storm
Portland (WFL)
St. Louis (MISL)

Strikers
Fort Lauderdale (NASL)
Minnesota (MISL)
Minnesota (NASL)

Studebakers
Chicago (NBL)

Summit
Houston (MISL)

Sun/Suns
Phoenix (NBA)
Southern California (WFL)

Superbas
Brooklyn (NL)

Supersonics
Seattle (NBA)

Surf
California (NASL)

Tams
Memphis (ABA)

Tapers
New York (ABL-3)
Philadelphia (ABL-3)

**Tate Stars (*See also* All-Stars,
Cuban Stars, North Stars, Stars)**
Cleveland (NNL-1)

Tea Men
Jacksonville (NASL)
New England (NASL)

Team
America (NASL)
Hawaii (NASL)

Terrapins
Baltimore (FL)

Terriers
St. Louis (FL)

Texans
Dallas (AFL-4)
Dallas (NFL)
Houston (WFL)

Thourots
North Hudson (ABL-2)

Thunder
Portland (WFL)
San Antonio (NASL)

**Tigers (*See also* Bengals, Bengal
Tigers)**
Brooklyn (AFL-2)
Brooklyn (NFL)
Buffalo (AFL-3)
Chicago (APFA)
Cincinnati (NFL)
Columbus (NFL)
Detroit (AL)
Detroit (APFA)

Hamilton (NHL)
Philadelphia (ECL)
Rochester (AFL-2)
Toledo (NNL-1)
Trenton (ABL-2)

Timbers
Portland (NASL)

Timberwolves
Minnesota (NBA)

Tip Tops
Brooklyn (FL)

Titans
New York (AFL-4)

Tornado/Tornadoes
Dallas (NASL)
Newark (NFL)
Orange (NFL)
Racine (NFL)

Toros
Miami (NASL)
San Diego (NASL)
Toronto (WHA)

Trail Blazers
Portland (NBA)

Triangles
Dayton (APFA)
Dayton (NFL)

Trojans (*See also* Gallagher Trojans)
Boston (ABL-2)
Troy (NL)

Troy
Troy (ML-1)

Turfs
Columbus (NSL)

Twins
Minnesota (AL)

Unions
Baltimore (UA)
Boston (UA)
Chicago (UA)
Kansas City (UA)
Milwaukee (UA)
Pittsburgh (UA)

U. S. Tires
Indianapolis (MBC)

Vagabond Kings (*See also* Kings)
Detroit (NBL)

Vikings
Minnesota (NFL)

Virginias
Richmond (AA)

Visitations
Brooklyn (ABL-1)
Brooklyn (ABL-2)
Brooklyn (ML-1)
Brooklyn (ML-2)
Paterson (ABL-2)

Vulcans
Birmingham (WFL)

Wanderers
Montreal (NHL)

Warriors
Golden State (NBA)
Philadelphia (ABL-1)
Philadelphia (BAA)
Philadelphia (NBA)
San Francisco (NBA)

Washington
Washington (AA)

Westchesters
New York (ABL-2)

Westerns
Keokuk (NA)

Whalers
Hartford (NHL)
New England (WHA)

Whales
Chicago (FL)

Wheels
Detroit (WFL)

Whips
Washington (NASL)

Whirlwinds
Boston (ABL-1)
Paterson (ABL-1)

(Jim) White Chevrolets
Toledo (NBL)

White Horses
Cleveland (NBL)

White Stockings
Chicago (NA) 1871
Chicago (NA) 1874-1875
Chicago (NL)

White Sox
Chicago (AL)
Louisville (NNL-1)

Whitecaps
Vancouver (NASL)

Whys (*See also* YMHA)
Muncie (NPBL)

Wildcats
Los Angeles (AFL-1)

Wind
Chicago (WFL)

Wingfoots (*See* Goodyear Wingfoots)

Wings
San Antonio (WFL)
Wichita (MISL)

Wolverines
Detroit (NFL)
Detroit (NL)

Wolves
Los Angeles (NASL)

Wonders
Brooklyn (PL)

Worcesters
Worcester (NL)

WPEN A. C.
Philadelphia (EL)

Wranglers
Arizona (USFL)1983
Arizona (USFL) 1984

Yankees (*See also* Black Yankees)
Bronx (ABL-2)
New York (AAFC)
New York (ABL-2)
New York (AFL-1)
New York (AL)
New York (NFL)

Yanks
Boston (NFL)
New York (AFL-2)
New York (AFL-3)

New York (NFL)

Yellow Jackets
Frankford (NFL)

YMHA
Pittsburgh (MBC)

Zephyrs
Chicago (NBA)

Zollner Pistons (*See also* Pistons)
Fort Wayne (NBL)

Bibliography

Many of the documents that proved most helpful in doing research for this book are to be found at the Halls of Fame in Cooperstown, NY (baseball) and Springfield, MA (basketball). Media guides, letters, and clippings in vertical files, correspondence, publicity releases, programs, etc. were very valuable. Also of great help were the data collected by Colin Jose (for his book on the North American Soccer League) and the inexhaustible files and data collected by Bill Himmelman, the NBA historian.

For those who wish to secure items mentioned in this bibliography, the following may be helpful:

For information concerning the Society for American Baseball Research (**SABR**) or its publications, write to SABR, Box 93183, Cleveland, OH 44101.

For information concerning the Professional Football Research Association (**PFRA**) or its publications, write to Bob Carroll, 12870 Route 30, North Huntingdon, PA 15642.

Books

Allen, Lee. *The National League Story.* New York: Hill and Wang, 1961.

Anderson, Dave. *The Story of Basketball.* New York: Morrow, 1988.

Barnett, C. Robert. *The Spartans and the Tanks.* PFRA, 1983.

Baseball Encyclopedia. New York: Macmillan, 1969 (and later editions).

Basloe, Frank J. *I Grew Up With Basketball: Twenty Years of Barnstorming with Cage Giants of Yesterday.* New York: Greenberg Publishers, 1952.

Benson, Michael. *Ballparks of North America.* Jefferson, NC: McFarland, 1989.

Bruce, Janet. *The Kansas City Monarchs: Champions of Black Baseball.* Kansas City: University Press of Kansas, 1985.

Byrne, Jim. *The $1 League: The Rise and Fall of the USFL.* New York: Prentice-Hall, 1986.

Carroll, Bob. *The Tigers Roar: Professional Football in Ohio: 1903-09.* PFRA, 1990.

Cohen, Richard M., Jordan A. Deutsch, Roland T. Johnson, and David Neft. *The Scrapbook History of Pro Football.* Indianapolis: Bobbs-Merrill, 1976.

Cope, Myron. *The Game That Was.* New York: Crowell, 1974.

Davidson, Gary, with Bill Libby. *Breaking the Game Wide Open.* New York: Atheneum, 1974.

Devaney, John. *The Story of Basketball.* New York: Random House, 1976.

Diamond, Dan, and Lew Stubbs. *Hockey—Twenty Years.* Toronto: Doubleday Canada, 1987.

Dickey, Glenn. *The History of Professional Basketball since 1898.* New York: Stein and Day, 1982.

DiClerico, James M., and Barry J. Pavelec. *The Jersey Game.* New Brunswick, NJ: Rutgers University Press, 1991.

Eskenazi, Gerald. *Hockey.* Chicago: Follett, 1969.

_____. *A Thinking Man's Guide to Pro Soccer.* New York: Dutton, 1980.

Falls, Joe. *Detroit Tigers.* New York: Macmillan, 1975.

Fischler, Stan, and Shirley Fischler. *Fischler's Ice Hockey Encyclopedia.* New York: Crowell, 1979.

Fox, Larry. *Illustrated History of Basketball.* New York: Grosett & Dunlap, 1974.

Gill, Bob. *Best in the West: The Rise and Fall of the Pacific Coast League, 1940-48.* PFRA: 1988.

_____. *A Minor Masterpiece,* Volume I: *The American Association, 1936-41.* PFRA, 1990.

_____. *A Minor Masterpiece,* Volume II: *The American Football League, 1946-50.* PFRA, 1990.

Gill, Bob, and Tod Maher. *The Outsiders: The Three American Football Leagues of 1936-41.* PFRA, 1989.

Gipe, George. *The Great American Sports Book.* Garden City, NY: Doubleday, 1978.

Gluck, Herb. *While the Gettin's Good—Inside the World Football League.* Indianapolis: Bobbs-Merrill Co., Inc., 1975.

Gold, Eddie, and Art Ahrens. *The Golden Era Cubs: 1876-1940.* Chicago: Bonus Books, 1985.

Halas, George. *Halas by Halas.* New York: McGraw-Hill, 1968.

Henshaw, Richard. *The Encyclopedia of World Soccer.* Washington, DC: New Republic Books, 1979.

Hershberger, Charles A. *Sports Hall of Oblivion.* Pleasant Ridge, MI: Hershberger, 1985. (Available from: 9760 E. Houghton Lake Drive, Where [Houghton Lake], MI 48629.)

Heward, Bill. *Some Are Called Clowns.* New York: Crowell, 1974.

Hill, Bob, and Randall Baron. *The Amazing Basketball Book: The First 100 Years.* Louisville, KY: Devyn Press, 1988.

Hollander, Zander. *The American Encyclopedia of Soccer.* New York: Everest House, 1980.

_____. *The Modern Encyclopedia of Basketball.* Rev. ed. New York: Four Winds Press, 1973.

_____. *The NBA's Official Encyclopedia of Pro Basketball.* New York: New American Library, 1981.

Hollander, Zander, and Hal Bock. *The Complete Encyclopedia of Ice Hockey.* Rev. ed. Englewood Cliffs, NJ: Prentice-Hall, 1974.

Holoway, John B. *Black Diamonds: Life in the Negro Leagues from the Men Who Lived It.* Westport, CT: Meckler Books, 1990.

Horrigan, Joe. "National Football League Franchise Transactions." *PFRA Annual, 1982* pp. 11-33.

Isaacs, Neil D. *Checking Back.* New York: Norton & Co., 1977.

Jares, Joe. *Basketball: The American Game.* Chicago: Follett, 1971.

Johnson, Chuck. *The Green Bay Packers.* New York: Thomas Nelson, 1961.

Jose, Colin. *NASL—A Complete History of the North American Soccer League.* Derby, England: Breedon Books, 1989. Available from: Soccer Learning Systems, Box 277, San Ramon, CA 94583.

Kaese, Harold. *The Boston Braves.* New York: Putnam, 1948.

Klein, Gene, and David Fisher. *First Down and a Billion.* New York: William Morrow, 1987.

Koppett, Leonard. *24 Seconds to Shoot*. New York: Macmillan, 1968.

Lang, Jack, and Peter Simon. *The New York Mets: Twenty-five Years of Baseball Magic*. New York: Holt, 1986.

Leitner, Irving. *Baseball: Diamond in the Rough*. New York: Abelard-Schuman, 1972.

Lessiter, Mike. *The Names of the Games*. Chicago: Contemporary Books, 1988.

Lieb, Fred. *The Baltimore Orioles*. New York: Putnam, 1955.

_____. *The Boston Red Sox*. New York: Putnam, 1947.

_____. *The Detroit Tigers*. New York: Putnam, 1946.

_____. *The St. Louis Cardinals*. New York: Putnam, 1944.

Lowry, Phillip J. *Green Cathedrals*. Cooperstown, NY: Society for American Baseball Research, 1986.

_____. *Green Gridirons*. PFRA, 1990.

Maher, Tod. *The All-Time United States Football League Register*. Researched by Tod Maher and Jay Langhammer. PFRA, 1986.

Mead, William B. *Even the Browns*. Chicago: Contemporary Books, 1978.

Menke, Frank G. *Encyclopedia of Sports*, 4th rev. ed. Revised by Roger Treat. South Brunswick, NJ: Barnes, 1969.

Moreland, George. *Balldom*. New York: Balldom Publishing Company, 1914.

Morse, Phillip M. *Hoosiers: The Fabulous Basketball Life of Indiana*. New York: Vintage (Random House), 1986.

Neft, David, Roland T. Johnson, Richard M. Cohen, and Jordan Deutsch. *The Sports Encyclopedia: Pro Basketball*. New York: Grossett & Dunlap, 1975.

Obojski, Robert. *Bush League*. New York: Macmillan, 1975.

Okkonen, Marc. *The Federal League of 1914-1915*. Garrett Park, MD: SABR, 1989.

Orr, Frank. *The Story of Hockey*. New York: Random House, 1971.

Orr, Jack. *We Came of Age: A Picture History of the American Football League*. New York: The Lion Press, 1969.

Peterson, Harold. *The Man Who Invented Baseball*. New York: Scribner's, 1973.

Peterson, Robert W. *Only the Ball Was White*. Englewood Cliffs, NJ: Prentice-Hall, 1970.

_____. *Cages to Jump Shots: Pro Basketball's Early Years*. New York: Oxford University Press, 1990.

Pluto, Terry. *Loose Balls: The Short Wild Life of the American Basketball Association*. New York: Simon & Schuster, 1990.

Povich, Shirley. *The Washington Senators*. New York: Putnam, 1954.

Puff, Richard, and Mark Rucker, eds. *The Empire State of Base Ball*. Northeast Chapter of SABR, 1989.

Rathet, Mike, and Don R. Smith. *Their Deeds and Dogged Faith*. New York: Rutledge Books/Balsam Press, 1984.

Riffenburgh, Beau. *The Official NFL Encyclopedia*, 4th ed. New York: New American Library, 1986.

Rogosin, Donn. *Invisible Men: Life in Baseball's Negro Leagues.* New York: Atheneum, 1983.

Rote, Kyle, Jr. *Kyle Rote, Jr.'s Complete Book of Soccer.* New York: Simon & Schuster, 1978.

Rust, Art, Jr. *"Get That Nigger off the Field!"* New York: Delacorte Press, 1976.

Salzberg, Charles. *From Set Shot to Slam Dunk.* New York: Dutton, 1987.

Seymour, Harold. *Baseball: The Early Years.* New York: Oxford University Press, 1960.

Spencer, David, and Barbara Spencer. *The Pocket Hockey Encyclopedia.* New York: Scribners, 1976.

Styer, Robert A. *Encyclopedia of Hockey.* South Brunswick, NJ: Barnes, 1970.

Sugar, Bert Randolph. *Hit the Sign (and win a free suit of clothes from Harry Finkelstein).* Chicago: Contemporary Books, 1978.

Sullivan, George. *This Is Pro Soccer.* New York: Dodd, Mead, 1979.

Thorn, John, Pete Palmer, and David Reuther. *Total Baseball.* New York: Warner Books, 1989.

Treat, Roger. *The Encyclopedia of Football,* 15th ed. Revisions by Pete Palmer. South Brunswick, NJ: Barnes, 1977.

Vincent, Ted. *Mudville's Revenge: The Rise and Fall of American Sport.* New York: Seaview Books, 1981.

Voight, David Quentin. *American Baseball.* 3 vols. University Park: Pennsylvania State University Press, 1983.

Ward, Arch. *The Green Bay Packers.* New York: Putnam, 1946.

Whitehead, Eric. *Cyclone Taylor: A Hockey Legend.* Toronto: Doubleday Canada, 1977.

Wilkins, Charles. *Hockey, the Illustrated History.* Dan Diamond, ed. Garden City, NY: Doubleday, 1985.

Magazines and Periodicals

Baseball History
Baseball Magazine
Baseball Research Journal (SABR)
The Coffin Corner: The Official Newsletter/Magazine of the PFRA
Colored Baseball & Sports Monthly
Harper's Weekly
National Pastime (SABR)
PFRA Annuals
Police Gazette
The Unofficial PF Journal (PFRA)

Newspapers

Arizona Republic (Phoenix)
Atlanta Constitution
Atlanta Journal
Baltimore Sun
Birmingham News
Boston Globe
Boston Herald

Chicago Tribune
Cleveland Plain Dealer
Detroit Free Press
Hartford Courant
Indianapolis Star
Louisville Courier-Journal
Milwaukee Journal
Nashville Tennessean
Newark News
Newark Star-Ledger
New York Clipper
New York Times
Philadelphia Bulletin
Philadelphia Inquirer
Pittsburgh Press
Providence Daily Journal
Rocky Mountain News (Denver)
St. Louis Post-Dispatch
San Francisco Chronicle
Seattle Times
Sporting Life
Sporting News
Springfield Republican (MA)
Toronto Globe and Mail
Troy Times (NY)
Washington Post (DC)
Washington Star (DC)
Washington Times (DC)

Index

Citations are keyed to alphabetically arranged items in Section 1.

232